'I don't know if there is another big club
where the supporters have a love like the
supporters have a love for this club.'
Gordon Strachan

Acknowledgements

The Herald/Evening Times Newsquest Media Group are acknowledged for their permission to reproduce the Neil Lennon and Aiden McGeady images. Ricky Fearon provided the memorabilia for the front cover.

The author would like to thank the many people who have contributed to this book in so many different ways. Thanks to colleagues and friends who have provided numerous comments on drafts, and the numerous followers of Celtic and other clubs who have offered their wisdom, advice and support during this process.

Lastly, a word of appreciation to all the contributors who have made this work possible. Go raibh maith agaibh.

Contents

Symbols of the largest Celtic supporters associations

Foreword

NEIL LENNON

Celtic Football Club became a part of my life from a very early age. Although Gaelic football was dominant in County Armagh and I was also very much part of that great sport, an awareness of Celtic Football Club seemed inevitable and I soon realised that the idea of Celtic played a significant role in the life and identity of my community in the north of Ireland.

Newsquest (Herald & Times)

The club was like an extension of my community – watching highlights of the match on television and eagerly awaiting the return of the travelling supporters to hear their reports of the game and their weekend escapades were the highlights of many Saturday evenings. It quickly became obvious to me that the influence and importance of the club was much greater than simply a question of football. Many people around also had their eye on English football but mention of Celtic brought people to life and references to Celtic appeared to evoke emotions other clubs failed to.

Having finally realised a lifetime's ambition in joining this world-famous club it is only now that I understand and appreciate the uniqueness of the club and the Celtic fan base. Indeed, it might be argued that it is the Celtic support and Celtic culture that distinguishes this great institution. As a player I have had the privilege of travelling with Celtic and have met many people amongst our worldwide support.

This network of like-minded people continues to affect me in a very positive way since the members of this Celtic family, no matter where they are, share a kindred spirit: a spirit that is the heartbeat of the club. Their unfailing devotion to the Celtic cause through good times and bad, their desire to proclaim the values of the club, the preservation of its history and culture along with the sharing of humour, craic, story and camaraderie – this I firmly believe represents and spirit and soul of Celtic Football Club.

Major occasions such as Lisbon and Seville exemplify this and make this easier for the rest of the football world to witness. Although taking place before I was born, I often feel as though I was in Portugal's capital that memorable evening in 1967 owing to the numerous stories of that generation of Celtic fans that I have eagerly listened to. Stories that have been proudly passed from friend to friend, mother to son, father to daughter, grandparent to grandchild. Although these stories can recount the action on the pitch it is the value of actually winning football's greatest prize and how that reflects an important part of the story of the Celtic support in Scotland and beyond that really makes an impression. The joy, the experience and the celebration of the Celtic family gathered in Lisbon and in front of their TV sets around the world in the name of this club still reverberates today. The power of this supporting community continues to make its presence felt.

Celtic supporters' tremendous contribution to the world of football was in recent years publicly acclaimed when the Club's supporters received the UEFA and FIFA 'Fair Play' awards after their impeccable behaviour in Seville. These accolades are of even greater value when one considers that they are usually kept for teams and their players.

The heritage and culture of the club is proclaimed from the stands week in week out at Celtic Park and wherever the support collects. What this means to many players who grace this club can never be underestimated. Even if new players from outside of the traditional Celtic community come to play for the club they very quickly realise that this is a special club and it is an honour just to pull on the green and white hooped jersey.

Despite the passion that is part and parcel of being a football supporter there has long existed a difficulty in exploring and explaining the phenomenon that is not only football, but the phenomenon that is Celtic FC. As fans and as players we can often even be part of this without any real reflection on what this is all about: why football, why a particular football club and, what does this football club represent in the larger scheme of life itself?

There are many books about football and many books have been written about Celtic. However, 'Celtic Minded 2' is a book with a difference. Its capacity to explore what is usually unexplored or left to lazy and uninformed commentary distinguishes it. Dr Joe Bradley and his team of writers do not shirk the issues that make Celtic and its support unique. Having read this book of 'Celtic Minded' stories I am convinced that its contributors have captured the true essence of Celtic and articulated the very soul and passion that constitutes this great club's support.

This is also a book that will appeal to those interested in the meaning of football to its many fans across the globe. For Celtic supporters who have a passion and love for the history and identity of this great institution, you won't fail to be impressed by the collection of writings that make up 'Celtic Minded 2'.

Representing the diaspora in football.
Celtic and Irish internationalist, Aiden McGeady

Newsquest (Herald & Times)

Difference and distinctiveness in Scottish football and society

Over the last 150 years Scotland's largest immigrant group has been comprised of Catholics and their offspring from Ireland. A few thousand Irish Catholics migrated to Scotland in the early part of the nineteenth century but the highest concentration of immigration occurred in the wake of the Great Irish Famine of 1845-51 and during the decades thereafter until around 1920. Most migration from Ireland to Scotland took place during this time although thousands more Irish have also arrived in the post-Second World War period, continuing until the present day. Although they reside in various parts of Scotland the progeny of this immigrant community has essentially settled in the west central belt, mainly in an around cities and towns like Glasgow, Greenock, Port Glasgow, Dumbarton, Coatbridge, Motherwell, Airdrie, Hamilton and Cumbernauld and in villages such as Glenboig, Carfin, Clelland, Plains and Croy.

Michael Davitt (1846-1906)
Member of the Fenians, Land Leaguer, human rights activist, Member of Parliament and patron of Celtic Football Club

There are Scottish, Lithuanian, Italian, Polish and other influences upon Catholicism in Scotland, but the vast majority of Catholics in the country originate from Ireland. There remains an Irish-born population in Scotland of around 50,000 people and more than 100,000 others have an Irish-born parent and thus constitute the second generation Irish. Nonetheless, most of the 'Irish community' is now third and fourth generation whose grandparents and great-grandparents migrated from Ireland during the second half of the nineteenth and early part of the twentieth centuries. The Irish in Scotland are a multi-generational community.

Although suffering much hardship and oppression in Scotland the Irish community has enhanced many aspects of modern Scottish society. It has contributed to the rise and establishment of the Labour Party, the building of the country's industrial infrastructure in the shape of roads, railways and shipping, as well as iron, coal and steel production, it has been a significant contributor to the establishment and development of the National Health Service, particularly through nursing, and has helped character the artistic and sporting practices and expressions of Scotland in the shape of acting, popular song, comedy, art, football and boxing. The education sector has been developed in Scotland with a significant contribution from Catholics of Irish descent. These are some of the features that form the principal contributions of the Irish to Scottish life.

Two other areas are significant for this book. The first is religion. It is likely that Catholicism in Scotland would have remained as a missionary Church, diminutive in significance and status, but for the influx of the Irish and their offspring in providing the clergy, service and laity that have been necessary for the survival and strengthening of a re-born post-Reformation Catholic Church in Scotland.

The second contribution of course has been the establishment of Celtic Football Club and its surrounding supporter culture in Scotland. This Irish Catholic immigrant and refugee community gave birth to Celtic Football Club in Glasgow and its offspring forms the vast majority of its modern support. Only for the influx of Irish Catholic migrants there would be no Celtic Football Club. Without Celtic, missing from Scottish sporting history would be founders and patrons of the club such as Brother Walfrid, John Glass and Michael Davitt, past directors like Willie Maley, Robert Kelly and Tom Grant and players such as Jimmy Quinn, James McGrory, Jimmy Delaney, Jimmy Johnstone, Paddy Crerand, Paul McStay and Aiden McGeady. These are only a few who have represented their immigrant community on the field of play in Scottish football. Without Celtic, also absent in Scottish life would be the colour, celebration, culture, beliefs, and ethnic and national identities that Celtic supporters bring to the sport and to Scotland generally. But for the Irish influence in Scottish life, Celtic and its supporters would not be because the very rationale for founding, sustaining and supporting the club would not have existed.

These influences partly reflect the way Irish Catholics and their offspring have integrated into Scottish and British societies. Nevertheless, these points are rarely stated so obviously in Scottish academic books, via relevant parts of the school curriculum or in political, economic, historic, cultural, social accounts and commentary. Similarly, these omissions mean that the history of the struggle of this migrant community to integrate into Scottish life has been largely silenced. Such lack of commentary, even among the offspring of the Irish themselves, reveals stories largely untold or long since silenced and privatised. Nonetheless, these chronicles and accounts are beginning to come to light mainly as a result of the work of the offspring of migrants who endeavour to explore and explain – sometimes in the face of opposition – aspects of the histories of their own community.

This book is part of that unfolding and largely untold narrative. When *Celtic Minded* was published in 2004 the vast majority of the Celtic reading public responded positively. *Celtic Minded 2* has emerged as a result of further work and discussions with numerous *Celtic Minded* as well as other insightful authors. The book's contributors are people who are beginning to find a way, beginning to find the words and language, beginning to discover what has been hidden as well as to ask questions as to why these have been hidden and with what consequences. They are beginning to articulate what has until now been silent or distorted. They represent the first generation of writers to explore, explain, reveal, reflect, record and narrate the meaningfulness of Celtic Football Club in historical, religious, social, cultural and national terms.

Celtic Football Club can be imagined as an Irish football club and a Scottish institution. It exists as a hybrid of Irish and Scottish influences: Irish because that explains the history, roots, ethos, soul, heart, composition and identity of the club and its support. Scottish because that is where the club and most of its modern support have been born, where they have learned to live as the offspring of the Irish in Scotland and where the context for their being, as individuals and as a community, is largely shaped. It is also an international club. It has a totemic value because its history has an inspiring and welcoming appeal and because in the minds

Celtic Park in the wake
of the death of Jimmy
Johnstone

of many of its supporters, players, custodians and employees, the club has long stood as a symbol of solidarity for other migrant groups in Scotland and elsewhere. The club is a symbol for marginalised peoples, and is an institution with supporters that in the spirit of Brother Walfrid, pride themselves on the Catholic and Christian principles of charity, neighbourliness and openness towards fans, as well as players or employees, from other national, religious and cultural origins and identities.

The contributors to this book inspire by giving attention to that which has previously been suppressed. They seek to take ownership of their own identities and refuse to have them shaped by elements in society that lack knowledge and awareness and are hostile, aggressive and intolerant towards matters in Scotland that are Catholic, Irish, Celtic or indeed, simply reflect a more plural and broad-minded Scotland. They speak in a way that few have been able or willing to in the past. They admirably reflect one of the aspirational declarations of the new Scottish parliament of the third millennium: 'One Scotland Many Cultures'.

ONE SCOTLAND MANY CULTURES?

The advent of a devolved Scottish parliament in 1999 has resulted in a number of important issues being addressed. One of these has been the issue of 'racism' in Scotland. The first part of this book will address aspects of racism and multiculturalism in relation to Celtic Football Club and its supporting community, a community substantially composed of the descendants of Irish Catholic migrants to Scotland.

Although racism in Scottish life has a long history, recognising and acknowledging this as a problem is a relatively recent occurrence. Indeed, in a recent article in an academic journal, one author wrote that:

> It is often argued that racism is not an issue in Scotland because there is a small black and minority ethnic population, and the Scottish people are thought to be tolerant of difference.[1]

Finn and Dimeo also note the traditional failure to acknowledge racism in Scotland despite a range of evidence to the contrary. Importantly for this essay, they emphasise that:

> The historic racialisation of the Catholic Irish by significant sections of the dominant Scottish Protestant population is

Guayaquil, Ecuador – Father Martin Chambers of the Society of St James disperses some of the Celtic jerseys left at Celtic Park after the death of Jimmy Johnstone

1 Hopkins 2004.

15

usually disguised when discussing Scottish society and football, discursively masked by the use of 'sectarianism' and the implicit failure to recognise inequalities of power between majority and minority group.[2]

We can also note that Hickman, Miles and Muirhead, Mac an Gaille, *et al*, stress that the longest established racism in British society is anti-Irish racism.[3]

One way the Scottish Executive has addressed and challenged 'racism' in Scottish society has been through the creation of the 'One Scotland Many Cultures' campaign. Through several ongoing phases, the campaign intends to raise awareness of the issue of racism in Scottish society. In this context, racism is essentially depicted as negative attitudes, behaviour and language towards people in Scotland who do not have white skin, who are not indigenous to Scotland and/or who have origins in another country. With this in mind, Scottish Labour Minister for Communities Margaret Curran said:

> We now want to encourage everyone to speak out if racist behaviour or language offends them and to challenge those who think it is acceptable to undermine people's race and culture, at work or anywhere else. . . Young people are our future and they should be given the confidence and every opportunity to embrace and celebrate Scotland's diversity.[4]

The campaign has run periodically since 2002 using billboard and bus shelter sites, radio advertising and programming and water cooler cups in offices. Websites have also been constructed to target young people and the workplace. Leading voices have added their support to the campaign including the Head of the Commission for Racial Equality in Scotland who said:

> The campaign underlines the need for everyone in Scotland, our public institutions as well as all individuals to play an active part in challenging racial discrimination and helping to build a fair and just Scotland.[5]

In 2005 the website created by the Scottish Executive to alert and educate people on racism in Scotland stated that, 'Racism can be defined in different ways, but for the purposes of this website we have used the following definition':

> Conduct, words or practices which disadvantage or advantage

2 Finn & Dimeo 1998.

3 Hickman 1998, Miles and Muirhead 1986, Mac an Gaille 2001.

4 'One Scotland Many Cultures' is accessible on http://www.onescotland.com/onescotland/. This quote from a related site http://www.youngscot.org/onescotland/, 18/01/2005, p2.

5 http://www.scotland.gov.uk/News/Releases/2004/02/5072.

people because of their colour, culture or ethnic origin. It can be subtle or overt, intentional or unwitting.[6]

Scotland's First Minister Jack McConnell reiterated this definition arguing:

This campaign promotes a Scotland of many cultures. It highlights the need for all of us to examine critically our attitudes. It urges us to challenge racism, whatever form it takes.[7]

A survey of the various Scottish Executive and 'One Scotland Many Cultures' websites demonstrates the range of information offered that aims to educate people to recognise racism and to be actively against it: indeed, as stated by the First Minister, for many people to change their attitudes with regards racist practices 'in whatever form it takes'. For example, the 'Racism and Colonialism' section of the official website refers to the origins of racism explaining that:

Scotland took part in the colonial exploitation of parts of the African, South American and Asian continents. . . Racist beliefs and attitudes became widespread during this period.[8]

Further, these beliefs and attitudes:

. . . served to justify the exploitation of the 'black' indigenous people of these continents by 'white' western Europeans. . . These ideas have changed over time and been modified to fit into changing circumstances. They still exert a powerful influence in the minds and resultant behaviour of many Scots.[9]

The Executive website also reproduces an interpretation of the most recent ethnic data resulting from the 2001 British census.

Pakistanis were the largest minority ethnic group representing just under one third (31%) of the minority ethnic population in Scotland. Over 70% of the ethnic minority population were Asian (Indian, Pakistani, Bangladeshi, Chinese or Other South Asian). For all ethnic groups, Scotland is either the most common or the second most common country of birth. However, the percentages vary greatly between different ethnic groups: 47% of Pakistanis were born in Scotland compared to only 18% of Africans.[10]

From these calculations racist crime, reported racist incidents and discrimination in the workplace are all determined. A single deviant or unusual reference emerges when health questions are addressed and the negative health statistics for 'white Irish people'

6 One Scotland Many Cultures website, 'Racism in Scotland' section. P1.

7 The Daily Record, 8/04/04.

8 One Scotland Many Cultures website, 'Racism and Colonialism' p1.

9 Ibid.

10 One Scotland Many Cultures website, 'Racism section, ethnicity data'. p1.

is given as a section of society that is least likely to report good or fairly good health. This reference is essentially a result of published research carried out by academics Williams and Walls *et al*, which has received some public attention and is included as a reading reference in Scottish Executive literature. Notably this research refers not only to those born in Ireland but also to the diaspora, the offspring of Irish migrants to Scotland. Had these two academics not carried out this research the Irish would almost certainly be completely omitted from the information offered.

Linked to the 'One Scotland Many Cultures' campaign is the 'YoungScot' website aimed towards young people aged 12 to 26. The 'YoungScot' website declares that the 2001 census showed that Scotland has 'many different communities including; Indian, Pakistani, Bangladeshi, Chinese, Caribbean, African' and that 'just over 100,000 ethnic minority people live in Scotland, about 2% of the population'. In this account recognition of the Irish presence in Scotland is ignored.

In relation to multicultural Scotland, the Executive's website contains numerous images of people wearing clothes that have Asian or Islamic connotations, have black skins or derive from south-east Asia. There are also people whose images denote recent migrants/refugees from Eastern Europe. There are no images that imply Irish origin and the presence of a multi-generational Irish community in Scotland. This focus, mainly on non-white skinned immigrants as well as on more recent migrants from Eastern Europe, contributes visually and textually to the creation of invisibility and silence with regards Irishness in Scotland, delineates the history and experience of the Irish within a banner of white homogeneity and incorporates and assimilates their offspring as Scots or British.[11]

Mac an Ghaill suggests that such texts are important in how they facilitate society's construction of 'knowledge about nation, race and ethnicity'. In other words these texts or narratives assist in the 'development of conceptual frames (structures) that organise our perceptions and understandings of the social world'.[12] This is also important for the development of privileged or dominant narratives as well as common sense and generally understood notions and representations concerning nation, race and ethnicity.

11 As described by Mac an Ghaill and Hickman et al.

12 Mac an Ghaille 2001, p181.

It can also be argued that they also have a role to play in the development of stereotypes as well as the often consequential racism and sectarianism that can follow.

On the Executive's website of information a history of migration to Scotland is also offered in short note form. This section identifies Chinese, Flemish, Italian, Lithuanian, Asian, African and Caribbean, French, Gypsies and Travellers, Jewish, Polish and present-day refugees and asylum seekers in Scotland. Migration from Ireland, by far the biggest single, and in many ways most significant group to originate from out-with Scotland, is covered by a single paragraph:

> The majority of these migrants were Catholic and had been largely confined to unskilled areas of the Irish economy. They filled similar jobs in the rapidly expanding Scottish economy, building the roads and railways, digging ditches and bringing in the harvests. They encountered discrimination in many areas, particularly in employment and housing. Smaller numbers of skilled Protestant workers also arrived at this time, finding employment in the new shipyards and workshops. Today the Irish and their descendants are the largest minority ethnic group in Scotland, and have made significant contributions to Scottish life and culture.[13]

The last sentence of this reference is an indication of the size and significance of the Irish presence: the Irish are conspicuously and specifically referred to as 'the largest minority ethnic group in Scotland'. This reference stands out in public narratives concerning the Irish in Scotland because it is unusual. It is atypical because it contradicts much of the Scottish Executive's other website materials in that it represents one of the only references to the Irish presence in Scottish life. It also specifically contradicts and confuses the assertion on another part of its website that 'Pakistanis were the largest ethnic group representing just under one third (31%) of the minority ethnic population in Scotland' as well as the notion that 'just over 100,000 ethnic minority people live in Scotland, about 2% of the population'.

In fact, including the Irish descended, approximately 15% of the population of Scotland can be categorised as being part of ethnic minority groups: that is, approximately 800,000 have origins outside of Scotland and the rest of Britain. Such contradictions, confusion, lack of knowledge and misinformation are indicative of

13 One Scotland Many Cultures website, 'History of Migration section. p1.

the dominant thinking behind notions and ideas concerning ethnicity, particularly the status of Irish descended people, in modern Scotland. Importantly, this defective and often prejudiced information also helps inform popular, media and political under-standings and representations with regards anti-racist and anti-sectarian matters.

That textual, oral, historical, social and other such omissions apply in countless accounts and across many time spans is unarguable. Significantly, and with few exceptions, the Irish, or more specifically the Irish Catholic experience, is largely absent from research, novels, histories and stories of life in modern Scotland. MacMillan points out that similar to the Executive's website, the Collins Encyclopedia of Scotland:

> . . . has no entry for the Irish in Scotland or the Catholic Church. Foreign visitors to Edinburgh attended an exhibition a couple of years ago at the Scottish Record Office, recounting the history of immigration to Scotland. Large displays set out the history of the immigration of Flemish weavers, Jewish traders, Italian peasants, Asian shopkeepers, Chinese restaurant owners, black bus conductors, and rightly praised the contribution they had all made to Scottish society. The massive Irish immigration in the nineteenth and early twentieth centuries was dealt with in something like three sentences as follows:

> 'in the mid-nineteenth century an increasing number of seasonal Irish farm labourers who worked in the summers in lowland Scotland stayed over due to poor economic conditions in Ireland. Many of them became a burden on the local Parish Poor Laws.'[14]

Likewise, an academically produced website telling the story of Glasgow and its new communities has a section looking at post-1950s immigration. Here the authors speak of pre-1950s migrants.

> By 1950 the Jewish, Italian, Lithuanian, Polish and a small number of Greek immigrants who had come during the previous sixty years had settled comfortably in Glasgow. . . The numbers of Asians began to grow rapidly after 1950 . . . [15]

In this account no mention is made of the substantial Irish migration to the Glasgow area – including Lanarkshire – during the period referred to. Indeed, although declining after about 1920, Irish migration to the Glasgow area remained higher than any other ethnic migration until the 1950s. In addition, many later migrants

14 MacMillan 2000.

15 www. theglasgowstory. com

settled, married and lived amongst older Irish migrant communities, thus continually adding to amongst other things, the Irishness and the Catholicism of this already established community.

These examples, and many more, correspond with academic work such as that of Hickman et al, on how the Irish and their descendants can be construed as invisible in British society.[16] For the purposes of this chapter, what is 'invisible' is understood as the origins, experiences and 'the Irishness' of those born in Scotland whose parents, grandparents or great-grandparents etc, arrived in Scotland from Ireland at varying points over the last 150 years.

To be able to recognise the omission of Irishness from popular and public forums and symbolisms, or to recognise the disapproving, demeaning and derogatory nature of representations of Irishness when they do emerge, it is important to have knowledge of the basic facts of Irish migration and settlement in Scotland. By way of parallel, it would be more difficult to understand racism against non-whites in North America without knowledge of the Slave Trade and the Black struggle for emancipation. Similarly, South Africa's racial problems cannot be understood without knowledge of British and Dutch colonialism. The same also applies to the experiences of the Irish in Scotland and Scotland's role in the colonisation of Ireland.

Popular, official and educational texts that omit, deny or limit the significance of the Irish presence in Scotland are important in creating, nourishing and sustaining Irish diasporic invisibility. This omission also lends itself to the construction of negative and inadequate expressions to describe this group when it is referred to. Importantly, having little or no knowledge of, the economic contribution of the Irish to emerging industrial and subsequently post-industrial Scotland, their contribution to the advancement of the Scottish health services, to Christianity, to education provision, to political life (particularly through the Labour Party) and of course to Scottish sport, means also that the sectarianism and racism faced by the Irish and their descendents is largely unrecorded and undocumented. In effect, it has been silenced through being excluded from these accounts. This is repeated throughout much of the contemporary Scottish media: a matter that is in part addressed in this book.

16 Hickman, 1998.

INVISIBLE IRISHNESS

Apart from the research of Handley (1943 & 1947) and Gallagher (1987), it took until 1991 before the first substantial work on the Irish in Scotland was produced as edited conference proceedings. Editor Professor Tom Devine stated in his introduction that despite having a significant presence since the mid-nineteenth century:

> Irish immigrants . . . have not until recent years been effectively integrated into the wider study of Scottish historical development.[17]

At another relevant conference held at the University of Stirling in January 1997, two 'leading' academic speakers expressed the view that the Irish could be referred to historically but not as a living or identifiable group or identity in Scotland. The Chair of the conference, as well as his supporting professorial colleague, offered a view that talk of the Irish in contemporary Scotland was illusory and that the offspring of the greatest single immigrant grouping in society over the past 150 years had 'ceased being Irish'.[18] This assertion reflects and correlates with the comparatively few academic or popular books and articles that address historical, cultural, economic and religious issues in relation to the Irish in Scotland and that a significant amount of published sources do so only within the boundaries of a 'sectarian discourse'. Such a declaration also reflects, as well as creates and sustains, a popular outlook that is founded upon a lack of knowledge, awareness and consciousness about the offspring of Scotland's largest ethnic and cultural immigrant group as well as reflection on Scotland's recent past history. These perspectives construct Irishness in Scotland at the periphery of social, cultural and political narratives and this also contributes to the production of Irish 'invisibility' in Scotland.

This ethnic invisibility is reinforced by the Scottish Executive's website materials relating specifically to Scotland as a multicultural society. In ideological terms, such perspectives reflect and substantiate, but also lend themselves to, other related views, including for example, that 'sectarianism' in Scotland is not really a problem, but is essentially an issue confined to certain geographical areas or is primarily an issue for football, especially alcohol induced hooliganism. Consequently, a perspective that refuses acknowledgment and esteem to Irishness will conspire to refuse recognition of anti-Irishness and anti-Irish racism and indeed, will invariably repudiate these.[19] Such a course of events may also

17 Devine 1991, introduction.

18 'Out of the Ghetto? The Catholic Community in Modern Scotland', University of Stirling, 24th January 1997.

19 At a public meeting at the University of Aberdeen, February 2005, Professors Tom Devine and Steve Bruce debated sectarianism in Scotland. Bruce denied its existence and its seriousness. Devine argued that it was a serious issue in Scotland as evidenced by a long list of Government-backed bodies, public figures, politicians, the police, newspapers, social and other organisations and prominent individuals who agree. Other academics such as Graham Walker offer polemical support to the arguments of Bruce et al. For example, see review of Bruce's work in Fortnight November 2004, 'The Myth of Scottish sectarianism'. See numerous publications, including 'Why Scottish Catholics should not live in fear of religious abuse' in the Scottish Catholic Observer, 10th December 2004.

reflect the old (British-Irish) couplet 'that the Irish can't forget and the British can't remember'.[20]

However, this has serious implications in relation to questions of culture and identity and is a reminder of the notion of what constitutes legitimate knowledge, especially its reproduction as power. It is also a reminder that colonialism 'signifies modes of domination' that do not simply disappear once colonisation – sometimes partial, re-cycled or re-located – takes place. In studying the work of Franz Fanon, Ahluwalia and Zegeye have explored some of these issues.

> The colonisation of the mind is manifested in the manner in which a people's history is denied and they are made to feel inferior and incapable, , , in this way, the national identity of a people is denigrated and made non-functional.[21]

This idea can be seen to have significance for Finn and Dimeo's reflection on Murray's work on football and sectarianism. They believe that author's perspectives are particularly revealing in relation to dominant and accepted views of racism and sectarianism in Scotland. Murray states:

> Anti-Catholicism is part of Scotland's history and can be understood in these terms. [However], Racism is totally odious and foreign to all that Scotland stands for.[22]

Finn and Dimeo conclude that as far as Murray is concerned:

> Anti-Catholicism is to be seen as essentially Scottish, part of what it means to be Scottish, but Scots are not racist: in an ill-judged choice of word, racism is 'foreign' to Scotland.[23]

Like Hickman, Mac an Ghall (2001) and Miles, Finn and Dimeo also observe:

> The avoidance of the issue of anti-Irish racism often presupposes an acceptance of the racist essentialism that 'races', itself a racist construction, come colour-coded.[24]

Giulianotti's reflection on racism against non-whites in soccer is further evidence of this erroneous assumption. Importantly it prompts consideration of the omission of accounts of racism against Catholics of Irish descent in many educational, media and public texts and representations in Scotland, including in explanations that originate with the Scottish Executive. In a similar sense,

20 Mac an Ghaill and Haywood 2003.

21 Ahluwalia & Zegeye 2001.

22 Murray 1988, p175.

23 Finn & Dimeo 1998, p125.

24 Finn & Dimeo 1998, p125.

Giulianotti argues that accounts of soccer's racialised past have been 'air-brushed from football's histories even though they have a long lineage'.[25]

Citing a number of authors Huckin makes the point that they have shown how silence can be used to convey information while fulfilling other communicative purposes. This 'air-brushing out of history' was also referred to by Huxley in *Brave New World*:

> The greatest triumphs of propaganda have been accomplished, not by doing something, but by refraining from doing. Great is truth, but greater still, from a practical standpoint, is silence about truth. By simply not mentioning certain subjects. . . propagandists have influenced opinion much more effectively than they could have done by the most eloquent denunciations, the most compelling of logical rebuttals.[26]

By largely ignoring the Irishness of many Irish offspring in Scotland and conflating this with a native Scottish 'white' category and assuming 'ethnicity' as a largely colour based notion, racism is perceived and shaped as an essentially black/white issue. As Mac an Ghaill, Finn and Dimeo note, the standard 'colour paradigm' of British race relations.[27]

In a Scottish context, this also means that the related question of 'sectarianism' is reduced to questions of 'religion', based on narrow understandings and representations of creed, while crucially important ethnic and 'racial' dimensions of sectarianism are ignored. Although the Scottish Executive's website acknowledges the country's role in the creation, building and management of the British Empire stating that 'racist beliefs and attitudes became widespread during this period' and that these beliefs and attitudes 'still exert a powerful influence in the minds and resultant behaviour of many Scots', Scotland's critical role in the colonial exploitation of Ireland, particularly Ulster, is absent from these texts. This might be partly accounted for because of the relevance of religion to the colonisation of Ireland, the contemporary and contested nature of not only the ongoing Irish-British conflict itself, but interpretations of this, as well as the relevance of ethno-religious identities in contemporary Scottish society. In other words, in Irish-British terms relevant histories of conflict and contestation exert an influence in modern Scotland and are historical questions with contemporary relevance and meanings.

25 Jones 2002.
26 Huckin 2002.
27 Mac an Ghaill 2001.

Having knowledge of Ireland's conquest, exploitation and domination by Britain is crucial to understanding the position of the Irish and their offspring within British society, particularly in Scotland. This arrangement has traditionally been one of subordination resulting from the imperialism of the English throne towards Ireland with a series of military and political invasions from the twelfth century onwards. Edward Said has stated that from that time a process began which engendered a persistent cultural attitude towards Ireland as a place whose inhabitants were perceived as a barbarian and degenerate race thus justifying invasion and subordination.[28] With the Union of the Scottish and English crowns in 1603 (and in 1707 the Union of the Scottish and English Parliaments), the English colonisation of Ireland became a British process. This resulted in a further more successful plantation of Ireland by British Protestant settlers who came mainly from Scotland and who were settled in Ulster under favorable terms:

> in exchange for swearing allegiance to the Crown and agreeing not to inter-marry or learn the language of the native Irish.[29]

While such conditions can be seen as the introduction of colonial inspired sectarianism into Ireland, for one sociologist, British colonisation in Ireland has also been as 'imperialistic as anything the great powers have done anywhere in the world'.[30]

Reference to the colonisation of Ireland is important to a contextual understanding of issues of 'racism' and 'sectarianism' within Scottish society. First, the descendents of the people who were colonised and subjugated are now either living on the island of Ireland or are part of the worldwide Irish diaspora that includes Scotland's community of Irish descent. Second, and more important for understanding the position of the Irish and their descendents in Scottish society, is the fact that almost all the relevant political, popular and academic literature, including from the Scottish media industry and the developing anti-sectarian industry, do not acknowledge this colonisation in any relevant commentary.

The lack of acknowledgement stands in contrast to an awareness that the colonial exploitation of parts of the 'African, South American and Asian continents' has contributed to racist beliefs and attitudes, the legacy of which remains as 'racism' within

28 Ibid.

29 Audrey 2000.

30 Jacobs 2005.

Scottish society, as stated by the Scottish Executive's 'One Scotland Many Cultures' campaign. The lack of knowledge and awareness about, as well as the omission and accompanying acknowledgement regarding the colonisation of Ireland in popular, educational and public discourses, is fundamental to understanding the denial of anti-Irish racism within contemporary Scottish society.[31] It is also essential to an understanding that 'racism' is not simply a black-white issue.[32]

Mac an Ghaill, talks of a degree of acknowledgement of the racialisation of the Irish in late nineteenth and early twentieth century Britain but the systematic absence of the Irish from most late twentieth century representations of racism and ethnicity.[33] This is partly akin to the relatively recent widespread denial of 'colour' or black/white racism in Scotland when its presence and effects began to have a significant influence on (public) social relations and non-white ethnic minorities themselves began to bring attention to the problems they faced.[34]

One consequence of this is that for Scotland, whiteness has traditionally been a defining characteristic of its history and collective identity, but so also since the sixteenth century has Presbyterianism, which was,

> not just a state religion but, for more than three centuries, defined the Scots to one another and to the rest of the world.[35]

Since the Reformation, a significant anti-Catholic culture has existed in Scotland, one that has varyingly infused many aspects of social and political life. Muirhead opines that: 'in Scotland anti-Romanism had become a religion and a way of life'.[36] Despite increasing secularisation in Scotland, the creation and expansion of a varying range of identity sources and expressions, and although Protestantism is multi-dimensional, involving social, political, moral, philosophical and spiritual aspects, it is the relationship between Scottishness and Protestantism, the anti-Catholic dimensions of Presbyterianism and the role of British/Scots in the colonisation and exploitation of Ireland, that have had a significant impact on relations between Scottish Protestants and Catholics of Irish descent in Scotland. Partly reflecting the significance of anti-Catholicism even before Irish-Catholic migration to Scotland took place, two statistics singularly demonstrate this in the city of Glasgow in the

31 See Jackson 1963, Curtis 1984 & Miller 1998

32 Back, Crabbe & Solomon 1999.

33 Mac an Ghaill 2001.

34 White on black racist crime in Scotland has been increasing in the new millennium and this is partly put down to the rise in 'reported' instances of these crimes. In addition, a new 'black literature' has emerged in recent years articulating the racism that non-white people face in Scotland and Britain more generally. See The Herald, 8/3/04, p1 and for academic writing on racism in Scotland see Hopkins, 2004

35 Gallagher in T M Devine (ed) 1991, pp19-43

36 Muirhead 1973

1790s where there were only thirty-nine Catholics in the city (and less than a handful in Lanarkshire) but forty-three anti-Catholic societies (Devine notes sixty anti-Catholic societies in 1791).[37] The Catholicism of Irish migrants arriving in Scotland has been a crucial factor in the development of social relations in modern Scotland.

PROBLEMATISING IRISHNESS IN SCOTLAND

The Economic and Social Research Council funded Irish 2 project in 2002, and other research that specifically reflects on popular football discourses, demonstrates that although Irishness in Scotland is frequently ignored, marginalised, labeled as negative, deviant and sectarian, Irish distinctiveness and character is important to the mosaic of identities that constitutes twenty first century Scotland.[38] Nonetheless, the denial and denigration of Irishness in Scotland rejects specified difference, is a form of enforced assimilation and is a refusal to recognise and confer esteem to Irish diasporic personal, family and community history, culture and identity.

Regarding a lack of understanding with regards Scotland's most significant ethnic minority and the pressures of rejection and simultaneous incorporation, Mac an Ghaill believes that as for Britain, the dominant black-white colour paradigm, the selective forgetting of Empire (and its consequences) and the assimilation that develops from a myth of cultural homogeneity and questions of difference/sameness, are at the core of Britain's problematising of the Irish in Britain. In Scotland, problematising the Irish and their offspring, and of course Irishness itself is further exacerbated by the 'religious' questions commonly referred to 'sectarian' issues.

Irish immigrants to Glasgow founded Celtic Football Club in 1887/88 and in the process established the club and supports' defining characteristics, culture and identity, as Catholic, charity and Irishness. Though important and defining features of Celtic and Celtic football culture, these have not been rigid or unaccommodating and from its birth the club has been an open one, welcoming as staff, players or supporters, people from a non-Catholic or non-Irish background. Thousands of people from other backgrounds have become Celtic supporters. Hundreds of players, including a number of the club's most famous footballers (for

37 Murray 1984, p93 and Devine 1988 p154

38 This project was financed by the Government-sponsored Economic and Social Research Council in 2001/02 and essentially looks at questions and issues of identity, focusing on people born in Britain of at least one Irish-born parent or grandparent. The work was carried out by Dr J Bradley, Dr S Morgan, Prof M Hickman & Prof B Walter. For further references see http://www.anglia.ac.uk/geography/progress/irish2/

example, John Thomson, Danny McGrain and Henrik Larsson) and its most successful manager (Jock Stein), have not been Catholic or of Irish extraction. Nonetheless, for many other Scots, Celtic's distinctive and significant Irish and Catholic character, married to its accomplishments on the field of play, has meant that the club and its supporters have been a focus for discontent, hostility, alienation and disadvantage. On the other hand, for the multi-generational ethnic Irish community, Celtic's hybrid identity as an Irish football club and a Scottish institution, a concrete expression of the diasporic Irish presence in Scotland, has offered security, celebration and success.

The problematisation of Celtic and its supports' Irishness is a discourse well established within the Scottish media. In a wider sense, reflection on some aspects of these discourses demonstrates that sport, particularly football, has the capacity to embody a multiplicity of identities – national, cultural, ethnic, religious, social, political, economic and community – in ways that few other social institutions and activities do. Such an examination also shows how the institution of Celtic demonstrates the fallacy of the polemic that the Irish in Scotland have 'ceased to exist'.

The previous volume of *Celtic Minded* discussed how Celtic's appearance at the UEFA Cup Final in Seville in 2003 provoked numerous disparaging commentary regarding Celtic and its supports' Irishness. It also noted that most media commentators marginalised or omitted positive mention of this and that in communications omission can be as important as inclusion. Such limiting, functionally prohibitive, and indeed, hegemonic discourses, can be considered dominant because they are pre-eminent, all-encompassing and recurrent in the Scottish media threading through editorials, letters pages, popular articles, news columns and football shows on radio. Indeed, positive reference to the Irishness of Celtic and its supporters' is virtually non-existent outside of the Celtic supporters' environment. During the period surrounding the match in Seville, one popular football commentator in Scotland contested Celtic and its supporters' Irishness:

> Celtic, a Scottish team whether some of their fans are willing to admit it or not. . . Celtic ARE Scottish so they belong to more than the supporters who follow them week in, week out

. . . This is Scotland against Portugal. . . right now Celtic, albeit unwittingly, are flying our flag. . .[39]

The *Daily Record* journalists' view was a popular one and some letter writers reflected this:

I was absolutely appalled and disgusted when watching the UEFA Cup Final. I am sure I am not the only non-Celtic supporter who was urged to 'get behind' the Scottish team. How many Scottish flags were in the stadium? I counted one but maybe I couldn't see the others due to the sea of Irish Republican flags on display. Isn't it about time that people like this decided which nationality they are?[40]

I could have sworn the UEFA Cup Final in Seville was between teams from Scotland and Portugal, but judging by the flags in the stadium I think it was actually Ireland against Portugal; there were more American, Canadian, or Australian flags than Scottish. . . I can't imagine what the rest of the world thought as they watched this disgraceful sight which was attended by some of our politicians who supposedly abhor this type of behaviour. This was not a good reflection on our culture and a bad night for Scottish sport.[41]

The head of the Dundee United Supporter's Association said with regards Celtic:

They need Scotland. I just wish you'd see a few more Saltires amongst their support, rather than [Irish] tricolours.[42]

Beyond the Seville event, a different Sunday broadsheet contributed to the ideology that views Celtic supporters' Irishness with hostility, complaining that Celtic's identity 'still contains a large Irish component'.[43] Another football columnist criticised Celtic and its fans' Irishness showing both the widespread nature of this criticism and how it is embedded in Scottish culture. This journalist referred to the diaspora in Scotland as the 'pseudo-Irish' who support Celtic as well as their penchant for 'diddly-dee music'.[44] The widespread nature of this hostility in Scottish culture is further demonstrated in a *News of the World* column that again reflected on Celtic and its fans' ethnic identity. For this football columnist, Celtic Park was full of:

Plastic Irishmen and women who drink in plastic Irish pubs and don't know their Athenry from their Antrim when it comes to Irish history or politics. . . Celtic must stop. . . flashing their Irishness

39 J Traynor, The Herald, Sport, 22/8/94, p9

40 The Daily Star, letters, 26/5/03

41 The Herald, letters, 23/5/03

42 See S Fisher, Sunday Herald, Sport, 18/5/03

43 A Massie, Scotland on Sunday, Week in Review, 29/7/01, p9

44 B Leckie, The Sun, 8/4/02, 50

... if Celtic are so keen to flaunt their Irishness perhaps they could do us all a favour and relocate to Dublin.[45]

Such antagonism, hostility and lack of tolerance towards Irishness in football have a long history in Scotland. In addition, outside of football similar discourses can be found at numerous junctures over the course of Irish settlement during the past 150 years.[46] During the inter-war period, a time when the Church of Scotland demanded the repatriation of the Irish in Scotland back to Ireland, a number of significant political figures, political parties and other influential people in Scottish society reflected these widespread feelings. During this time Conservative Member of Parliament, Lord Scone, expressed the view that:

... culturally the Irish population. . . has not been assimilated into the Scottish population. It is not my purpose to discuss now whether the Irish culture is good or bad, but merely to state the definite fact that there is in the west of Scotland a completely separate race of alien origin practically homogeneous whose presence there is bitterly resented by tens of thousands of the Scottish working-class.[47]

The unacceptability of Irish-Catholics to the Orange community in Scotland has been one of the most perceptible contemporary manifestations of this attitude.

Study the [Irish-Catholic] names of some of the 'Labour' candidates elected. . . What do Glasgow's Protestant clergymen think of this situation? What do the genuine patriots, in the SNP's rank-and-file, think about it?. . . There isn't a Scoto-Eirishman in Scotland, a Lally, a Murphy, or a Gaffney, who is not Eirish under his skin. Scratch them and their Eirish bit comes out. . . [48]

Similar sentiments have frequently been expressed by some of the Reformed Churches in Scotland. In 1986, in his address to the annual Assembly of the Free Church of Scotland, the Moderator's speech included criticism of the Catholic and Irish nature of those of immigrant extraction:

In 1755 there were no Roman Catholics in Glasgow. . . In 1786 there were about seventy and by 1830, they numbered 30,000, with 14,000 in Edinburgh. . . Today the Roman Catholic system is virtually triumphant in Scotland. Being allowed by its constitution to lie and cheat as long as its own ends are realised, its close organisation and its intelligence set-up has enabled it to infiltrate the whole educational framework of the land.[49]

45 G McNee, News of the World, 6/5/01, 15; Ibid, 7/10/01, p69

46 See Handley et al

47 Hansard, 261, 22/11/32, p245

48 Orange Torch, June 1984

49 Moderator's address to the Church Assembly, Church Records, July/August 1986

The ideology that gives rise to such comments, beliefs and identities is also evident in the contemporary discourses that have followed the decision of Celtic player Aidan McGeady to represent Ireland at international football. The denial and rejection of the distinctiveness of the Irishness of Celtic Football Club and its supporting fanbase can be partly examined through reflection on McGeady, one of the club's third generation Irish players. McGeady has chosen to play international football for Ireland, thus representing his family's and migrating community's country of origin, rather that Scotland, his country of birth and upbringing. This focus specifically looks at the popular and media reaction that has surrounded his decision as but one illustration of the denigration, denial and rejection of the Irishness of the Irish diaspora in Scotland. Such reflection contributes to an improved understanding of the central role that Celtic plays in Irish diasporic life and also shows Scotland as being socially, culturally and politically constrained and limited by sectarianism and racist attitudes and identities. The reactions to McGeady's decision personifies, embodies and reflects much of Scotland's problem-atising of the Irish diaspora in Scottish society – and at a time that coincides with the Scottish Executive's campaign, 'One Scotland, Many Cultures'.

AIDEN MCGEADY:
IRISH DEMON IN THE SCOTTISH MIDST

The public airing in 2004 of McGeady's decision was met with much negative media comment as well as abuse from the opposition fans of almost every team in the Scottish Premier League during the football season 2004-05. At Celtic Park in August 2004, the visiting Motherwell fans abused McGeady and subsequently sang the popular Scottish anthem 'Flower of Scotland'. At Tynecastle, the home of Hearts, in April of the same year a BBC Scotland football commentator stated that he was to interview McGeady after the match, adding: 'I'll need to take down a bottle of whisky and some shortbread to Scottify him'. Previously this comment-ator's fellow broadcaster, himself a former professional footballer, denied the player's national and cultural identity, and others like him in Scotland, by arguing that McGeady 'was Scottish', adding:

He may well have chosen to play for Ireland, as far as I'm

concerned the boy was born in Scotland and that makes him Scottish and that's the end of the matter.[50]

Leaving aside this former player's ignorance of the complexity of national and cultural identity and citizenship and how this is manifest in sport, there are other elements of discourse worth examining in relation to anti-Irish racism in Scotland. Hearts supporters' abuse of McGeady during the match was viewed as legitimate, acceptable and understandable, as far as one football commentator and newspaper columnist was concerned. He believed that McGeady had turned his back on Scotland, showed a lack of patriotism (despite his patriotism in choosing Ireland) and he was disloyal to Scotland. He further hoped that 'McGeady has a miserable career as an Irish internationalist'.[51] A Scottish football fan agreed stating:

> It's a disgraceful situation. McGeady has chosen to play for a foreign country rather than represent Scotland. He's getting stick for it and rightly so.[52]

A *Daily Record* sports writer also supported the abuse of McGeady believing that:

> This isn't about sectarianism, this is about being Scottish and proud of it. McGeady has been educated here, used our health service and learned all his football in Glasgow. But thanks to his mum, he has now chosen to play for the Irish national team. Its heartbreaking. Its time all Scottish Celtic fans got over their obsession with Ireland. The fact that Glasgow sports shops sell as many Ireland football tops as Scotland football tops is both pathetic and ultimately unhelpful.[53]

Another *Record* reporter stated:

> Celtic's new boy wonder insisted he would prefer to play for the Republic of Ireland, his grandfather's birthplace, ahead of his own country [and] that has been met with widespread fury from some Scottish football fans and could result in him being the target of abuse.[54]

Neither of these reporters contemplated the possibility of their own sectarian or racist mindsets and their capacity for inflaming such attitudes in others. Their lack of education and knowledge in matters ethnic in multicultural Scotland is thus exposed in a blatant fashion. During the same period, complaints regarding McGeady dominated on radio phone-ins and on many Scottish football

50 G Smith, BBC Radio Scotland, 25/4/04

51 S Cosgrove, The Daily Record, 30/12/04, p67.

52 The Daily Record, 31/12/04, p79.

53 J McKie, The Daily Record, 1/1/05, p11

54 The Daily Record, 2/5/04, pp72-73

websites, widely used and accessed forms of modern football supporter communication in Scotland. On the Glasgow Rangers fanzine/website, *Follow Follow*, one of Britain's most significant and popular football websites, many fans reiterated the abuse of McGeady.

> A wee traitor of the highest order. Should be booed at every ground he appears at.

> Sums up the mentality of the F*nian player. Rather ditch his roots to pick up tatties in terrorist country instead.

> He honed his skills dodging police whilst shopping.

> I can only assume that the Republic of Ireland will be sending over the dole money to pay for him and his like minded friends not to mention the contribution for their schooling et al.[55]

A *Scotland on Sunday* broadsheet sports writer discussed McGeady's choice to play for Ireland suggesting the young player might have a 'twisted streak' in relation to not choosing to play international football for the country 'both he and his parents were born and bred in'.[56] As with other commentary over several years prior to this outbreak of attention on the Celtic player another sports columnist in the same newspaper anticipated the McGeady case when he referred to the Irishness of the Celtic fanbase and his perceptions of what Scotland should represent to them. The columnist expressed the view:

> . . . there is a section of the Celtic support, in particular, who turn my stomach with their allegiance to the Republic of Ireland in preference to the nation of their birth.[57]

In a more cryptic but similar fashion to this polemic, during 2006 Celtic and its supporters were taken to task over their lack of perceived affinity for the Scotland international side. One sports columnist on Radio Clyde's Superscoreboard stated:

> I think we should all be proud to be Scotland fans and we should all be hoping that the nation should get back to major finals. . . I'm a passionate Scotland supporter and I would like to see other people have that same passion for the Scotland team.[58]

One of Scottish football's most well-known media commentators, who hosts a BBC radio phone in, appears on Scottish Television's football programmes and writes several football

55 Follow Follow, Glasgow Rangers supporter website fanzine, http://www.followfollow.com/ 26/4/05

56 A Smith, Scotland on Sunday, 2/5/04, p7.

57 R Travers, Scotland on Sunday, 9/11/97,13.

58 9/5/06.

columns, also contributed to the debate surrounding the player. This *Daily Record* sports writer frequently conveys negativity towards the Irish diaspora in Scotland expressing Irishness within football culture as well as other related matters. The tone of this narrative is consistent with many others throughout the Scottish football media and beyond. Its hostile and disapproving tone states that expressions of Irishness in football in Scotland are wrong. In one column, this commentator attempted to pre-empt accusations of ignorance, prejudice and racism by stating that his hostility was not based on 'an anti-Irish agenda', only that he was a proud Scot who made:

> No apologies for that and this fixation with Ireland which so many Scots have makes my blood boil.[59]

In a further dimension of this dominant popular discourse, those who publicly supported McGeady's choice were also criticised. Celtic footballer, Neil Lennon, who had defended McGeady's choice in international football was criticised by *The People* columnist who stated:

> Lennon's reasoning – if such it was – was that McGeady will incite the wrath of Scottish football fans because the Glasgow youngster has snubbed the land of his birth to play instead for the Republic of Ireland, for whom he qualifies as his dad is Oirish.[60]

The use of the word 'Oirish' by this columnist is particularly revealing and may be considered racist, the term used frequently by people being derogatory towards Irishness, especially in hostile football websites and fanzines and other outlets. As with a number of other sports columnists this particular writer also expressed concern over the possibility of Jim O'Brien, another young third generation Irish Celtic footballer, playing for Ireland in international soccer and accused Ireland of being a 'foreign power'. In an article indicatively titled, 'Why O Bro do people suffer a national id crisis', the writer criticised both O'Brien and McGeady. The columnist opined that:

> What is puzzling is the current trend of some Scots, born and bred here, who want to pledge their allegiance to a foreign power.[61]

These articles reflect a dominant narrative that is hostile, demeaning, prejudiced and accusatory towards Irishness in Scotland – and indeed, Irishness per se – within Scottish football

59 J Traynor, The Daily Record, 2/5/05, p24.

60 D Leggat, The People, 26/12/04, p10.

61 D Leggat, The People, 8/5/05, p17. Leggat has written numerous similar items including a denunciation in 2005 on SPL sponsor Irish company Setanta Sports (The People, 9/10/05, p15) using descriptions like 'the Irish TV company', 'same tricks', sitting in their boardroom in the Irish Republic', 'Irish TV paymasters', 'murkier agenda', 'the same Irishmen', 'Setanta's Blarney Bhoys', 'Who are their SPL scared of. Their Setanta Paymasters in Ireland? Celtic?' 'Setanta, an Irish organisation'.

culture and society. Prior to the emergence of McGeady at Celtic in an article describing Celtic's supporters, a former 'Young Scottish Journalist of the Year', criticised them for seeing:

> No inconsistency in packing their ground to wave the flag of another country. They flap the Irish tricolour and sing sad Irish songs and roar of the Irish struggle. There's a country called Ireland for goodness sake, why don't they go and live there?[62]

Indicatively, given the widespread commentary regarding McGeady's Irishness, the booing and verbal abuse of the player has been generally ignored by the media when reporting Celtic games, despite this (to a greater or lesser degree) taking place at almost every match McGeady has played for Celtic in Scotland – even against lowly opponents Clyde in a Scottish Cup tie in February 2005.[63]

This silence has also extended to a prominent sports writer on Scotland's biggest selling broadsheet, the *Herald*: a columnist who frequently addresses controversial subjects in Scottish football, including sectarianism and racism. In terms of the issues surrounding McGeady, strikingly, this journalist remarked only briefly that:

> McGeady is a single minded young man, as made evident in his bold and controversial decision to play for Ireland instead of Scotland.[64]

Revealingly, at a lecture in 2005 this journalist stated that with regards Celtic and its fanbase, he found the 'Irish-Catholic thing too difficult to address' though ironically this did not preclude him having a hostile attitude towards the 'Irish-Catholic thing' when he stated that this:

> over-egging of we're Irish and, these third and fourth generations . . . I can't help feeling uncomfortable with this – this over-emphasis on Irishness.[65]

On reviewing a book by Celtic supporters, some of whom purposely addressed this subject, the journalist declared that the book contained too many examples of 'drooling, dripping Irishness'. He believed that Celtic fans expressing these significant aspects of their history, experience, culture and identity was 'upsetting' because in the book,

> I find people who were born in Scotland, who live in Glasgow, and

62 J MacLeod, The Herald, 18/2/02. p12.

63 The Herald, 27/2/05, Sports, p1.

64 G Spiers, Newman Lecture, University of Glasgow, 17/3/05.

65 G Spiers, The Herald, Arts, Books and Cinema, 1/5/06, p6.

who support the world-famous Glasgow Celtic, yet for whom being Scottish is just about the last thing they desire.[66]

The journalist later admitted to reading only three of twenty-one chapters, approximately 10% of the book. Of the chapters missed he had ignored the first third of the book written by the editor which contextualised the work of the Celtic supporting contributors who were Catholic, Protestant, non-believers, as well as from North America, Germany, Ireland and Scotland. In his review, this leading sports journalist demonstrated a lack of knowledge about, and acquaintance with, immigrant life in Scotland as well as ethnicity, Irishness, community and cultural identities. He reproduced a standard interpretation of seeing Irishness as the opposite of, or, as being opposed to Scottishness, – but not as a legitimate identity in its own right.

Such views raise questions regarding the roots, origins and nature of prejudicial perspectives – especially those passed as objective and neutral commentary but which manifest themselves as racist and sectarian views and opinions. They also invite an important question regarding a similar book that might purport, through the window of sporting activity and culture, to explore the offspring of Asians in Scotland, Scots in Canada or Turks in Germany. Would those books have been criticised for 'drooling' with Asianness, Afro-Caribbeaness, Scottishness or Turkishness? Or would those descriptions have invited accusations of 'racism'?

Problems and hostility arising from Irish differentiation in Scotland reflect an inability to use reflective, accommodating and positive language in describing the Irishness of the Irish diaspora in Scotland. Reflecting aspects of the hostility and confusion over how to describe a Scots-born Irishman, or even criticise the abuse he attracted, an *Express* sports writer called McGeady an 'Irish kid',[67] while a *Herald* sports columnist called him a 'Scot'.[68] A *Sunday Herald* writer referred to McGeady as being 'as Scottish as the rest, even if he seems to think otherwise', while a *Sun* columnist stated that McGeady was '100 per cent Scottish. . . but the bad news is that he is just about to turn Irish'.[69] In the latter descriptions identity is imposed and constructed through discourse upon someone who is not what these writers negatively, aggressively and thoughtlessly assert. McGeady's assumed, experienced and chosen Irish identity is ignored and little or no

66 G Spiers, The Herald, Sport, 11/12/04, p2.

67 I MacFarlane, The Scottish Daily Express, 8/12/04, p85.

68 D Broadfoot, The Herald, Sport, 2/8/04, p2. .

69 M Grant, The Sunday Herald, Sport, 9/1/05, p2 & The Sun (Scottish edition), R Grieve, 21/9/02, p70.

reference is made (apart from negatively in the wider discourses) to how he actually sees himself and how he values and imagines his country of origin.

Nevertheless, despite this hostility towards diasporic Irishness, the print media in Scotland is not unfamiliar with the concept of having a national or cultural identity reflecting family and community origins rather than those of the country of birth. This partly indicates that it is 'Irishness in Scotland' that invites particular opprobrium. In 2005, the *Herald* described a person as a 'Nigerian, born in London'.[70] A *Herald* writer described US born actor and singer Frank Sinatra as a 'skinny little Italian boy' in his younger days[71] and announced that Coatbridge born and bred Ayesha Hazarika, 'a second generation Indian comedian', had become young achiever of the year at the Asian Women of Achievement Awards in London.[72] The same newspaper described boxer Michael Gomez as a Dublin-born Englishman[73] and London-born singer Rod Stewart as a 'veteran Scottish rocker'.[74] The *Herald* also spoke of Eric Liddell (Chariots of Fire) as 'Scotland's best known athlete' and as having 'always remained in his nation's heart' when referring to his place in the Scottish Sports Hall of Fame. Scotsman Liddell was of course born in Northern China of Scottish parents.[75]

Scottish tabloids have also been able to extend themselves conceptually in relation to questions of national and cultural identity. The *Daily Record's* sister paper, the *Sunday Mail* described former Celtic footballer Mike Galloway as an 'English-born Scot'[76] while throughout the 1970s and 1980s, Scottish international footballers Richard Gough (born in Sweden and brought up in South Africa from mixed nationality parentage) and Stuart McCall, Andy Goram and Bruce Rioch, were almost always individually or collectively referred to as Scots despite all being born in England or elsewhere. Likewise, the same applied to the language used to describe John Beattie of British and Irish Lions rugby fame in the same period, though Beattie was born in Asia and spent the first twelve years of his childhood in Borneo before returning to Scotland with his family.[77]

Scottish sports columnists and reporters have also been required to produce commentary on players in comparable circumstances to McGeady. This has included other footballers

70 The Herald, 12/7/05, p1.

71 5/8/05, p25.

72 The Herald, 27/5/05, p19.

73 The Herald, 3/1/05, p32.

74 The Herald, 2/5/05, p1.

75 The Herald Sport, 27/8/05, p10.

76 Sunday Mail, 28/11/99, p34.

77 See R Boyle, P Lynch, 1998, p108.

eligible to play for Scotland but who choose to play for another country. The two most high profile cases in Scotland in season 2004/05, thus corresponding to the period when McGeady was widely abused, were those of English based footballer Nigel Quashie and former Livingston player Burton O'Brien.

INTERNATIONAL SOCCER ALLEGIANCES: PERSPECTIVES

Quashie was born in England and has a maternal Scots-born grandfather. He is of mixed descent with English, Scottish and Afro-Caribbean constituting his national and cultural background. Although Quashie had played several times for the English junior and 'B' teams, he was invited to play for Scotland in 2004 on the basis of his Scots-born grandfather. The then Scotland manager Bertie Vogts commented that Quashie 'feels Scottish'.[78] This statement was unquestioningly reported in the *Herald*. The *Express*, and several other newspapers, reported that Quashie was extremely proud of his Scots-born grandfather. Quashie's grandfather was born in Glasgow, and the player said he was 'privileged' to play for the team. He continued this would fulfill:

> his grandfather's dying wish. . . My late grandfather Andrew McFarlane. . . was a full-blown Scot and a Rangers fanatic. Although he lived in London for a long time he never lost his Scottish accent. He has passed away now, but I am very proud to be given the opportunity to represent my country through my mother's side. When I was growing up I was always aware I could play for Scotland and I am chuffed to bits now it is finally happening. It will be a great honour.[79]

Burton O'Brien was born in South Africa. He moved to Scotland aged four after his family decided to relocate, his parents having lived and worked there for the previous six years. O'Brien played for Scotland at junior level but subsequently let it be known that he wished to play for South Africa. This attitude has seemingly developed in response to his perception of a lack of opportunity to play for Scotland. In 2003, O'Brien was reported as saying that with regards Scotland:

> I got called in at the last minute, which was a bit of a surprise, but I was really happy to be involved. Even though I never got on it was good to know I'm in the plans. . . It's really good for your

78 The Herald, 21/4/04, p34.

79 21/4/04, p78.

confidence. Hopefully I can get a run in the team and try to force my way back into the Scotland set-up again. . . [80]

However, as O'Brien failed to be further rewarded with an international honour for Scotland and as South Africa pursued him for their team, he looked to the country of his birth to play international football and possible World Cup competition. The *Sun* newspaper subsequently reported:

> Burton O'Brien is set to turn his back on Scotland and accept a shock call-up for South Africa's World Cup squad. [81]

The *Sunday Mail* then reported that O'Brien had not been called up to either the 'Future Scotland' squad or the full international team and the player had said that: 'as it stands I still intend to play for South Africa'. [82]

The *Sunday Herald* believed that despite the wrangling taking place over the player's international future, which was uncertain due to South Africa not following procedure, 'The player refuses to talk about the issue in detail, other than to say he regards himself as South African and not Scottish'. [83] At the same time, The *Daily Record* carried a report of one of O'Brien's team mates saying that if South Africa failed in its bid to have O'Brien play, then:

> South Africa's loss would-be Scotland's gain. . . I would love to see him turn out for Scotland. . . I think it is sad to see players go and play for other nations instead of their home country. . . Burton has taken a real ribbing about in the Livi dressing room but we have to respect his decision.

The *Record* further reported:

> Scotland manager Walter Smith confirmed last week that the door remained open for the 23-year-old to turn out for the Scottish national side. However, it seems O'Brien has set his heart on playing for South Africa. Livi manager Richard Gough, who faced a similar tug of war between the same two countries, believes O'Brien has all the credentials to be a top-class international player. Gough said. . . I want the lad to play for Scotland and I spoke to him about that when I first came. [84]

By July 2005, the *Sunday Herald* reported that O'Brien had said:

> I would be delighted to play for Scotland. I was very pleased with what the Scotland manager Walter Smith said about me, that the

80 Daily Record, 1/11/03, p46.

81 The Sun (Scottish edition) 11/6/04, p78.

82 Sunday Mail, 12/6/05.

83 Sunday Herald, Sport, 15/5/05.

84 Daily Record, 2/5/05.

door would remain open if things didn't work out with South Africa.[85]

In light of the reporting around the cases of Quashie and O'Brien the hostility and maltreatment that McGeady has faced can be seen and understood in a context that would not be relevant if he had chosen to play for Norway, Japan or Australia: that is, if his family background and origins were Norwegian, Japanese or Australian. The media and supporter commentary that frequently and obsessively assails Celtic and its fans' Irishness, outside and beyond of the McGeady context, reflects that it is Irishness which is viewed negatively in Scotland.[86] Indeed, it is only in its wider social, cultural, religious and political contexts that McGeady's case can be understood.

'STICKS AND STONES MAY BREAK MY BONES'

While the cases of McGeady, Quashie and O'Brien are each in their own way distinctive, they are similarly rooted in issues involving birthplace, family ties, identity and choice in international football. What is conspicuous about all three cases is how the Scottish sports media has dealt with Quashie and O'Brien compared to McGeady, even allowing for McGeady's promising stature within the Scottish game and the role of his club as one of the two biggest names in Scottish football. In addition, the public debates that have followed newspaper reports on football websites, radio phone-ins and spectator reactions at Scottish football stadia reinforce the social, cultural and political perceptions and meanings attached to Irishness in a Scottish context. The widespread opprobrium that has ensued in the wake of McGeady's decision is significant because it partly reveals how embedded and tolerated this is within Scottish football and, to a degree, wider Scottish society. After all, there has been no notable or articulate reaction (except by Celtic supporters') in support of McGeady – including even from McGeady himself. Likewise, there has been little demonstrated by way of an understanding or acceptance of McGeady's desire to play for 'his country'.

Attitudes towards McGeady, as well as Celtic and its fanbase, is specific in that these can only be understood in their historical and cultural contexts which offer meaning to contemporary

85 Sunday Herald, Sport, 24/7/05.

86 See Celtic Minded, 2004.

identities, attitudes, affinities and prejudices. This is of course, partly what the Scottish Executive website maintains in its anti-racist educational role in reflecting on the development and evolution of white on non-white racism in Scottish society. However, no such context is utilised to explain anti-Irish hostility in Scotland, the longest established of Scotland's racisms. Indeed, it is clear that such racism is barely mentioned, if at all. Key to understanding this omission is the fact that the Irish diaspora does not experience any substantial or positive public recognition in Scottish society. The case of Aiden McGeady is but one example of this.

Importantly for anti-racism, this omission also applies to the Scottish Executive's own 'One Scotland Many Cultures' campaign. As previously discussed in this chapter, the anti-racist website associated with the campaign includes little or no recognition of the Irish diaspora as the longest established, numerically most significant, ethnic group in the country. In addition, and more significantly in terms of popular football and newspaper reading cultures, media commentary surrounding McGeady (and in relation to other similar examples noted elsewhere) constructs a prism through which Irishness in Scotland is viewed as a disloyal, malevolent, irrational and divisive presence. Paradoxically, at the same time the Irishness of those born in Scotland is seen as not real or genuine. This prism dominates in Scotland when Irishness is publicly addressed. In the eyes of some of the newspapers quoted, the Irish in Scotland should 'do us all a favour and relocate to Dublin', 'there's a country called Ireland for goodness sake, why don't they go and live there'? and, 'it's time all Scottish Celtic fans got over their obsession with Ireland'. Such sentiments are mirrored by Aberdeen fans who taunt Celtic supporters with the cry of 'you're in the wrong country'. Several choices seem to dominate for those in Scotland who esteem their Irish origins, history, community, symbols and identity: return to the land they have a strong affinity for; privatise their Irishness to such an extent that they do publicly display it, or, be socially reconstructed as Scottish and become more acceptable to the wider Scottish society. This is important to understanding past and present Irish identities in Scotland while such hostility towards Irishness also links to Hickman's thesis on the 'denationalising' of Irish people and their offspring in Britain. [87]

87 Hickman 1995.

Some people in Scotland believe that the worst days of anti-Catholic and anti-Irish racism, sectarianism and prejudice are much diminished.[88] Certainly, the period described by Professor Stewart Brown, from around the time of the Education Act (Scotland) 1918 until the outbreak of the Second World War, when there was an 'official' Presbyterian campaign against the Irish Catholic community in Scotland, has not been repeated in the past sixty years and it is highly unlikely that such campaigns would be popular in modern Scotland. That particular campaign was both institutional and popular, and is viewed by Brown as an attempt at:

> marginalising, and even eliminating an ethnic minority whose presence was regarded as an evil, polluting the purity of Scottish race and culture.[89]

However, as Finn argues elsewhere, such obvious manifest-ations of anti-Catholicism and anti-Irishness can also be re-cycled and manifest in less obvious ways in the present. Finn believes that one of the ways that this becomes manifest in Scotland is in the football environment.[90] The case of Aiden McGeady demonstrates that despite anti-racist campaigns such as that on the part of the Executive, anti-Irish racism persists. Likewise, a review of McGeady's experience reveals that this is popular, widespread and embedded to the extent that it forms a hegemonic, though often disguised and unrecognised aspect of culture and identity in Scottish society. This dominance and its incipient nature are referred to by Huckin who notes:

> Much public discourse is ideologically shaped, drawing on well-established social orientations, attitudes, values and other group beliefs.[91]

McGeady's case is a metaphor for Irishness in Scotland. His experience and the absence of public expressions in defence of his Irishness aligned with his maltreatment within Scottish football circles and the media more generally, reflects this. Nonetheless, despite a denial of Irishness within Scotland, research demonstrates that there are many second, third and fourth generation Irish in Scotland whose cultural and/or national identities are characterised to a greater or lesser extent by Irishness. This includes those who see themselves as Irish rather than Scottish or at least view their Irishness as primary or important. Like McGeady, the evidence also demonstrates that many of these people also suffer the indignities

88 For example see The Herald 20/3/2000 for quote by Catholic Church spokesperson, Monsignor Tom Connelly

89 Brown 1991.

90 Finn 1991 & 1991.

91 Huckin 2002.

and pressures that he has attracted, though these are rarely, if ever, made public.

This experience largely constitutes an internal narrative within the Irish descended community in Scotland. For many, being Irish or viewing Irishness as a primary identity means attracting a range of negative comments and experiences. However, a collective silence in Scottish society surrounding this negativity means that they rarely find public expression or are ridiculed when they surface. In addition, the evidence also demonstrates the place of Celtic Football Club in the formation and expression of Irish ethnic identity in Scotland, and Celtic's position as a public and popular face of Irishness in Scottish society means the club is also confronted by similar antagonisms. Like McGeady, the Irishness and Catholicity of Celtic Football Club and its support have been largely rejected within Scotland and both have been racialised and sectarianised in a derogatory fashion. This problematisation of Irishness and other distinctive features of Irish Catholic immigrants and their offspring in Scottish society can be viewed as a legacy of the problematisation of the Irish and the Catholic faith that has taken place over centuries in the context of Britain's association with colonial Ireland and Irish migration to Britain. Such a legacy is not unusual in post-colonial relationships.

A commentator in a British-based Irish community newspaper had a different perspective on McGeady from that which characterised and dominated the Scottish press. Writing in the *Irish Post* and being critical of how Scottish sports writers addressed, created or reflected the 'McGeady controversy', Birmingham born Irishman Joe Horgan wrote:

> So Aiden McGeady has to be Scottish, feel Scottish and represent Scotland just because he was born there. There is to be no account of his formative years, his own society within Scotland.

More incisively, Horgan notes:

> Though born in Britain, it cannot be assumed that individuals are having the same relationship with their place of birth as those growing up in a British family next door. . . They have been raised in an Irish family and though they stay by and large in Britain and have British accents they are Irish. That is how they see themselves. Their parents or grandparents, the music, the long summer holidays in Ireland, their names and their religion all

combine to create an identity for them that is inherently Irish. That is the nature of identity too.

Finally, the writer makes an assessment concerning McGeady's experience:

> . . . because bigotry deals in simplistic stereotypes and identity is superbly complex, an expression of identity is so often met with derision or objection.[92]

Such perception, understanding and reasoning seem beyond most of those Scottish media commentators for whom McGeady appears to personify and represent a green tinted Beelzebub.

RACISM AND IRISHNESS IN SCOTLAND

Racism can only be understood in relation to histories and cultures of imperialism and colonisation. Exploration of hostility towards Irishness and reflection on Scotland's past in relation to the British Empire evokes recollection of, until recently, widely accepted racist understandings and representations of Irishness in Britain. Such an exploration means that we re-expose anti-Irishness in Scotland to questions of context and meaning rather than undermining and ignoring this by simply seeing sectarianism as a problem 'between' two different religious traditions – or, as a problem caused by one particular strand of the Christian faith. This also means re-exposing Scotland's past as the junior but vital partner in the exploitation that parallels the building and sustaining of Empire with the reminder that colonisation inherently equates with the inferior-isation and domination of indigenous peoples and forcing them to change their ways, cultures and identities.

Further, using this approach also means that we can see more clearly that the selective use of the history of colonisation to explain some aspects of racism and not others can be seen as conceptually important in constructing knowledge of racism in modern Scotland. Current approaches to education and knowledge provision, for example that of the Scottish Executive's 'One Scotland Many Cultures' campaign, but particularly the knowledge imparted through the educational sectors and by the media, serve to deny the racism experienced by the offspring of the Irish in Scotland. They also function to shift that experience into a bland sectarian terminology used to describe any cleavage, indeed difference that

92 Irish Post, 21/5/05, p20.

appears to exist or is represented as existing between Protestants and Catholics.

To change this one must transform the language, questions, tools of analysis and sources of reference in the quest to understand racism and sectarianism. This might also lead to a genuine and serious addressing of Scotland's 'sectarian' problem, as well as a rejection of the assimilationist strategy that dominates amongst information providers, academics, educationalists and those empowered through their positions and roles in the media.

Focus on Aiden McGeady brings to light the revealing but unrecognised practice of people within the Irish Catholic descended community who, over several generations, have determined that to be accepted within Scottish society, they must forfeit – consciously or unconsciously by a process of learning or rejection – much of their Irish and Catholic distinctiveness and, adopt more visibly Scottish choices, including those pertaining to personal, community, cultural and national identities. Internally as well as externally this concerns denial or marginalisation of their actual ethnic identity as well as its common or dominant concomitant cultural and attitudinal attributes. Some change in national and cultural identities invariably takes place (all identities remain in flux and are never absolutes), where they are located outside and outwith their more 'natural' (eg, in this case the island of Ireland) cultural, historical habitat and geographical location, though this is not contingent on time as a factor nor does it equate with a decrease in 'native' identity. Nevertheless, this does not detract from the arguments here or indeed of Phinney *et al*, that in:

> . . . the face of real or perceived hostility toward immigrants or toward particular groups, some immigrants may downplay or reject their own ethnic identity; others may assert their pride in their cultural group and emphasise solidarity as a way of dealing with negative attitudes.[93]

Phinney *et al's* comment is relevant to the Celtic-Irish-Catholic supporter experience over the past century in Scotland while this commentary also becomes more revealing when partly reflected upon by Burdsey who has looked at British born Asians who achieve success in English football. Burdsey's work shows that those who have either consciously or unconsciously under-emphasised their Asianness and in some cases, 'sought to decrease the degree to

93 Phiney, Horenczyk, Liebkind & Vedder 2001.

which their cultural difference is apparent', are the most successful of young aspirant British born Asian footballers.[94] This means that increasingly, practices and attitudes more acceptable to the mainstream are adopted as cultural capital or are imposed upon Asianness without comment, reply or resistance. Burdsey also implies that regardless of how ethnic the privatised family and social life are, the required cultural passport can only be acquired or achieved if this compliance is adhered to. This point is emphasised through the stress on the 'Britishness' of at least three highly successful athletes in Britain since the 1990s, boxer Frank Bruno, footballer Ian Wright and sprinter Linford Christie. In all three cases the public image and persona attached to these athletes was 'British' in the extreme with little personal or public recognition of their African roots, heritage or culture.

> All shared a common tendency to underplay the degree to which their ethnicities were prominent within the sporting arena, together with an inclination to openly embrace elements of nationalist sentiment, such as the St George or Union flags, when celebrating sporting victories.[95]

Acceptance was thus easier and facilitated by such public gestures and being seen as being less black, Afro-Caribbean, Asian, etc. The hybrid nature of the 'Black British' identities that these particular athletes adopted were sufficient to offset any significant damage to their image as successful sports people. One can only wonder at the media and public treatment and perceptions of a similarly successful – never mind unsuccessful – athlete who would have stressed that despite being born in Britain, their primary identity was not British but Nigerian, Jamaican or African?

Burdsey also talks of Sikh Asian footballers who have been exempted from wearing a turban or have not attended a Sikh temple for many years, thus acquiring the cultural capital (perceived as more Britishness and less Asianness) to become professional footballers. As this author intimates, it may also be indicative that few successful Black or Asian athletes are ever seen to be at the forefront of anti-racist work, though some might be drawn to this as a result of their non-white skin and high public profile. In addition, we cannot take it for granted that because a person has a non-white skin that they do or are willing to understand and articulate in a meaningful way the racism they experience.

94 Burdsey 2004.
95 Ibid

The media portrayal of McGeady as having to choose 'between' Scotland or Ireland is a public manifestation of an internal community experience that has often faced the Irish diaspora in Scotland, though few of these experiences can be witnessed beyond that community or make headlines the way McGeady's has. In sub-text, McGeady's story encapsulates important aspects of the Irish Catholic diasporic experience in Scotland. As a Catholic, supporting and now playing for the Irish descended Catholic community's favoured football club (Celtic), and, choosing to represent Ireland in international football, he has done what few others in his community have been able to. In being a successful footballer, he has publicly announced his cultural allegiance, his ethnicity and that his affinities in sport and beyond lie with his country of familial origin rather than the country of his and his parents birth. McGeady's chronicle also demonstrates the 'great narrative of dispossession and belonging' as referred to by former Irish President Mary Robinson.[96]

Likewise, reflection on his experience echoes the maturity of developing academic notions regarding identity, ethnicity and diaspora, and shows that Ireland and Irishness are not bounded by an island of Ireland context: indeed, in its diasporic context, Irishness is re-formulated and re-contextualised. In a related sense Irishness in Scotland, as with elsewhere in the diaspora, is marked by hybridity and syncretism. In this way people with origins in Ireland can become Boston Irish, Birmingham Irish, London Irish as well as Glasgow Irish or Coatbridge Irish. Irish descended people who are able to make such choices and understand, recognise and withstand the numerous pressures to conform to the dominant identities, are participating in and 'doing' Irish culture and identity. In doing it, they become 'it' and therefore, are 'it'. In doing, such people expand notions of cultural belonging marked by 'multiplicity, historicity and dynamism' and show how cultural, ethnic and national identities are not categorically 'fixed'.[97] McGeady is an example of those of the Irish diaspora in Scotland, many connected through fandom to Celtic Football Club, who:

> identify themselves as Irish with a strong sense of tradition about who they are and where they are coming from.[98]

96 Address by Uachtarán na hÉireann Mary Robinson to Joint Sitting of the Houses of the Oireachtas, 2/2/1995.

97 Mac an Ghaill & Haywood 2003.

98 Ibid.

ACQUIRING UNDERSTANDING:
LOOKING OUT AND SEEING MORE

Media reports on football cannot be relied upon to offer informed social and cultural commentary. However, the media is an important reflection of the society with which it originates. Therefore, it would be a mis-reading as well as mis-leading to simply take football reporting in Scotland (or elsewhere) merely as 'football reporting'. Media references to football reveal much about a society in terms of culture, attitudes and identities.

> Like all individuals, players and fans are also social and political actors born into a particular historical epoch and political community.[99]

We can of course add club owners, custodians, employees, as well as the media and others, to this.

Textual detail of football coverage alone is not enough to offer insight and understanding of what is often occurring in terms of supporters, players, match officials, in relation to the media, and for the purposes of this work, particularly in terms of the representations that dominate with reference to Irishness and sectarianism. For an understanding that is less prone to bias and prejudice, like any other subject matter, it is essential to have knowledge of context and history and an awareness of the origins of sources of information before a more accurate critical evaluation can develop. In particular, football fandom can be a complex matter, but for a number of clubs with social, cultural, religious and political attributes, it is about more than just football. Indeed, for their respective supporters, that is what offers football clubs like Barcelona, Ajax and Sydney United, in particular amongst many others, meaningfulness. Not only at club level, but in international football, matches such as those between Iran and the USA, Holland and Germany and England and Scotland, demonstrate how football can become representative and symbolic of social, cultural, religious and political attributes. For matches between these countries, history and even past wars offer an intensity that rises above the mere act of kicking a ball. Football is more than a straightforward field sport and as such, can offer an important window into an understanding of the rest of society.

99 Bar-On 1997.

For the sports print media in Scotland as well as many others connected to Scottish football and society, McGeady stands out and encapsulates much of the popular imagery of a third generation west of Scotland 'Tim' or 'Fenian'. He is seen to be a traitor or labelled sectarian because of the decision he made, he does not fit in, he is not prepared to let go of his past, he remains Irish and he refuses to become a Scot, and, he demonstrates this (and he does not pass the test and acquire the requisite credentials) in one of the most significant ways possible, by representing in sport what those hostile to him consider to be 'his country'.[100] Despite this perception, as far as McGeady and those like him are concerned (indeed as far as football's governing bodies, UEFA and FIFA are also concerned), he is in fact doing precisely that: he is representing 'his' country.

McGeady's experience highlights the historical and contemporary position of many second, third and fourth generation Irish in Scotland who have implicitly understood – consciously and unconsciously – the consequences of remaining 'Irish' in the eyes of belligerent and confrontational elements in Scotland. This has often meant that for those of Irish descent who wish to progress and have as few social and economic barriers placed in their way as possible, socialisation 'out' of Irishness and 'into' Scottishness comes around even before they are born or, in early childhood. Where a decision is subconsciously or consciously made, denial, shame, confusion, contestation and deception can assist the formation and characterisation of subsequent identities – Irish, Scottish and otherwise. For Aiden McGeady, life might have been easier if he had chosen to be Scottish as opposed to being 'Irish in Scotland'. If that choice had been made, he may well have abjured himself of his heritage, history and identity and subverted these to a new and more acceptable course in the narrative that is identity. Such a choice would have been shaped by the experiences and accounts of other members of the Irish descended in Scotland, including the socialisation processes that eventually contribute to and constitute what and who we all are and become as well as a response of fear and hesitation regarding public reaction to the choice to be Irish in Scotland. For McGeady, his Irish background, heritage, culture, community and identity all assisted him make a choice which reflects who and what he perceives himself to be: a member of the Irish diaspora in Scotland and a member of the

100 Tim is the diminutive of Timothy, a considered Irish Catholic forename. It can be used positively as a label or statement of address by those within the group of Irish Catholic descent in Scotland but used as a negative term and label by those outside of the group. In the north of Ireland this is often used as 'Taig' which is similar to the Irish language version of Timothy which is Tadhg. Taig is usually a derogatory term aimed towards Irish Catholics. The 'Fenians' (The Irish Republican Brotherhood or the Fenian Brotherhood) was the name given to tens of thousands of Irish in the nineteenth century who engaged in revolutionary military struggle against Britain. As well as in Ireland, many thousands of Fenians existed amongst the Irish communities of Britain and the North America. These included Michael Davitt, one of Celtic's principal patrons. Today in west-central Scotland and Northern Ireland it is often used derogatorily – though not by those who claim the label with pride – to describe Roman Catholics of Irish descent.

Irish nation as imagined within and beyond the shores of the island of Ireland.

Many people do not recognise, understand nor acknowledge the anti-Irish and anti-Catholic experiences of the Irish Catholic-descended in Scotland. This is demonstrated clearly in numerous academic works, the 'One Scotland Many Cultures' website and the popular media. Of course, the Irish descended in Scotland are not the only minority grouping to have such experiences and reflection on the experiences of other minority groups can assist us better understand racism in Britain and beyond. Moran reflects on the perceived widespread racism against non-whites that exists in English soccer and English society generally. He believes:

> . . . many white people involved in the English game have no conception about racism or what may constitute racist remarks. [101]

He particularly notes how so called 'banter' and 'jokes' are often used but which only disguise the real racism being perpetuated. It may be indicative of a similar problem in Scotland that 'sectarianism' in society, generally perceived as division 'between' Protestants and Catholics, was only recognised as a significant social issue from around the early 1970s. Few references to 'sectarianism' can be found within the Scottish media before this time — especially outside of a Rangers' — Celtic or football context. Sectarianism's gradual recognition and addressing is partly indicated by the increasing number of questions asked of Glasgow Rangers from the early 1970s for its refusal to sign or employ Catholics. Up until this time there was virtually no reference to this policy in political circles or in the media. Indeed, until the 1960s and 1970s it is recognised that many other institutions in Scotland participated and colluded in the practice of anti-Catholic discrimination in the workplace (including a number of other football clubs) such was the embedded nature of this custom. The entrenched character of this prejudice was so significant that few people, including Catholics who were accustomed to this and accepted it as a cultural fact of life, publicly challenged it. [102]

To a degree the 'Scottish and Protestant' challenge to sectarianism partly emerged as a result of the anger and shame brought upon Scotland by rioting and hooligan sections of Glasgow Rangers fans in cities like Barcelona and Birmingham in the 1970s. Some

101 Moran 2000.

102 See Bradley in Devine 1995.

of the social, political and media analysis that arose from these episodes and Rangers signing policy elevated 'sectarianism' as an issue in Scotland. Nonetheless, despite the raising of certain questions, the Scottish media continued to blame both 'sides' of the perceived same coin (as interpreted by commentators in the media). When discussion of Rangers fans and football hooliganism took on a sectarian dimension, the Scottish press frequently balanced discourse of Rangers' 'no Catholics' policy with mention of Celtic's symbols. Comment even extended to criticism of Catholic schools. In the wake of Rangers supporters rioting in Birmingham in 1976, the *Daily Record,* recognised that too strong a criticism might antagonise its mainly Protestant readership, ignored the fact that events had taken place in England, and tempered its editorial criticism of fans by stating that Celtic should be: 'willing to be recognised as a sporting bastion of Catholicism. They must bear a share of the guilt'.[103]

In a similar sense to the way sectarianism had been previously unrecognised and unacknowledged in Scotland, Moran reviews how instances of racism in English football have also been ignored. Moran's example is remarkably similar to the furore surrounding Aiden McGeady and for those in Scotland who esteem their Irishness and express this through football.

> The France '98 [World Cup] tournament was one of the best examples of black communities in England visibly supporting the countries of their heritage. Jamaicans and Nigerians wore their national shirts with pride in many towns and cities up and down the country. During the championships I was having a drink in a pub watching Nigeria on television when I was asked in a somewhat unfriendly tone why I was supporting Nigeria. I was asked where I was born, to which I replied London, and what passport I had (British), and my 'accuser' leaned back in 'triumph' thinking that he had won the argument by 'proving' where my loyalties should really be.[104]

Football captures and reveals a similar set of issues for the Irish diaspora in Scotland. Research demonstrates that the community in Scotland whose ethnic, cultural and national origins are in Ireland, utilise different narratives from their non-Irish or non-Celtic counterparts to reflect their distinctiveness, but also their divergent and unaccounted for experiences in the face of opposition and hostility towards their faith and ethnic origins.[105]

103 Daily Record, editorial, 13/10/76, p. 2

104 Moran 2000.

105 See Irish 2 Project, Celtic Minded (2004) and forthcoming research.

The sports media narratives in Scotland around Celtic's third generation Irishman, Aiden McGeady, is indicative of how Irishness, Catholics and Celtic are widely understood, perceived and represented within Scottish society. Generally, these are 'inferiorised' identities. Specifically, the more Irish, Catholic or the more one is viewed as supporting the football club that culturally and in popular terms encapsulates both these identities, the more one is likely to be confronted by deeply embedded hostility and prejudice. In many ways McGeady publicly encapsulates and embodies these identities and this is demonstrated by not only the attention he attracts, but also, the nature of that attention. McGeady is popularly viewed as not complying with what would have been an easier choice: to be recognised as visibly Scottish rather than Irish. He has chosen to publicly reveal his identity and to make his Irish ethnicity visible in the most public of forums. His actions have also raised questions about how the Irishness of the multi-generational Irish community in Scotland that he has aligned himself with, particularly those who esteem their Irishness, is seen beyond that community. McGeady is seen to represent 'the other' as opposed to the norm, mainstream and acceptable common sense identity of Scottish.[106] McGeady's identity is popularly viewed by those hostile to him as one of defiance and is not only perceived as disloyal, but as an act of betrayal. Further, such manifestations and continuation of Irishness in Scotland is perceived as evidence of the prejudice of the Catholic community of Irish descent he comes from and whose ways and differences are seen as a prime cause of sectarianism. These include 'their' different football club, 'their' different names, 'their' different faith and schools, even sometimes a different moral code or life philosophy arising from these.[107] It is an act that 'keeps these things going' as far as many people in Scotland are concerned.

Ironically, ideologically this thinking links to not only the Scottish Executive website but also to the campaigns of bodies in society that strive to have Scotland perceived as open, plural and multicultural. At one level, this might best be explained through Shaw's contention that such ideological connections and links means referring. . .

> . . . not simply to attitudes but to systems of perceptions that act to conceal inequities, contradictions and antagonisms'.[108]

106 Shaw 2005, pp37-40.

107 Numerous football focus groups and other interviews in Scotland reveal frequent references to these differences when Catholics or sectarianism is a topic of debate. Particular focus is recurrent with regards to the existence of Catholic schools in Scotland. See forthcoming research.

108 Shaw 2005.

Here concealment is key to understanding a number of matters pertaining to identity in Scotland and subsequent social relations, including those of a 'sectarian' nature. Shaw also argues that such ideologies reinforce structured relations of power. This means that a critical analysis of the Scottish sports media can indicate its power to shape and affect individual and community identity, but also in:

> . . . the development of prejudiced attitudes and discriminatory behaviour [and that such] information. . . cannot be assumed to be 'neutral'. Rather information is likely to be imbued with ideological components.[109]

In this sense, the Scottish sports media reproduce and perpetuate these notions and ideological components – which reflect as well as construct – and serve to create and reinforce – rather than challenge – racism, sectarianism, prejudice and discriminatory behaviour and attitudes. This in turn makes such behaviour seem normal, acceptable or even appropriate, because it has 'always been so'. Such embedded thinking and manifestations dominate socially, culturally and politically. Indeed, as far as McGeady is concerned, such abusive behaviour can even be justified and advocated as is evidenced by much of the unchallenged commentary around football in Scotland. In this context, Brubaker discusses the idea of the:

> . . . tacit, taken-for-granted background knowledge, embodied in persons and embedded in institutionalised routines and practices, through which people recognise objects, places, persons, actions or situations as racially, ethnically or nationally marked or meaningful, and are thereby in a position to orient their action meaningfully to such cues, and to invest their own action, in turn, consciously or unconsciously, with interpretable racial, ethnic or national signals or cues.[110]

Elias has studied the connections between identity and national character. In his work on Germans he notes how deeply embodied aspects of German habitus, personality, social structure and conduct emerge out of history and patterns of social development and give rise to ideas of 'I' and 'we' in national or imagined community terms. What becomes 'second nature' is partly accounted for by the term 'habitus'. Likewise, the embedded nature of anti-Irishness in the Scottish print media and beyond suggests that this is a part of the Scottish habitus that has emerged from history, culture and

109 Ibid.

110 Brubaker, 2001.

social development.[111] To make sense of anti-Irishness and anti-Catholicism in Scottish society, to accept this as a norm or as part of a national code of reference, means that deeply embedded meanings and understandings are being evoked and tapped.

Negative references towards Irishness in Scotland would have no meaning if made in China or Mexico. Only in Scotland, or Britain more generally, where such stock knowledge already exists in relation to established dominant perceptions of the Irish, Irishness, Ireland and Catholic migrants and their offspring in Britain, can such references find meaning, through connotations and a significance that emerges from history, culture and social development. In this way this tradition in Scotland results in a habitus code of widespread hostility to Irishness.

A sports field or stadium provides a site of contestation, a space for the social construction, maintenance and expression of identity, a place and environment where teams are imagined as representative of a community, people or nation. It is here that such codes and discursive practices become more sharply defined and explicit. A sporting event can transcend the field of play and generate social, cultural and political meanings far beyond the immediate event and world of sport generally. In Scotland, as in many other countries, football – and its resultant discourses – has the capacity to reveal feelings, emotions, behaviours, attitudes and identities in a way that many other locations or situations either do not, or, which serve to disguise such human characteristics.

Racism, sectarianism, prejudice and discriminatory behaviour are themselves socially constructed identities, attitudes and behaviours. As they mature, people become aware and conscious that they are white or black, but importantly, the relevance and meaning of skin differentiation requires to be socially constructed in a particular context: that is, it requires to be taught, learned and experienced – consciously or unconsciously. In other words, a body of knowledge requires to exist and to be drawn from in order to construct identity. There was little known racism on the basis of skin colour before the onset of colonialism and consequent slavery of recent past centuries and, Communists and Socialists did not exist to oppose Capitalism until people like Marx and Engels explained, labelled and identified such an 'iniquity'. Further, these

111 See Maguire &
Poulton, 1999.

are human made positions and identities and are therefore social constructions. Likewise, racism, sectarianism, prejudice and discriminatory behaviour against Catholics of Irish descent in Scotland are learned: they are social constructions and identities located within a broader historical, social and cultural context.

For people like Maley, the language of 'sectarianism' utilised in Scotland has only obfuscated the racism the Irish have experienced:

> [The issue] remains above all a cultural and political one. It affects all aspects of national identity. Anti-Irish racism and anti-Catholicism are inseparable in a Scottish context.[112]

In the context of an essentially minority Irishness being omitted or misrepresented this may be considered in a broader context where the dominant narratives and representations pursue cultural homogenisation in Scottish society, driving the seemingly centrifugal tendencies of Scottishness and its primacy at the expense of other cultures and identities whereby Scottishness becomes the 'natural' and 'common-sense' identity. As Lewis states more generally:

> Tension between tolerance of diversity and a desire to instil a disciplining and normalising regime of governance runs through the whole panoply of social policy in the UK.[113]

Maley opines that the Scottish media has persisted in its refusal to stand up to the realities of anti-Irish racism.

> Scotland is a country which does not respect cultural difference. Only the cloistered academics and other privileged professionals, cushioned from the vicissitudes of economic deprivation could fail to see that sectarianism rather than religious bigotry is the product of national and social discrimination.[114]

The discourses around McGeady, Celtic and its supporters' culture and identity, and upon other cultural and ethnic issues that have a Catholic or Irish connotation, reflect that football in Scotland, as with many other countries, is penetrated by cultural and political ideologies. Such media comment also shows how sport is enmeshed in the media's reproduction and transmission of ideological themes and values that are dominant in society.

Lewis speaks of 'a degree of rhetorical commitment to tolerance and respect for diversity', thus implicating Governmental

112 Maley, Glasgow Herald, 26/9/91

113 Lewis 2005.

114 Maley, Glasgow Herald, 26/9/91.

bodies, educational establishments as well as those of the media in their omnipotent roles as information providers in modern societies.[115] As Crabbe asserts, 'football exalts assimilationist sentiment' while the same author also talks of a 'self perpetuating 'feel good' multiculturalism'.[116] Lewis refers to multiculturalism taking place in a postcolonial society. She notes the unequal relations between erstwhile coloniser and colonised and recognises the difficulties that are presented as,

> the children and grandchildren of natives [or coloniser] are speaking and living in [many or most of] the same linguistic and cultural idioms as the children and grandchildren of the once immigrant.[117]

Lewis further acknowledges that it is in the terrain of culture that these 'difficulties' are played out, for example, in terms of national and sporting identities within the sports media. This is an apposite observation in relation to the Irishness of those descended from Irish immigrants in Scotland.

Although historical accounts of the Irish in Britain show them as a racialised minority, and as an inferior people as defined by the British, a shift in the racialised discourses meant that in late twentieth century Britain, a paradigm emerged that constructed 'racism' as an issue defined by colour – black or white – as opposed to a social, political, religious or ethnic 'other'. Mac an Ghaill suggests that this paradigm is an importation of an American model of thinking and ignores the recent past as well even as the racialisation of other white groups such as the Jews in European history. This common-sense dominant understanding of racism in Britain has meant that other racisms are unacknowledged, unrecognised or forgotten, due often to prevalent political circumstances (eg, for Irishness, circumstances such as the Northern Ireland 'Troubles'). Consequently, such limited representations of racism means anti-racism is also restricted as the black-white dichotomy becomes prevalent and privileged.[118] In this process, in being almost solely white, the offspring of the Irish Catholic diaspora in Scotland is unmarked by skin colour, is constructed as ethnically invisible and, therefore, racism against them, goes unrecognised and denied.

This denial and lack of recognition is also among the reasons

115 Lewis 2005.

116 Crabbe 2004.

117 Lewis 2005.

118 See Mac an Ghaill 2000.

for the importance of Celtic to the Irish diaspora in Scotland. Since its very foundations, Celtic has been for many Catholics of Irish descent, the primary environment where Irish confidence, celebration and assertion takes place and where Irishness becomes manifest. For those of Irish descent who recognise the club in its historic cultural and national terms, Celtic has remained 'the' primary public focus for Irishness in Scotland.

EDUCATION, KNOWLEDGE, RECOGNITION AND ACKNOWLEDGEMENT

In one sense the Scottish Executive website materials reflects the dominant discourses and ignores the more complex, nuanced and subtle forms, manifestations and expressions of racism in Scotland as well as related issues of power relations and arrangements in society. Refusing or being unable to recognise and confront Scotland's racist and sectarian past is significant and underlies the consequences that reproduce and sustain this hegemony in the present.

The dominant views and ideas of the wider public in relation to Irishness in Scotland are partly reflected in and simultaneously created by the media. The potential educational role of the media is a powerful one. With this in mind, Long and McNamee's assertion seems particularly appropriate:

> The near universal acceptance that racism is wrong somewhat ironically brings its own problems. There is an unwillingness to acknowledge certain practices, within and outside sport, as racist because that might require us to recognise, at least potentially, the racism within ourselves.[119]

Although this comment is a general one without regard to creed, colour or origin, in the context of this work, this idea is particularly relevant in addressing anti-Irishness in a Scottish context. The kinds of anti-Irish racism that occurs and flourishes within the Scottish sports media environment, perpetuated by numerous football writers and by their adherents in the form of letter writers, radio contributors and readers, is both reflective and a determinant of social relations in Scotland. It is almost entirely negative in how it affects, re-produces and represents these problematic social relations, institutions and processes. In short,

119 Long & McNamee 2004.

the production of a lack of knowledge, understanding and awareness regarding Irishness has a pernicious effect upon Scottish life.

Long and McNamee note that 'we all have embedded racial constructions affecting the way we think and behave towards each other'. They also agree that 'all forms of racism relate to two general themes or paradigms: 'inferiorisation and antipathy'. Referring to Blum, both stress attitudes and actions are key, especially those characterised by disrespect, contempt, derision, derogation and demeaning.[120]

For football supporters in Scotland the narratives that surround Aiden McGeady, Celtic and Irishness are situated within an ideology and identities that are deeply embedded in Scottish culture: McGeady provides but one example. The normalised and widely accepted nature of discourses hostile to McGeady is reflected in the fact that so few commentators deviate from the most common and culturally significant notions and images projected. In these dominant discourses the Irish in Scotland experience an identity that is marginalised, abused and ultimately, more often than not, silenced and concealed. Racism in Scotland is shown to go beyond a black-white colour dichotomy: focus on football and the print media demonstrates this.

The continual pressure on those of Irish descent in Scotland to change, to become Scottish, has contributed to a process whereby many Irish become Scots and many others negotiate their Catholic and Irish identities by, 'keeping their heads down'. Conroy suggests that in human relations social progress may indeed be best bought by, 'keeping one's head down'.[121] Horgan posits the enquiry in another way. He asks the question, were the Irish so defeated and crushed that to survive, especially in a hostile social and political environment in Britain, 'they had to, in effect, cease to be'. He suggests further that like native Americans and Australian Aborigines, have the Irish been told to 'stop being who they are or were and become somebody else'.[122]

Assimilationist, marginalising and sectarian accounts directly contribute to the invisibility of the Irish in Scotland. For Hickman, this is also about 'forced inclusion' and the 'myth of homogeneity'.[123] In addition, being frequently confronted with representations (especially in the media) of your community, heritage, origins

120 Ibid.
121 Conroy, 2003.
122 Irish Post, 5/11/03.
123 Hickman 2005.

and identity, that are destructive and filled with ridicule, and, simultaneously making Scottishness appear right, proper and the norm, and thus negatively hegemonic, assists in the creation and sustaining of an Irish identity typified by negative imagery. 'Keeping one's head down' may more often than not lead to assimilation and even invisibility as opposed to integration. This also raises questions regarding aspects of the purpose of anti-racist and anti-sectarian campaigns and whether their quest is partly for integration or assimilation.

Negative labelling, silence and an ideological process of sectarianising Irishness is a manifestation of a contest that has a depressing and diminishing effect on the identities of individuals, families and communities who choose to esteem their Irishness. Contrary to this, the evidence suggests, that as far as migrants and their offspring are concerned, integration, that is, 'simultaneous ethnic retention and adaptation to the new society', is the best model for their well-being while 'marginalisation' is the worst. This might also be viewed as a positive model for social relations in Scotland. [124]

DIASPORA, IDENTITY AND MULTICULTURAL SCOTLAND

Important to understanding the Celtic experience in Scotland, we can also see that the importance of sporting representation and linkage with diaspora is not exceptional to Celtic or those of Irish descent in Scotland and can be observed in other countries and amongst other diasporic communities. This can be illustrated in the case of the many British born Pakistanis for whom cricket provides an ethnic space, a source and a manifestation of their connections and links with the country of their forefathers and families. Cricket is part of popular culture and provides the Pakistani diasporic community with a public arena to display distinctiveness and otherness. Like football and Celtic in Scotland for the Irish diaspora, cricket might also be considered a space for empowerment and public celebration where these may be lacking for many British born Asians in British society.

In April 1992 the Pakistan international cricket team, captained by Imran Khan, won the World Cup Limited Overs Cricket Competition in Sydney. A young Pakistani, born and bred in Britain,

124 Phinney,
Horenczyk,
Liabkind & Vedder
2001.

told his English friends, 'I'm proud to be British but when it comes down to the hard core, I'm really Pakistani'. Another celebrating young man told a *Guardian* reporter, 'if you cut my wrists green blood will come out'. The Pakistani flag is green, the colour of Islam. When young British born Pakistanis go to see the Pakistan national team play cricket in Britain their cry is often, 'Pakistan zindabad, Islam zindabad, Pakistan forever, Islam forever'.[125]

A similar set of social constructions and meanings arises for the Croatian diaspora in Australia in relation to football. Jones and Moore state that for the Croatian community in Australia:

> The soccer ground becomes a focus for a dispersed ethnic community. . . For the normally residentially dispersed supporters, it is the soccer fixture that has become a major rationale for coming together as a group and publicly expressing their shared ethnicity.[126]

The Croatian sports centre based on soccer provides a sense of place where the person belongs 'as an individual and as a member of a community'. The importance of soccer for the community network was highlighted by one member who said:

> In the Croatian community everything is tied together, church, family, social functions, football – whether or not you're interested in football you're interested in Sydney Croatia's result.[127]

For those of the Croatian diaspora in Australia who build much of their social life around soccer and in particular Sydney United-Croatia, this environment provides and sustains a social setting based on kinship, friendship, shared experience and mutual understanding. Within Australian soccer such people exercise their Croatian ethnicity as a central characteristic of the existence and nature of such clubs. In one sense the involvement of Croatians in Australian soccer allows them to enjoy a communal experience, 'a home from home' as one fan put it.[128] As John Bale might say, the Croatian sports centre based on soccer is a much loved space that provides a sense of place where the person belongs 'as an individual and as a member of a community'.[129] This is important given their existence as a diaspora community. This is a primary manifestation of the Croatian diaspora in Australia and is further evidence of the way sport can become an expression and reflection of ethnicity and communal solidarity.

125 Werbner 1996

126 Jones & Moore 1994.

127 Hughson, 1997.

128 Ibid.

129 Ibid.

The silence and invisibility that has been learned by and imposed on the Irish diaspora in Scotland although dominant, is also incomplete and, as many Celtic supporters and individuals like Aiden McGeady repeatedly demonstrate, Irishness is not entirely obscured in Scottish life. Football in Scotland makes the Irish in Scotland publicly manifest and identifiable, to themselves as well as others.

Nevertheless, for Scotland to flourish, to be seen as multi-cultural and to resolve racist or sectarian issues that have long had a detrimental effect on social relations, many in Scotland will be obliged to learn to recognise the distinctiveness and the legitimacy of having identities that are not Scottish or British but which reflect the multicultural imagery that many of the country's public representatives and outlets project. If campaigns such as 'One Scotland Many Cultures' intend integration as opposed to assimilation, then this has to be explored, explained and projected more forcibly if success is to be achieved. Inclusion might be realised when the hegemonic anti-Irish and anti-Catholic attitudes and (other racist) identities within Scottish society are discarded owing to improved education, knowledge and morality. This would also allow for the Irishness of the offspring of Irish immigrants in Scotland (including Celtic and its supporters) to be maintained, celebrated, esteemed and promoted. In this context, these would not be viewed or contrived as being disloyal or 'against' Scottish identity; this would not be seen as a symptom of a community's failure to achieve the required passport of 'Scottishness'; and Irishness might instead be perceived as part of the mosaic of a modern Scotland, where 'Scottishness' prevails and is primary for many if not most people, but where there exists social and cultural space for others who choose not to be Scottish, despite birth or residence there. Positively contributing towards society's well-being and social, cultural and political life need not require adherence to the symbols and discourses of Scottishness – including playing for or supporting the Scottish international football team – for this to be achieved.

Irishness in Scotland is a hybrid identity of Irishness drawn from the island of Ireland as well as from Irish community life in Scotland, with inevitable aspects of Scottishness acquired through this experience. It is not the same as Irishness in Ireland or Irishness in Boston, Sydney or London. Like those versions of Irishness, it is specific, it is Irishness in Scotland developed and constructed via the Irish community experience there. As Edward Said has stated:

> all cultures are involved in one another; none is single and pure, all are hybrid, heterogeneous, extraordinarily differentiated and unmonolithic.[130]

The Irishness of Aiden McGeady, Celtic and its supporters, challenges notions of assimilation that can exist amongst the children, grandchildren and great-grand children of Irish migrants in Scotland. A pre-requisite to understanding racism in Scottish/ British societies is the deconstruction of 'whiteness': a matter omitted on the Scottish Executive information websites and elsewhere. This points to the need for more nuanced understandings of 'white' diasporic identities, as well as Scottishness and Britishness. In addition, crucial to helping 'solve' Scotland's racism problems is a deeper understanding:

> of the ways in which everyday racism is experienced, who perpetuates such racism and the influences this has on how people feel about their identities.[131]

Such improved, tolerant and accepting understandings hold hope for Scottish society as it seeks non-aggressive, non-prejudiced, non-sectarian and non-racist Scottish identities, while accepting the identities of those not of Scottish origins and who do not consider themselves as Scottish but who live in Scotland as a result of historical circumstances and often, contemporary choice.

The *Irish 2 Project* interviewees and others believe that hostility towards Irishness is not confined to the Celtic environment but also extends beyond football. They frequently perceive hostility manifest in the workplace and in everyday social life. In some instances this antagonism can also be evidenced within the diaspora itself. In turn this can be viewed as a reaction towards hostility and antagonism from out-with the community and, as a response to the pressures to assimilatate.[132] This also suggests that there are members of the Irish diasporic community in Scotland who have chosen and learned to adopt other more acceptable identities: identities which are not, or are at least diminished or privitised, Catholic, Irish or Celtic 'minded' ones. Despite the contestation over Irishness and the assimilative and conforming pressures

130 Said 1994, pxxix

131 Hopkins 2004, pp88-103.

132 Hickman 1995

The Coloniser's Breastplate

We must seek to deny them access to knowledge of
their history and culture.

We must create for them an environment where
they can't remember who they are.

We must re-direct their passions and allegiances.

We must demean and degrade their faith and
distort its understanding.

We must blame them for that which we have
created.

We must make them hang their heads low.

We must make them keep their silence.

We must make them different from what they really
are.

We must prevent them from not only reaching the
truth, but from seeking it.

perceived and experienced by many second, third and fourth
generation Irish to become Scots, or more acceptable Scots by
divesting themselves of their Irish identities, the *Irish 2 Project*,
Aiden McGeady's decision to play for Ireland, as well as other
research, reflects that Irishness can be significant and manifest in
Scotland. This evidence further demonstrates Celtic's foremost
cultural importance for the Irish diaspora in Scotland.

Support for Celtic Football Club discloses otherwise hidden
and, in the eyes of their possessors, repressed aspects of the
Irishness of the Irish ethnic minority in Scotland, while simultaneously reflecting experiences and identities frequently marginalised,
unheard, ignored and denied. This hostility demonstrates the
marginalisation, denial, sectarianism and racism, faced by those
within the community of Irish Catholic descent, particularly by
those who are conscious of, and esteem, their family and community
origins and identities.

In Scotland, football is bound up and inherently linked with
the process of community construction. For those descended from

Ireland in Scotland who acknowledge Celtic as intrinsic to their Irishness, as from its inception and throughout its life, the club remains a site for the preservation and celebration of their cultural traditions, customs and political preferences. Linking with the ideas of the founders of Celtic Football Club, it functions as a site for a sense of community born from the majority of these supporters sharing familial and kinship origins in Ireland. It constitutes a setting for friendship and association with people often inter-married, having experienced the same denominational school format, sharing similar geographical spaces in Scotland (frequently in the Glasgow and Lanarkshire areas, within a thirty mile radius of Celtic Park in Glasgow) and with a sense of belonging, to Ireland, Catholicism, Irish history and Irish culture. Celtic represents part of the history of the Irish in Ireland, of the Irish in Scotland and of part of the history of the worldwide Irish diaspora. It is for these reasons that for many within the Celtic fanbase, particularly to those who represent the core support, the club finds its meaningfulness and social, cultural and political significance.

Section 1
Value and Meaning

Celtic captain Billy McNeil lifts the European Champions Cup in 1967

The Lion Kings:
the Impact of Lisbon

Patrick Reilly

An interest, an activity, a pursuit need not be important in itself for it to be sociologically informative. We can learn about the world from things that are in themselves trivial or even worthless. To hear, for instance, that a majority of visitors to Stratford-upon-Avon are more interested in the home of the Teletubbies than in Shakespeare's birthplace tells us something about the state of contemporary culture, even if it is not a discovery to set the heart singing. Fifty years ago George Orwell wrote two long essays on *Boys' Own* comics and the saucy holiday picture-postcards of Donald MacGill. He knew very well that these productions had no significant artistic merit, but he insisted that they were worth investigating for the light they shed upon the society that produced them. Today he might be examining TV reality shows of the Big Brother genre to ask why far more young people take the trouble to vote in them than can be bothered to visit polling-stations during general elections. Trifles can be revelatory: the meanest door may open on unsuspected riches.

Confronting Scottish football, Orwell might have found it to be as rewardingly revealing of our society today as he found *The Hotspur* and seaside postcards to be of English society fifty years ago. Broadcaster Kirsty Wark expressed her baffled indignation at what she regarded as the excessive brouhaha over George Best's funeral – he was only a football player, she protested. So even those who despise professional football as a puerile activity or, worse still, deplore it as a plague with repulsive social consequences, must concede its significance in terms of the interest it generates and the numbers it enthrals – this is popular culture at its most potent. It is instructive, too, in opening windows upon certain aspects of Scottish society that are customarily kept firmly closed. There is an almost innocent indiscretion, touchingly honest, in the naked way it so uninhibitedly lifts the curtain on attitudes we normally prefer to keep hidden – people are less guarded in disclosing what they truly believe.

Consider, for example, the series of startling football developments. In 1998 the man hailed by many as the greatest ever Rangers manager announced his intention to resign in order to avoid being sacked. He had in the previous season equaled his great rivals' feat of nine domestic league championships in a row and was still very much in the running to surpass it, yet he preferred to jump rather than be pushed. Paranoia is a word easily and lazily bandied about by commentators on Scottish football, but in Walter Smith's case he had excellent grounds for believing that his time at Ibrox was almost over – he might well have been sacked at the end of a season in which he could have established a surely unbeatable record for an unbroken series of league championships.

> Domestic triumphs, however monotonously repeated, will no longer suffice for the manager of Rangers.

This is a mystery only for those unversed in the underlying, unspoken, ever-present realities of Scottish football. Domestic triumphs, however monotonously repeated, will no longer suffice for the manager of Rangers, as Scot Symon, also in his time the most successful manager in Britain, discovered when he was summarily dismissed in 1967.

Smith gave as his reason the old prophet-in-his-own-country reproach: neither he nor his team, he complained, had ever received their due credit for their achievements in Scotland and for this he blamed a carpingly unappreciative press. But even if this had been true, it was irrelevant. If he feared the sack, he knew it would not come at the hands of curmudgeonly commentators – the threat came from within Ibrox, not from the sports department of some newspaper. It was his own chairman, rightly or wrongly who was insufficiently impressed by what had been achieved in Scotland and who clearly demanded more than simply the routine annual delivery of a league pennant. For anyone still in doubt, David Murray made it crystal clear in his remark that Smith was almost certainly the last manager of his kind at Ibrox and that the era of long-term appointments was over. Henceforth, it was to be a matter of short-term contracts, which, de-codified, meant that the new man would be expected to win the European Cup in three years or make way for someone who could. It is a job description that might be replicated, if at all, only at the very pinnacles of European football. Deliver the European Cup or (in football terms) die: this seemed to be the covert ultimatum and it was an astonishing one to be issued to the manager of a team playing in the relative backwater of Scottish football.

No wonder Smith felt aggrieved. All his domestic triumphs were to count for nothing when set beside his European failures. However, in a classic move well known to psychology, he displaced his resentment from its real target onto a surrogate. He blamed the press for undervaluing him when the true culprit was his own chairman.

Why did Smith have real cause to fear for his job? Why did Murray ever contemplate sacking him? The search for answers to these questions takes us out of the realm of football altogether and into the religious, political and social recesses of Scottish society.

To solve the mystery we have to turn to the age-old myth subtending and informing the game in Scotland. Despite the brave efforts of provincial clubs (Hibs and Hearts in the fifties and sixties, Aberdeen and Dundee United in the seventies and eighties) football continues to be dominated by the Glasgow based giants. They simultaneously sustain and bedevil the game through the intensity of their rivalry and this rivalry is an expression of the old antipathy between Presbyterian Scotland and the descendants of the Famine and post-Famine immigrants from Ireland.

I have written elsewhere of the social problems that arose in Scotland from the arrival of a people whom the native Scots regarded, not simply as savages, but as Romanised savages. From the other side, the novelist, Patrick MacGill from Donegal, the first significant recorder of the post-1845 immigrant experience, described Scotland as 'the black country with the cold heart'. When the football team founded by the immigrants achieved early and great success, a cry quickly resounded throughout the land for a native team to beat the Irishmen.

> Deliver the European Cup or (in football terms) die.

What did this really mean in the 1890s? Was it purely racist, even if devoid of the poisonous animus usually associated with that word today? Or was it, in essence, a religious hostility, wearing a racist disguise with 'Irish' serving as a convenient synonym for 'Catholic'? Whatever the meaning was then, from a background where most football teams were of a similar ilk, Rangers were elected 'the' Scottish Presbyterian team: the team to beat the Irishmen. This was their historical mandate and mission and they have continued to be faithful to it right down to our own day. Celtic might continue to be a good team, but only on condition that Rangers remained the best: as a creditable second-best to Rangers, Celtic could be tolerated, patronised, even praised, but only on condition that this strict hierarchical subordination was firmly observed.

Patrick MacGill from Donegal, the first significant recorder of the post-1845 immigrant experience, described Scotland as 'the black country with the cold heart'.

Glasgow Rangers was an extension of much of the rest of Scottish society. Rangers have long been the establishment team, identified by many as one of the great pillars of modern Scottish society along with Scots Law and the Church of Scotland and, closely associated with the Union and as the epitome of Scottishness – although this latter view has changed somewhat in recent years. Celtic, with the tricolor flying over the stadium, have for just as long been linked with Irishness, Romanism, Republicanism and subversion – all of them historically viewed contemptuously in Scottish and British societies.

However, great changes have taken place in Scottish society. In the past, so long as the two teams clashed only in Scotland, the blues could consistently be relied upon to nose ahead of the greens and the land was, by and large, at peace, because this was how things were supposed to be, the expected, natural, almost god-given order – what else does that raucously threatening cry, 'we are the people', mean?

What happened in Lisbon on 25th May 1967 changed this forever and overturned all the norms upon which Scottish football comfortably reposed. The winning of the European Cup remains a feat for which Celtic have never been forgiven by important elements within Scottish football. Astonishingly, against all the odds and against all reasonable prediction, the 'Irishmen' became the first non-Latin team to conquer Europe.

The triumph was unique in another sense, achieved as it was by a team composed entirely of players all born within a thirty-mile radius of Glasgow. The English, Germans, Dutch merely followed where Celtic led. The team that establishment Scotland recognised, at best, as second in the land was now incredibly first in the continent. The achievement continues to rankle.

G.K. Chesterton quotes lines by Tennyson on the fall of Napoleon – he thought to quell the stubborn hearts of oak. Madman! – 'as if the defeat of an English regiment were a violation of the laws of nature'. Celtic's victory in Lisbon seemed to those who bellow that they are 'the people' an equally perverse and unnatural event. That these inferior, unwelcome, unwanted intruders, who ought never to have been allowed to enter the country in the first place, should succeed where Rangers fail is for a certain kind of mindset a humiliation demanding to be expunged and an insult to be avenged.

> The winning of the European Cup remains a feat for which Celtic have never been forgiven by important elements within Scottish football.

Celtic might be the representatives of immigrant Irish Catholics but none of the team that won in Lisbon was Irish-born and four of them, together with the manager, were Scots Protestants. Nevertheless, a call arose for the intolerable situation to be put right. Whatever Celtic achieve Rangers must surpass: it is the first axiom of Scottish football. It explains why the massive resources of the most powerful club in Scotland were mobilised to erase the insult by making Rangers Kings of Europe. Glasgow Rangers owner David Murray threw down the gauntlet by proclaiming that where Celtic spent five pounds he would spend ten, and he more than lived up to this promise.

But the Murray era came later and I am running ahead of the story. In 1967 there were other reactions to what was seen as the outrage in Lisbon. Scot Symon was dismissed as the Ibrox manager and a series of appointments followed to find the man to topple Celtic at home. The comments of the journalists were, as always, revealing. John Fairgrieve defiantly declared that Rangers would always be Scotland's leading team, regardless of what Celtic might or might not achieve. Jack Harkness more deviously suggested that if Rangers could follow up Celtic's Lisbon victory by winning the Cup Winners' Cup – in fact, they lost 1-0 to Bayern Munich days after Lisbon – they and Celtic should meet to decide who was the best team in Europe. Jock Stein (who was as clever a controversialist as he was a coach) acidly retorted that he had imagined that that question had already been settled in the Estadio Nacional on 25th May 1967. What needs to be remarked is that the underlying motivation for Fairgrieve's statement and Harkness's proposal reveals a mindset not primarily concerned with football at all — other factors were clearly involved — and both men were trying, in their different ways, to deal with the hurt that Lisbon had caused. Football was the vehicle for them to reveal their thinking.

> The underlying motivation for Fairgrieve's statement and Harkness's proposal reveals a mindset not primarily concerned with football at all — other factors were clearly involved.

Long before the Souness-Murray revolution, Rangers had re-established their leading position within Scottish football, winning leagues and cups with a reassuring regularity. But the memory of Lisbon continued to fester in the soul, and to be the unvanquishable cocks of your own midden was small consolation for the chagrin of remembering that your fiercest rivals had once been the Kings of Europe. Prior to 1967 domestic supremacy was all that any Rangers manager had to concern himself with — after 1967 it was no longer the acceptable standard.

When Rangers lose in Europe the pall of funereal gloom that envelops the media is striking enough, but it is the savagery of the backlash that is breathtaking. The fury and the sense of betrayal seem extravagantly excessive and must surely be bewildering to any outsider just newly arrived in Scotland. After all, Scotland's national champions, even when they are Rangers, are sure to be small fry in comparison with the leviathans cruising European waters. Why on earth should one expect, far less demand that they should triumph over the best of England, Italy, Germany and Spain? It would be in the nature of a miracle were they to do so.

Here, precisely, is the sore point. The trouble is that the miracle had been performed in Lisbon by the team historically designated to play second-fiddle to Rangers. Here, for many, is the affront and there can be no peace in the land, so far as football is concerned, until the wrong has been righted. Even if Lisbon is dismissed as a fluke, an aberration, astronomically unlikely ever to be repeated, nevertheless it did happen and the hurt is no less. A team from Scotland did once win the European Cup; the trouble is that, for many, it was the wrong team that did so. It is an outlook that transcends sport and that has its roots in certain notions of cultural and racial superiority prevalent in Britain for several centuries and particularly in Scotland since the coming of the Irish after the Great Hunger of 1845. It lingers to this day.

There was a feeling abroad after Lisbon that Rangers had defaulted upon their historical mandate: the team to beat the Irishmen had failed to do so, in Europe at least, and Lisbon was still unavenged. So when David Murray and Graeme Souness joined forces at Ibrox in 1989 they shared a common resolve that the time had finally come for the right team to triumph. The chairman put his enormous wealth and influence at the disposal of his new manager as a programme of radical transformation was launched. A batch of English internationalists had already been brought to Ibrox by Souness, the harvest of his long and extensive experience of football south of the border. England strips were seen at Ibrox for the first time and 'Sweet Chariot' was added to the repertoire of anthems. When Souness left after three league championships, two of them in successive years, to be succeeded by Walter Smith, the Ibrox revolution, if anything, intensified.

Under Souness the team ceased to be as Scottish as it once was while under Smith it, astoundingly, ceased to be as Protestant as it once was – at least in terms of the players on the pitch. True, the signing of ex-Celt Maurice Johnston had already taken place under Souness, but that was as much motivated by a desire to embarrass Celtic as it was to achieve European success. The Italians that came to Ibrox, most if not all of them at least nominally Catholic, was another thing altogether, underlining, as it did, that the new European demands necessitated an abandonment of the old de facto anti-Catholic policy. Smith dispelled any lingering doubts over this by proceeding to sign the Irish-descended Catholic Neil McCann – Rikki Fulton's celebrated sketch about a Rangers manager's dilemma after inadvertently signing a Catholic partly became a museum piece, a historical curiosity. Murray and Smith made it

> A team from Scotland did once win the European Cup; the trouble is that, for many, it was the wrong team that did so.

clear that they could not be expected to deliver European success while also restricting himself to native-born Protestant players. In addition, and crucially, that kind of policy was hardly politically correct in the new Europe.

The rescinding by UEFA of the three-foreigners rule opened the door to greater European recruitment, while the old traditional ban on Catholics was silently revoked. Celtic, too – surely reluctantly – were sucked into the new orbit and were compelled, to maintain a semblance of challenge, to search abroad for players who cost far more in transfer fees and salaries than Celtic wanted to pay: the alternative was to make do with the homebred players rejected by their rivals as inadequate. Celtic felt they had little choice as the club was towed along in Rangers' wake – and the Ibrox policy was proving invincible, at least within Scotland.

But, even had they wished, Celtic simply could not match, or come close to matching, the vast sums being expended by Rangers in their pursuit of that holy grail of football, the European Champions Cup. The figures are staggering when the millions spent by Souness, Smith and Advocaat are added together – and there is surely, no one, naive or impudent enough to maintain that this incredible expenditure (possibly as much as £140 million) had, as its prime objective, the winning of the Scottish League Championship.

It explains why Rangers soon found themselves in a parlous predicament. Advocaat became the convenient whipping-boy in the media for these financial difficulties and it is true that in his last days an element of reckless desperation characterised his recruitment policy, the signing of Torre Andre Flo being, perhaps, the most signal instance of this. But was Advocaat's policy so very different from that of his two predecessors? First there were the English, then the Italians, then the Dutch, but the same policy of buying big and paying high has continued throughout the Murray years – Advocaat may, at worst, have carried it to an extreme, but he did not initiate it. That decision was taken when Murray and Souness together resolved that, whatever the cost, Rangers must succeed in Europe and that domestic success would no longer suffice.

We have heard much in recent years about Advocaat's disastrous legacy and about his successor Alex McLeish as its prime victim, and, it is certainly true that no other Rangers manager in modern times was so hampered and hamstrung financially as McLeish, although his position seemed pitiable only in comparison with the riches made available to his three predecessors. The spending has been, arguably, excessive, irresponsible and, set against what it was intended to achieve, the holy grail remains as elusive as ever. How are we to explain the power and compulsion of this gambling mentality at Ibrox, the more so since its failure has had such dangerous and even potentially disastrous repercussions?

In hindsight, Celtic's triumph in Lisbon, acclaimed though it has been, may yet prove to be even more important for our football than anyone has ever hitherto imagined. Together, Jock Stein and David Murray have changed the face of Scottish football in a reprise of the situation back in the 1890s when the great rivalry was first born. Then a Celtic side sweeping all before it provoked the call for a team to beat the Irish and Rangers best responded to the appeal. Under Murray, Rangers again assumed their historic role as the team to beat the Irish, this time not only in Scotland, but, by winning the European Cup, thereby bringing to an end that painfully intolerable Celtic superiority. It may well be that the Murray reaction will, in the long run have a truly revolutionary impact.

> Together, Jock Stein and David Murray have changed the face of Scottish football in a reprise of the situation back in the 1890s when the great rivalry was first born.

The Stein years were gloriously unsurpassable and, for almost ten of them, Celtic were one of the great European teams, appearing in two European finals and losing at the semi-final stage on two other occasions. It is a considerably better record than that achieved by Sir Alex Ferguson during his fifteen years in charge at Old Trafford. At home, nine league championships in a row were won, along with eight Scottish Cups and six League Cups. But after Stein, Celtic reverted to what they had generally been, a good, sometimes a very good team, able to win trophies and give a reasonable account of themselves within Scotland.

After Stein, everything was as it had been before: only the unforgettable memories survived. But after Murray everything changed and it seems that there can be no going back. Celtic's nine-in-a-row achievement under Stein was matched by adding Souness and Smith together and domestic parity and pride were completely restored. But a football Rubicon had been crossed: the paramount prize of Murray's ambition, a glory to equal Lisbon, is still unattained and, despite more than two decades of crushing, recurring disappointment, he cannot, perhaps dare not, openly admit that it is a prize perhaps beyond attaining: not only the prize itself, but the status those great Celtic sides had for around ten years in European football. For what kind of reception would such an admission provoke among those who proclaim so bellicosely that they are 'the people'?

> Had you forecast that in a relatively short time Rangers would have at one point more Catholics in their first eleven than Celtic, people would have hooted with derision.

As always, Celtic has to be beaten, but that is no longer the raison d'etre of Rangers' existence, merely a necessary step towards qualification for Europe. The Lisbon triumph has had consequences impossible to foresee at the time and still in process of working themselves out almost forty years after the event. Little did Jock Stein realise at the time the remarkable chain-reaction he had set in motion. Had you predicted prior to 1967 that there would be a Rangers team without a single Scot in it, you would have been met with stunned disbelief. Had you forecast, even more absurdly, that in a relatively short time Rangers would have at one point more Catholics in their first eleven than Celtic, people would have hooted with derision. Yet so it proved.

Success in Europe was now seen as more important than pandering to the close minded and Murray was brave enough to see that such success was not compatible with the old traditional bigotry, however easily that bigotry – and in 2005 he publicly admitted himself that this is what it was – could fit in with domestic triumph. Were Rangers at some future date to win the European Cup with a goal scored by a player who had just announced his intention to study for the priesthood, does anyone seriously believe that the joy among their supporters would be any the less unconfined? This might not have happened only for what took place in Lisbon: no Catholic need apply is no longer the presiding axiom in Govan and Tommy Gemmell and Steve Chalmers can take great credit for this momentous change in policy.

The rivalry is still as fierce, perhaps fiercer, than ever, but certain irreversible changes have occurred and the process continues. The league championship is important now for the access it affords to European riches and glory. After the worst run of domestic results in Rangers' history in 2005/06, Alex McLeish temporarily escaped dismissal because he took the team to the last sixteen of the European Champions Cup – that's how important it is. This is what makes the present situation of Celtic and Rangers alike so unstable, so impossible of continuance. It seems inconceivable that either or both of them could simply decide to abandon their European ambitions and revert to being the purely Scottish-based teams they once were, content to make a token appearance in Europe before being rudely dismissed at the first hurdle.

Yet these are dangerous, maybe even ruinous ambitions if seriously pursued, as the present parlous condition of Rangers in particular so clearly demonstrates – living beyond one's means can be as disastrous in football as it is in life. The Ibrox predicament is deeper because the demands upon Rangers are greater – Lisbon again – but neither team can openly opt out of serious European involvement without risking the disaffection and possible defection of large numbers of their followers, for that would, in essence, reduce the domestic championship to a squabble between two baldheads for a comb.

Yet the Ibrox gamble for European success has so far ended in near-ruinous failure, the vast sums of money expended have not met their purpose. For Celtic, too, the position, if less critical, is equally unsustainable. Both teams are in limbo, wandering between two worlds, one dead, the other powerless (so far) to be born. Unable to go back, they are frustrated in going forward, yet they must somehow do one or the other – and go forward they must if they are to realise their dream of becoming major players in the European arena: hence the alluring vision of the English premiership with its promise of becoming instant sharers in its television pot of gold.

This ambition to move south has come in for much criticism since it was first made known. In recent years British Labour Government Minister Dr. John Reid, provoked a storm of

> The Ibrox gamble for European success has so far ended in near-ruinous failure, the vast sums of money expended have not met their purpose.

condemnation for saying, one, that Celtic and Rangers are known the world over in a way that their competitors in Scotland are not; two, that their future should accordingly lie furth of Scotland in a structure that reflects and enhances this global reputation. Why such truisms should cause outrage is puzzling – it's as if people were to get upset at hearing Sean Connery and Billy Connelly described as international stars whose stature demands stages greater than the Usher Hall or the Glasgow Pavilion. The facts about our national team sport are plain for all to see.

> Dr. John Reid, provoked a storm of condemnation for saying (Celtic's and Rangers') future should lie furth of Scotland in a structure that reflects and enhances (their) global reputation.

From all over Scotland many thousands of fans come to watch their chosen teams play at Ibrox and Celtic Park. They could stay where they are, at far less expense and trouble, to watch, on their own doorsteps, teams who play in the same league as Celtic and Rangers, but they choose not to do so: they choose to spend more time and money to see the teams they want to see: the teams that hold meaning for them. Those who deplore this must also say what they propose to do about it. We clearly cannot forcibly detain them within their own areas and compel them to follow their more local teams. We cannot impose pass laws as South Africa once did with its blacks, nor treat them as Mrs Thatcher once treated the miners, using flying squads of police to confine them to their own locales. In a free society they can come and go as they please: that where they choose to go displeases other people is neither here nor there.

Equally irrelevant is the fact that these other people find the motive for these journeys even more discreditable than the destinations. No one will deny that these two teams are so well supported in Scotland and abroad because they are the embodiments, inheritors and carriers within our society of traditions, allegiances and loyalties which many others within Scotland either do not understand, deplore or wish to see abandoned: that is another story of course. But John Reid did not create these traditions and allegiances: he simply called attention to the fact that they exist and that they explain the dominance exerted by these two teams over Scottish football.

Tom Devine did exactly the same in his admirable history and nobody called him insensitive and irresponsible. Facts are chiels that winna ding. If these are unpalatable facts, history is the culprit and it is pointless to blame any individual today who merely stays loyal or faithful to what everybody thinks they know.

The charge levelled at Dr. Reid by his critics, however, is that, instead of condemning these noxious and disruptive traditions, he seems to be endorsing and encouraging them by advocating the export of the 'sectarian' virus to other presently uninfected parts of the earth. Shameful enough that the plague exists among us, but who in his right mind wants to spread it to strangers?

But it is too late. The alleged disgrace of having large numbers of supporters throughout the world is already out in the open for all to see. If it ever was a secret, the 2003 UEFA Cup Final in Seville blew it wide open. Everyone now knows, if they didn't know before, that Celtic have more supporters in North America than many leading English teams have in England. It is too late to tell them that they should be ashamed of themselves and that they should be following the Dallas Cowboys or the New England Patriots – as well rebuke those fans from Fife for not being at East End Park or Methil.

> Celtic have more supporters in North America than many leading English teams have in England.

It seems difficult to challenge Dr. Reid's key assertion that Glasgow Rangers and Celtic have an international appeal that is irreconcilable with the limitations of Scottish football and the modern capitalist values that dominate European football. The two bestride Scottish football like colossi. Until 2005, they have won between them twenty of the past twenty leagues, thirteen of the past twenty Scottish Cups, and fourteen of the past twenty League Cups. This might reasonably be described as a duopoly. This implies no criticism of other teams. They do their best with the available resources, but this best is plainly not enough to break this stranglehold upon the Scottish game.

There are some pundits who believe that the departure of the Glasgow giants, far from being a disaster, would be a blessing for all concerned. The upas tree is a plant that voraciously absorbs all the available nutriment in its vicinity, thereby condemning the neighbouring flora to deprivation and death. These pundits regard the Old Firm as a kind of upas tree, far too powerful for lesser shrubs to flourish in their shade. The remedy is to transplant the upas tree and give the lesser growths a better chance to thrive. Restore genuine competition to the Scottish League and, in becoming exciting and unpredictable, it will cease to be the sham it has for so long been.

It is not a completely implausible thesis. Perhaps the going of the giants would be a boon for professional football in Scotland and a boon for society. The rivalry between the two, always intense, has become increasingly rancorous and fierce as the rewards for success become commensurately lavish. Often with no realistic outside challenge, everything frequently rides upon how each fares against the other. In yet one more vain attempt to devise a truly competitive set-up, the teams can now meet as often as six times a season, with each collision hyped as an armageddon upon which the whole season depends. Is it surprising that both sets of supporters, fed upon a diet of media hysterics, approach each game as if it were some final conflict for the possession of Valhalla?

Winner takes all, loser humiliated. Each side playing the other as many times as they do possibly brings out the worst in everyone. This is what John Reid and others are advocating.

In a better league, with more quality teams, the giants will dwindle to 'normal' size; the all-consuming business of beating each other – the sole determinant of Scottish success – will lose some of its urgency and their confrontations will shed the desperate, last-ditch, do-or-die element that bedevils them at present. Scotland is too narrow, too enclosed a country to contain these two giants without tension and turmoil – they need greater space, a wider expanse, where they will not be continually jostling each other. Of course, rivalry between the two will be around for as long as football is but it is this enforced propinquity in Scotland that makes this rivalry so intense.

There is a vociferous body of opinion in Scotland today that these traditions are inherently and necessarily disruptive, violent and pernicious, and that the only progressive course is to dismantle and eradicate them altogether.

There is a vociferous body of opinion in Scotland today that these traditions – however they are perceived and understood – are inherently and necessarily disruptive, violent and pernicious, and that the only progressive course is to dismantle and eradicate them altogether. Celtic seem to attract particular criticism for its Irish and Catholic origins, links and identities. At best, these are condemned as obsolete and irrelevant, at worst, as a barrier to social harmony. Yet the astonishing phenomenon of the Seville UEFA Cup Final – obviously and strikingly a game played outside of the Scottish environment – throws a very different light upon the subject of Celtic and its support's Irish and Catholic identities.

From start to finish Seville was an astonishing and unprecedented episode. What other team in Europe, not to say the world, could have attracted 80,000 supporters from all over the globe – the huge majority obviously ticketless – to a football match in a foreign city which they could have watched on television in comfort and at no expense by staying at home? What other team in Europe or the world could have taken such a multitude abroad, suffered a dramatically heartbreaking defeat, and not been tarnished by one single arrest for misconduct even after so bitter a disappointment? What actually happened was truly remarkable. Those who followed Celtic to Seville made such an impression upon the local people that they set up a Celtic supporters' club in tribute to their impeccably behaved, good-humoured visitors. Moreover, the Celtic support-ers got on so well with the followers of their conquerors, Porto, that they were officially recognised and rewarded by UEFA for being the best football supporters in all Europe.

> Something is plainly amiss in Scotland with the assumption that the Celtic tradition and identity is bound to provoke disorder.

Something is plainly amiss in Scotland with the assumption that the Celtic tradition and identity is bound to provoke disorder. It was, unarguably, Celtic's traditions and identities – maybe more so, the supporters' traditions and identities – all that the club historically represents and embodies, that brought the multitudes to Seville to see them play. Indeed, it might be argued that it was those very identities that made the event what it was and encouraged the Celtic support to behave and act as it did: behaviour and actions that were to win them accolades from all sides.

Those who accuse Celtic of clinging to and fostering traditions that are inflammatory and noxious must explain why the expedition to Seville, which was disappointing from the point of view of the result, was nevertheless in every other sense a triumph, one of the finest exhibitions of sportsmanship, celebration and good humour that football at the highest level has ever witnessed. The behaviour in Lisbon was equally exemplary as it has been in other European cities, but it's easy to be good when you're winning – to behave well when you are hurting is another matter altogether. If the Celtic tradition, so often maligned in Scotland, is as intrinsically productive of nastiness and violence as its critics in Scotland allege, how are we to account for the completely peaceful nature of the Seville adventure? The city's inhabitants and the UEFA authorities may have feared the worst as 80,000 converged upon the city. In the event, it turned out to be everything UEFA could dream of: the celebration of a loved football club and event given great honour by well-behaved supporters.

Seville made it inescapably plain that it is only in the pent-up, cramped, confined, intolerant pinfold of Scottish domestic football, tied down by an often bitter anti-Catholic and anti-Irish history and, amid conditions guaranteeing the maximum amount of tension and turbulence, that trouble occurs, or, is perceived as occurring. Celtic's distant triumph in Lisbon has already produced revolutionary changes within Scottish football. Perhaps the last and most momentous is yet to come, for if that triumph finally leads to their release from Scotland, it will be the single greatest, beneficial service provided by Lisbon.

'Singing when we're winning': but not only when we're winning

STEPHEN FERRIE

In football, where winning is generally perceived to be every-thing, you might be forgiven for thinking that what constitutes success is largely self-evident. It's surely about scoring more goals, amassing more points, collecting more trophies than the opposition. There can be little scope for debate: either you win or you lose. Success is an absolute thing. Or is it?

Monday 26th May 2003: the morning after the night before. Not so much the night before, as the week before. The dream of European glory lies wilted in the baking heat of southern Spain. We wake up to a further, awful, hangover pang. The domestic campaign that promised so much that season yields nothing but an oversize helping of humble pie. Wallets are empty, hearts are heavy and smug grins are etched on the faces of our greatest rivals: the League title, the Scottish Cup and the League Cup beam out at us from the Ibrox trophy cabinet. Rangers, with arguably one of their poorest teams in recent memory, have just completed the domestic treble for the seventh time in their history. It doesn't get much worse than this if you are a Celtic supporter.

As the week unfolds, however, things start to get perplexing. Via radio phone-ins, letters pages and websites, tales of pride begin to emerge and we hear claims of an achievement of sorts. The media are bemused. Rangers fans are beside themselves with laughter. They put it to us scornfully in the most straightforward and uncompromising of terms; 'how can you claim success, when not only did you lose in Seville, but you also won nothing domestically?' The logic seems irrefutable. The trophy cabinet lies bare. So, can we really claim success?

The answer to this question lies not only in examining the Seville experience, but also in delving deeper into the psyche of the Celtic community. Michael Grant, writing in the *Sunday Herald* the weekend after Seville, reflected on the club's achievement: 'It began the week as a football club' he said, 'and ended it as a social phenomenon.'[1] In this respect Grant is perceptive, but perhaps he is looking at the world through the wrong end of the telescope. Celtic haven't so much ended up as a social phenomenon, they began as one, and it is in looking at things in the context of that social phenomenon that we arrive at a far richer definition of what success means to Celtic and its supporting community.

Celtic haven't so much ended up as a social phenomenon, they began as one.

A great deal has already been written about the origins of Celtic Football Club; its quest to help alleviate the suffocating poverty of nineteenth century Glasgow and to serve as a focal point for the immigrant Irish who settled in the city. However, in order to understand how a seemingly absolute term like success might actually have a relative dimension, it is important that we keep the historical perspective at the front of our minds. Tom Campbell and Pat Woods in their acclaimed history – and a far less contrived one than many others – of the club provide what might be regarded as the ideal reference point against which the term 'success' might be judged:

> Celtic Football Club arose out of the needs, physical and emotional, of a whole community in Glasgow: the club's revenues were designed to alleviate the worst effects of chronic poverty among the city's Catholics, and its anticipated success was calculated to engender a feeling of pride within an Irish community suffering from persecution and cultural alienation.[2]

Note how the term 'success' is linked with engendering a sense of pride amongst the Irish Catholic community. Certainly, success on the field was anticipated, but the driving force was to provide a shared sense of identity and common purpose for the immigrant Irish and their offspring.

For Celtic therefore, the fortunes of the football club are inextricably linked with the past and ongoing experiences of the community that gave birth to it and that has sustained it

(1) Sunday Herald, 25/1/03. Michael Grant writes on the Celtic experience in Seville.

(2) The Glory and the Dream, The History of Celtic F.C. 1887-1986 by Tom Campbell and Pat Woods. Chapter 2, p. 15.

throughout its history. For some, particularly those from non-Celtic backgrounds, the connection between the club's origins and its current reality as a twenty first century football club represents a mere historical footnote with little or no contemporary relevance. The Irish influence is acknowledged only in the past tense. No account is taken of the ongoing and vibrant nature of that influence in a present-day sense. And yet Irish influences continue to permeate all aspects of the club's being. For example, a sizeable number of the club's season ticket holders travel from all parts of Ireland, the vast majority of the club's fan base can boast parents, grandparents or great-grandparents of Irish birth, and the songs and stories – the myth and legend – that are passed from generation to generation, are all deeply rooted in Irish culture and tradition. The relationship between club and community therefore is a dynamic one: never static, but evolving and undergoing a process of continuous regeneration. Memory is important for Celtic supporters of Irish Catholic descent and identity.

The experience of the Irish who sought refuge in Scotland from the hunger and poverty of their native land provides a useful psychological reference point for judging success. The key to understanding what success means in terms of the football club is rooted in the formative – and to some extent ongoing – experience of the community as it attempted to establish itself in its new environment. This experience was characterised by suspicion, exclusion and hostility. To compound matters, the Famine, poverty and religious and political repression that provided the motivating force to leave home proved to be an elusive shackle to break free from. For many, the coat of change bore an all too familiar resemblance. Des Dillon, a contemporary author whose writing is infused by Irish influences, captures the crushing disappointment facing the Irish who arrived in Glasgow:

> If the immigrants thought they were coming to a better
> life it was only relative to the Famine. It was a better way
> to die, coughing your lungs up on a bar floor than digging
> up the roots in the iron frost of a Donegal winter. From
> one hell to a slightly more bearable hell, helped on by the
> emotional anaesthetic of whiskey.[3]

Irish influences continue to permeate all aspects of the club's being.

(3) Six Black Candles by Des Dillon. p. 226.

For those nineteenth and early twentieth century immigrants the measures of success were rooted in basic, almost primal, aspirations; to be free of hunger and poverty, to have access to decent housing and education, to be allowed to participate on an equal footing in Scottish society and to be free to express their identity and culture without fear of persecution. Herein lies the key to understanding why success in the context of the modern day football club is far more complex than simply totting up the silverware nestling in a trophy cabinet.

The immigrant Irish were treated with hostility and suspicion by native Scots. The stereotypical economic and social threats often synonymous with immigrant groups in general were compounded by the cultural, political and religious differences between the two communities. It's not surprising therefore that the emergence of Celtic Football Club as a galvanising force for the Irish should also spark a counter reaction.

The almost instantaneous success that Celtic enjoyed on the field of play was the catalyst for calls from within the mainstream of Scottish society for a club to rise to the challenge of 'beating the Irish'. But this was more than a mere sporting objective. Many found the very idea of a football club founded by Irishmen and supported by Irishmen an effrontery; an effrontery that would not go unchallenged. Many football teams in Scotland experienced success but it was Rangers Football Club that eventually became 'the' team to answer that call and take up the mantle.

(4) 1873 and 1888 respectively, are the years that Celtic and Rangers are generally recognised to have meaningfully entered the football scene. Both clubs were, in fact, formally constituted in the preceding years: Celtic in November 1887 and Rangers in 1872.

Prior to Celtic's emergence onto the Scottish football stage Rangers were one of a number of clubs who regularly contested Scotland's football honours. Others among this elite included Renton, Vale of Leven and Queen's Park. Indeed, one might argue that Queen's Park were at that time the undisputed football force in Scotland. Between 1872/73 – when Rangers were formed – and 1887/88 – when Celtic was formed[4] – Queens Park won the Scottish Cup, the only meaningful national competition at the time, on nine occasions. Rangers, on the other hand, had failed to muster a single win in spite of contesting the final on two occasions. Other Scottish Cup winners during the period prior to Celtic's existence include Vale of Leven, Dumbarton and Renton.

The arrival of Celtic meant that the football landscape changed forever. The club made an immediate impact. It contested a Scottish Cup final in its first season and quickly established for itself a place at the top table that it has retained to this day. The glory days of Queens Park, Renton, Vale of Leven and many others would soon be consigned to the dustbin of history. The football map of the future would take on a distinctly two-dimensional format, and terms such as success and failure would have a far deeper underlying meaning for each of the protagonists.

For Rangers, success would become synonymous with maintaining the cultural status quo between the two communities. A status quo where the British and Protestant values of the majority were, and indeed to some extent still are, seen to be superior to the Irish and Catholic views of the minority. A quick dip into the supporters' repertoire of songs provides an insight into a community imbued with a strong sense of superiority. Songs such as, 'We are the People', 'Simply the Best' and 'Rule Britannia' serve to remind us who's dominant.

So ingrained has this siege mentality become that prizes offering greater prestige and wider recognition are often spurned out of a sense of duty, almost, to keep Celtic – and its supporting community – in its place. To illustrate this, an interesting debate occurred during the reign of the great Rangers nine-in-row team of the late-eighties and nineties that is worthy of note. As the possibility of matching Celtic's achievement of nine successive league titles grew closer Rangers also happened to be performing relatively well in Europe. An interesting question was asked of the Rangers support, most notably on radio phone-ins: if you had to choose between winning a European trophy or beating Celtic's record of nine consecutive league titles, which would you go for? The over-whelming response was in favour of beating Celtic's record.

For Rangers then, success has come to be defined by their position relative to Celtic. In the period prior to Celtic being formed they were simply one of a pack of leading teams. The arrival of Celtic changed all that, providing an impetus that would galvanise Rangers and see them, ultimately, become the pre-eminent force in Scottish football. One can only wonder how the Scottish football landscape might look today had the Irish not arrived and Celtic Football Club not been formed. Would Dumbarton perhaps have achieved nine consecutive league titles? Would Queens Park perhaps have become the first club from Britain to win the European Cup?

> One can only wonder how the Scottish football landscape might look today had the Irish not arrived and Celtic Football Club not been formed.

Another factor that further complicates any analysis of success is the emergence of a range of measures deriving largely from the commercial world. Whilst football clubs, none more so than Glasgow Rangers and Celtic, have always offered the potential to be examined in terms of economic criteria, the past 20 years or so has seen a sharpening of focus in this area, with commercial measures becoming widely referred to and used to benchmark status and success. Back page headlines are no longer restricted to matters on the field. Instead, one is equally as likely to read about success in terms of share price, balance sheet strength, or profit and loss. However, the adoption of the financial model and the general commercialisation of the game have resulted in a football landscape of haves and have-nots. We see this in terms of the clubs, where an elite band has emerged. They are referred to by UEFA as the G14,[5] directly mimicking the terminology of the wider economic world, where the term G8 is used as a collective noun for the world's richest nations. We also see it in terms of the players themselves, where a relatively small group of superstars command vast salaries that distance them from most other players and, more importantly, from the average football fan.

(5) In September 2000, fourteen founder clubs created the 'G-14 European Football Clubs Grouping', an Economic Interest Group registered in Brussels. In September 2002 they were joined by four new members, taking the number of clubs to 18.

In the modern era of satellite TV other measures of success have emerged and become part of the average football's fan's vocabulary. These measures, directly associated with the power of television, include brand and television ratings. The bigger clubs, including Celtic and Rangers, represent a huge commercial gravy train to be exploited as football becomes box-office on a global scale. Of all the commercial measures to emerge over recent times it is somewhat ironic that brand should come to the fore as offering perhaps the largest source of untapped potential. The term brand has long been synonymous with identity, but in recent times its use has been corrupted and it is now associated almost exclusively in commercial terms, narrowing its truer meaning.

Great brands encapsulate an emotional connection that unites the provider and the consumer. Celtic, when looked at in the context of an emotional and cultural connection, can claim to be a truly great brand in the purest sense of the word. That brand, however, risks being corrupted if it is manipulated to suit the narrow commercial interests of a limited few, reconfigured and dumbed-down to increase its mass market appeal. The baby really is in danger of being thrown out with the bath water as those who would repackage the club's identity peddle a pick 'n mix variety of the club's inherent Irishness to fickle paymasters who include within their ranks, shareholders, broadcasters and advertisers. What was once genuine and integral is in danger of becoming modular and built to order. The irony facing Celtic's current custodians is that they perhaps run the risk of undertaking from within a process of cultural re-engineering that was once advocated by hostile forces on the outside.

If we attempt to evaluate Celtic's success in relation to these commercial measures it would seem reasonable to conclude that the club, by and large, has achieved a great deal. By any standards, Celtic, like Rangers, can justifiably claim to be among the financial elite of Europe, though to boast of this seems to be very un-Christian and un-Celtic. We may be operating at the fringe of that elite, compared to the economic muscle of Real Madrid, Manchester United and the big Italian clubs, but we are nonetheless within touching distance. Indeed many have argued, including most of the club's current directors, that our financial prospects are constrained by operating in Scotland and that our full financial potential is yet to be realised.

However, to judge success on the basis of financial parameters is to mistake the menu for the meal. In microcosm, it is like a man who boasts of the commercial worth of his house when what is really of value is the degree to which that house is a home, nurturing relationships, providing security and comfort and offering a sense of belonging. The heart and soul of Celtic Football Club goes far deeper than the empty shell of a mere public limited company.

Success, as we have seen, has come to mean something different to either half of the so-called 'Old Firm'. Whereas for Rangers success might be viewed in terms of domination, for Celtic and its support it might be seen more in terms of a struggle for participation, an underlying determination not to be marginalised and respectful recognition of their difference and distinctiveness within Scottish society. Des Dillon, encapsulates the essence of that struggle:

> Paradise was where the Irish were allowed to become Irish again, together. Instead of the scum that they were in the rest of Scotland.[6]

Little wonder then, given the circumstances of the immigrant Irish, that success should come to be viewed in terms that are relative to constraining factors such as hardship and oppression, rather than in absolute terms such as victory or defeat.

Let us keep in mind this broader historical perspective and return to the example of Seville. Re-examined in this context, it becomes clearer, not only why many Celtic fans view the Seville experience as a success, but also why the entire concept of success has to be considered in a different light. Whilst the cold truth remains that Porto lifted the UEFA Cup that night, defeating Celtic 3-2, the Seville experience and, indeed, the entire European campaign that season, from a cultural perspective represents a significant achievement.

The campaign leading up to the final and the climactic experience in Seville in the days immediately surrounding the event proved to be a triumphant outcome for the Celtic community. If we relate events in Seville to the original aspirations that led to the founding of the club we see success in relation to a range of deeper measures; success in terms of pride, success in terms of a celebration of culture and success

We see success in relation to a range of deeper measures – pride, a celebration of culture and in terms of a community coming together and seeking to reach out to be part of something bigger.

(6) Six Black Candles by Des Dillon. p.226.

in terms of a community coming together and seeking to reach out to be part of something bigger.

It seems fitting to conclude our thinking on the issue of success by reflecting on the recent project to erect a monument at Celtic Park to serve as a permanent reminder of the contribution of Brother Walfrid, the Club's most important founding father. Eddie Toner, Chair of the Memorial Committee, outlining his thoughts on Brother Walfrid's legacy, had this to say on the subject of success:

> Success on the football pitch is important to any club. But is it crucial to its existence? I would argue that in Celtic's case it should never be. Success can be measured in different ways and how it is achieved can vary also. Walfrid gave us a vision, it was Christian, it was charitable, it was about never forgetting our roots and indeed, maintaining them. It was about being happy, about celebrating and about making our fellow man and woman welcome. It was about openness and inclusiveness.[7]

Evidence, if it were needed, that, in the cultural sense at least, success is very much a relative, rather than an absolute, term. Whilst it would be naive in the extreme to claim that winning matches and trophies matters nothing to Celtic fans, it is nonetheless clear that the struggle to establish and to nurture Celtic as a focal point for the dreams and aspirations of a community represents a success that is, arguably, of far greater significance.

Booker T. Washington, one of America's leading educationalists, offers an insight on the matter of success that could well have been written with Celtic in mind. Success, he argues, is to be measured not so much by the position reached, as by the obstacles overcome.[8]

(7) Extract from Eddie Toner's speech at the unveiling ceremony for the Brother Walfrid statue on Saturday 5th November 2005.

(8) Booker T Washington, born into slavery, went on to become one of America's leading educationalists and champion of the rights of African Americans. The full version of the quotation on success reads, 'Success is to be measured not so much by the position that one has reached in life as by the obstacles which he has overcome'.

Commemorative booklet of Requiem Mass for Jimmy Johnstone 17th March 2006

Legends

Tom Campbell

I listen to radio phone-ins only when driving home from a match but I can't be the only one who gets upset at much of the content. My friend in the car often assures me that AM Radio means Absolute Moron: so far, I have resisted telling him what I think FM stands for.

In the first place it's a wholly artificial situation where a football pundit can sit in a studio with all the advantages: a time-switch which can cut off any caller, prepared notes to strengthen his arguments, and the psychology of the last word, patronising, rarely humorous, sneering or brutal. Usually the caller is a fan emotionally involved in the topic and, therefore, at a considerable disadvantage with an alert journalist, intent on winding him or her up. In a battle of wits too often the caller is virtually unarmed – and that annoys me.

Of course, callers can also irritate. Do they like the sound of their own voices that much? Why don't they just bore their friends to death in the pub like the rest of us? Yes, yes, I know that football is all about opinions but I would suggest that might be a 'democratic myth': one of those often taken for granted notions in modern society. Some people should not have opinions – or should utter them only in a darkened room with padded walls, and preferably sound-proof ones at that.

A problem is that too many of them have no sense of perspective and are concerned only with the most recent match. Sometimes journalists too have no sense of history. I received a call from one asking me to tell him about Bobby Evans. For God's sake how could anybody, pretending to write about football for a so-called quality newspaper, not know about Bobby Evans of Celtic and Scotland? The fact that the reporter in question is under forty years of age cuts no ice with me at all. Many of the world's greatest thinkers and revolutionaries have been under forty when they made their mark.

Language in the tabloid sports pages has become overblown with hyperbole, debased and distorted, totally devalued by mindless repetition and meaningless phrases. If a player is not a success at either Celtic or Rangers, he is permanently labelled a flop: for example, Cascarino or Flo. Read accounts of the games and you will see that every save by a goalkeeper brilliant, every goal spectacular, every fightback thrilling, every defender resolute, and the man who scores the winning goal a hero. Presumably, if he does that two or three times in a season, the hero becomes elevated to the status of a legend. What nonsense and so lacking in contextualised understanding, assessment and intelligence.

Halls of Fame present another problem. Not the idea of them, but the actual selections. Too often the emphasis is on current performers or recent players whose exploits can be viewed on film or videotape. If you don't appear on TV, you have a problem; if you can be detected on black-and-white film, you have a faint chance; if you played before the advent of film, TV or video, you simply don't have a hope. The dice is loaded in favour of the current crop of players. Look at the players eligible to be members of the SFA Hall of Fame with an entrance requirement set at fifty caps. In that case, Billy McNeill, the first club captain in Northern Europe to hold up the European Cup, won't be there; even more to be regretted neither will Jimmy McGrory, the greatest goalscorer in the history of Scottish football, but a man who was granted a miserly seven caps for Scotland.

The camera is invaluable but sometimes it makes memory irrelevant. Last season's goals – even last month's – fade away from the mind because we know we can see them again and again on TV. We no longer need to remember, and I'm as guilty as the next person. But I can still remember every detail of the goal that John McPhail scored in the Scottish Cup Final against Motherwell at Hampden Park on April 21st 1951. Memories were treasured in those days because there was to be no other record of the events; no TV, no video, no playback time and time again (and from all angles). A schoolboy then, I had to memorise all four of Hamlet's soliloquies for my Higher English and, if prompted, I can still quote them extensively.

What sense of perspective – or history – does a present-day member of society have whose memory has not been trained or at least alerted to the value of the past and of history generally? Who can judge the Celtic players of times that went before? How can he or she assess what constitutes a Celtic legend? Logically, the only person fit to judge should be in his mid one hundred and thirties, be of active mind and memory, have seen every Celtic match season after season, be astute enough to separate wheat from chaff, be a football follower and current season-ticket holder, in full possession of all his mental faculties, knowledgeable and objective, un-swayed by sentiment or emotion. There are none like that around I'm afraid.

So it does come down in the end to a matter of opinion. When I was invited to write this chapter, I accepted the invitation without any hesitation – and then the problems began. It boiled down to a matter of choice, and Celtic throughout their history have been blessed with genuine star players. How could I possibly miss out Sunny Jim Young, Celtic's hero for so many seasons between 1903 and 1917? Or Patsy Gallacher, the Mighty Atom, a shrimp of a player who thrilled Celtic Park with his skill and courage between 1911 and 1926? Or Malcolm McDonald? Malcolm who could play any position and who has been described by many reliable judges as the purest footballer who ever pulled on a Celtic jersey?

Teams are recalled with pride, individuals with affection – and, by definition, a legend is a one-off, a unique performer, elevated above his colleagues by ability, performance, achievement and character. This last one is probably the most important to those who are steeped in the ways of Celtic Football Club and the meaningfulness of the club to the Irish diasporic community, Celtic's core supporter.

Football is a collective sport, managers often declaring that no player is bigger than the team and directors insisting that no individual is bigger than the club. Thus, sometimes a grouping of men, indelibly bound in the folk memory and whose names trip lovingly on the tongue, spring to mind: Shaw, McNair and Dodds – a goalkeeper and his two full backs, a trio who perfected – if not invented – the passback as a football tactic, a threesome who played in aggregate more than 1,500 games for Celtic; Evans, Stein and Peacock – a half-back line to savour, and no doubt many recall that all three of these stalwarts were not Catholics. Something that would not need even to be stated only for the troubled society Celtic has found itself in. Nevertheless, those three players formed the turbine that fuelled the Celtic side that emerged to win the league-and-cup double of 1953/54.

Then there was Bennet, McMenemy, Quinn, Somers and Hamilton – a forward line for all time. Alec Bennett and Davie Hamilton were clever and speedy wingers, goalscorers too; Jimmy McMenemy and Peter Somers were the classic Scottish inside-forwards, controlling the tempo of the game and providing the ammunition for the goalscorers; Jimmy Quinn, the greatest centre forward of his day and the spearhead of the line and, when required, the battering ram. Among them they scored 591 goals for Celtic in their years at Parkhead.

Or, Delaney, McDonald, Crum, Divers and Murphy – the forward line in the Empire Exhibition Trophy triumph over Everton in 1938, a match that could be described justifiably as the British Championship. It was a forward line which dazzled, and one that seemed to operate as if by mental telepathy as they interchanged frequently at speed, but never lost their edge and danger. A glorious forward line, sadly broken up at the start of World War II.

What a side those units would make, if they could all be fielded at the same time! To be a legend at Celtic Park is to be a member of a very exclusive club – and what might be the criteria? Talent surely? I must admit a fondness for the likes of Tommy McInally and Charlie Tully but it must be agreed that they were often tiresome and frustrating in their bouts of petulance. They could – and should – have contributed more to Celtic's history than an endless fund of anecdotes. I note also that the same stories, virtually word for word, have been attributed to both of them in some histories although they played a quarter of a century apart.

Talent alone is not enough: we must also have solid accomplishment. One-season wonders, no matter how talented need not apply. Bobby Templeton was probably the most charismatic and dazzling of performers on Celtic's left wing and the story – apparently true – is often told of how he entered the lions' cage at a travelling circus and tweaked a tail for a bet. In his season and a bit (1906/07) at Celtic Park he won both league and Scottish Cup medals but was that enough? Similarly with Paolo di Canio, he of the volcanic temper, the warrior courage and the monstrous ego. In his season (1996/97) with Celtic he thrilled the crowds with his virtuosity but Celtic won absolutely nothing with him in the side. He played for the jersey, but like so many others these days, he also played for himself and a huge wage packet

Accomplishment then? Despite the protestations of the Corinthians, winning is the important thing otherwise why bother keeping the score? A famous victory, if an isolated one, can be a hollow triumph. Poor Willie Miller who had to play for dreadful Celtic sides in the unofficial seasons of World War II and who played so heroically – well enough to win six caps for Scotland – just doesn't qualify, although I think he has been the best goalkeeper I've personally seen playing for the club.

Length of service: surely a very important factor in the equation? A player such as Alec McNair must be considered. He joined Celtic from Stenhousemuir in 1904 as an inside forward, but he played every defensive position for Celtic as well until he retired in 1925. After almost twenty-one seasons at Parkhead he is Celtic's longest-serving player with 604 appearances in major competitions and has a claim to being the club's most versatile player. He was one of the greatest full backs who ever played in the Scottish League, adroit in steering opposing wingers into corners where they could do no damage. He could have played as a sweeper while sitting in a rocking chair, so well could he read the game.

Bobby Evans comes into this long-serving category too. He joined Celtic from St. Anthony's in 1944 and left for Chelsea in mystifying circumstances in 1960, having pulled on the green-and-white jersey 535 times. In the last match of the 1947/48 season, when Celtic flirted with relegation and faced Dundee at Dens Park, Evans was chosen for the first time to start a match at right half and, as the expression goes, the rest is history.

He became a magnificent wing half, a wonderful competitor: nobody ever played better week after week, season after season for so long as Bobby Evans. In the inconsistent Celtic sides of that time Bobby Evans was scrupulously clean and the epitome of reliability and performance. However much both McNair and Evans deserve to be considered as Celtic legends, they are struggling against human nature. Spectators and supporters may admire defenders but the glory in football generally goes to the forwards.

Celtic is a unique football club. From the very start, even before its players kicked a ball, they carried the hopes and aspirations of a community, a community that has grown in recent years via the advancement of the Irish and Irish-Scottish diasporas and the development of modern communications, to being more than a local one. It has to be said though in qualifi-cation, that the local – as in the west of Scotland – will always provide Celtic with its very core as well as its meaningfulness and passion. Nonetheless, in those early years, Celtic's immed-iate success on the football pitch became a source of pride for their downtrodden Irish Catholic followers.

For this reason Celtic players have become heroes in a very different way to that which the modern media is often seen to promote. Celtic's heroes have become community represent-atives – playing for a cause – even when some of these players did not come from that community. So long as they became Celtic Minded that was the essential and only qualification for the support. But what sort of player and person have the fans taken to their heart, recognisable as a Celt, regardless of ethnic background, colour, nationality or religion?

'Heart' might be another key ingredient – the courage to face long odds and the will to succeed even in the most unlikely of circumstances. The men I have chosen as Celtic legends have all demonstrated heart, and have accordingly been rewarded with undying affection by the fans, their exploits recalled and perhaps enhanced by time and in the telling. And legends have accumu-lated a degree of myth about their exploits. When I was a child I was led to believe that Jimmy McGrory scored three goals in three minutes every other week: alas, he only did that once.

Celtic legends are home-spun, modesty still being regarded a virtue in Scotland (though modern entrepreneurs would like to have it otherwise): their skill, character, and achievements are real and not imagined. I was told recently that Ron Atkinson, the one-time TV pundit, had moaned that it was hard to be a legend. Compared to the Celtic men mentioned in this article, characters like Atkinson come across as legends only in their own lunchtimes.

Being a Celtic legend is different from being a legend at another club. We expect and demand other things from a player than talent and professionalism, more than effort and commitment. What is it, this extra dimension we demand? Character on the pitch, and hopefully off it too.

For me the following men represent aspects of the Celtic ideal: they are players to be identified with and to be honoured in the memory as among those who were truly great. They are not heroes because of what they did on the field of play – how can a human being be a hero for football ability or longevity or whatever alone? These particular players are however, legends of Celtic Football Club. They can be listed only in chronological order: Jimmy Quinn, Jimmy McGrory, Jimmy Johnstone and Henrik Larsson.

Jimmy Quinn was the first great Celtic centre forward, a thrusting, charging leader, fearless and single-minded in his pursuit of goals. He was the centre forward as spearhead, marauder, finisher – swashbuckling without any hint of flash. A gritty, courageous performer and a legend for all Celtic supporters, he was feared by opposing supporters and not just for the 217 goals he scored. Football in the early 1900s was a fiercely physical sport and Jimmy Quinn handed out a fair degree of punishment: old films showing goalkeepers gathering the ball and kicking it away in quick, jerky motions do not just reflect the antiquated movie technology as such goalkeepers were an endangered species struggling to survive. It was a rugged struggle in every match, but in those days that was

Jimmy Quinn – as Willie Maley his manager once stated, 'all the men killed by Jimmy Quinn are alive still, and doing well.'

acceptable; jarring tackles were made and accepted without complaint. As Willie Maley his manager once stated, 'all the men killed by Jimmy Quinn are alive still, and doing well.'

His performances against Rangers alone might well have qualified him as a legendary centre forward. He was the first forward to score a hat trick in a Scottish Cup Final, and it came against the Ibrox men in 1904 after Rangers had gone two goals up after only ten minutes. The winning goal was typical of Quinn – bursting through the middle, struggling to keep his feet while being tackled and shoulder-charged, and finishing with a blistering shot as he fell to the ground. Jimmy Quinn was ordered off more than once in matches against Rangers for violent conduct – and that, when added to the inevitable suspensions, earned him the status of martyrdom, endearing him even more to Celtic followers.

As a second generation Irish Catholic Jimmy McGrory was from Celtic's founding and supporting community, being born

Jimmy McGrory was the epitome of the never-say-die player. Celtic through and through

and reared only a few miles from the front doors of Celtic Park. Like Quinn (another second generation Irishman), he was short, stocky and powerful, tireless in his efforts, no matter how hopeless the situation looked. However, unlike Quinn he played for Celtic in lean periods as well as in triumphs. He also played when football was more physical, but he was a most honourable player, a genuine sportsman who was loved – and that is the correct word – throughout the football world. Jack Harkness, a famous Hearts goalkeeper and later a *Sunday Post* journalist, often told of the time he was barracked by the crowd at Celtic Park after he violently pushed McGrory aside in the penalty area. Harkness – incidentally a close personal friend of the Celtic centre – had realised that McGrory, while diving headlong for the ball, was on a collision course with the post: he went for McGrory instead of the ball and pushed him away from danger amid howls from the terracing for a penalty kick. McGrory made a point of telling the Celtic following that Harkness had stopped him from being seriously injured, and the crowd for Hearts next visit to Celtic Park gave Harkness a standing ovation.

Despite a loan period with Clydebank early in his career, he has to be considered a one-club man, even resisting a disgraceful attempt by Celtic to sell him to Arsenal in 1928, the transfer fee allegedly being earmarked to pay for Celtic's new grandstand.

During the dark days of massive unemployment in Scotland, Jimmy McGrory supported virtually single-handedly his entire family. Apparently he was so good-natured, Christian and charitable that he would give away the money in his pockets to the less fortunate who lay in wait for him as he walked to Celtic Park along London Road. Eventually his sister had to stealthily take the silver coins out of his pockets and replace them with coppers.

McGrory was the epitome of the never-say-die player, never better exemplified than in the 1931 Scottish Cup final against Motherwell. Celtic were two goals down and being outplayed by the classy 'Well side with only seven minutes left when McGrory slid in to get one goal back. In the dying seconds, his presence in the penalty box distracted Allan Craig and caused the Motherwell player to head into his own net for a most dramatic moment in Scottish Cup history.

Between 1921 and 1937, when he retired to become Kilmarnock's manager, Jimmy McGrory, the greatest goalscorer ever in senior Scottish football with 468 for Celtic, was an inspiration. Very many of these goals came from his head; he was able to hover in the air – in the manner of Larsson's goal against Porto in the 2003 UEFA Cup final – and it was claimed that not only was he defying the Law of Gravity but that he had repealed it. Despite his record – and success in a Scotland shirt – he gained only a miserly seven caps, a disgraceful state of affairs but one which gained him much sympathy from the Celtic support who considered the repeated snubs as evidence of anti-Catholic, anti-Irish and anti-Celtic racism and sectarian-ism before such words had taken their place in the English language and became an apparent concern to so many in modern Scottish society.

Jimmy Johnstone – his forte was dribbling but his greatest attribute was sheer physical courage after being treated brutally by many defenders unable to cope with his trickery

Then there was Jinky. Jimmy Johnstone was an often troubled wee man, plagued by insecurity despite his incredible talent. Even today, watching him on video dribble past much taller defenders, twisting and turning and bewildering the likes of the most sporting full back Davie Provan of Rangers, simply makes you smile. Humberto Maschio, the playmaker of the Racing Club of Buenos Aires, shook his head and told me in 2005: 'Jimmy Johnstone! Impossible to stop: estupendo, magnifico, superbo, the best'.

Troubled and often undisciplined, Jimmy nevertheless represents a West of Scotland type – and not really a nasty one. As a former schoolteacher I tend to see him as an occasionally wayward pupil, but an endearing one, a boy who wants to be good and tries – the sort of Catholic who goes to confession and is heartily sorry for his sins, does intend to reform – and sometimes fails: but the intention is there, the attempts are made.

Some of his greatest performances were on the big stage: in the European Cup and in matches against Rangers. Nobody could ever forget his play against Red Star of Belgrade when, prompted by a Jock Stein promise of being excused a flight to Yugoslavia in return for a four-goal lead against one of the great European sides, he simply ran riot. Also, his memorable jinks against the England full back Terry Cooper when Celtic outplayed Leeds United twice in the 1970 European Cup. Campbell Ogilvie, Rangers longtime secretary, confided to a Celtic director: 'my heart used to sink whenever I saw that wee man take the field against us'. A wee man, yes, but he scored quite a few goals against Rangers with headers by outjumping their defenders in a crowded penalty area.

As a player his forte was dribbling but his greatest attribute was sheer physical courage after being treated brutally by many defenders unable to cope with his trickery; but he would demand the ball again and face up to the bullying. Perhaps in recent years that courage was more than physical as he struggled against, and finally succumbed to, Motor Neurone Disease in early 2006.

Recently he was selected in a poll as 'Celtic's Greatest-Ever Player'. However, many thousands of Celtic supporters past and present did not vote. Personally I don't think he was the greatest, but I don't grudge him the accolade: I can understand the emotional attachment felt by the Celtic support towards Jinky and therefore the vote in his favour. He was certainly one of the greatest.

Take those first three players; Quinn, McGrory and Johnstone. All of them were quite typical of many second and third generation Irish Catholics who were born into humble circumstances (indeed, often very poor circumstances) in the Scottish west central belt; Quinn in a miners' row in Croy, McGrory in a Garngad tenement, and Johnstone in a deprived Lanarkshire council estate: all around ten miles from each other too. They all improved their lives through football and playing for Celtic and their community. All of them were modest, humble men. Jimmy Quinn was reluctant to sign senior forms and insisted he was meant to be only a junior, Jimmy McGrory never wanted to play for any other club and did so for £9 a week, a pound less than most of his colleagues whom he had carried for seasons. Jimmy Johnstone, when eventually he left Celtic, was never the same player: in Celtic and its supporting community he found a strong identity.

Whenever these men took the field in a Celtic jersey the supporters knew they were going to get 100% effort from one of their own. The fans identified with them completely: they sensed that these men, if they were not playing for Celtic, would be actively supporting them. They were not idols placed upon a pedestal and out of reach: they were down-to-earth and approachable. Their gifts as players might have been sublime but their lives were ordinary and I note that all three of them share the same Christian name, and that it has been changed into the Glasgow vernacular as 'Jimmy', and with some affection.

The last player chosen is a different breed altogether, but like all the good and great who come to Celtic and become 'Celtic Minded', a very welcome man. Henrik Larsson came from Feyenoord as a gifted player and he developed at Celtic Park into a world-class player. More importantly, he stayed at Parkhead for seven years – the best seasons of his football career. Born of a Swedish mother and a Portuguese father, Larsson's early life in Sweden could not have been easy but he became a thoroughly modern professional footballer: always fit, always active, always trying his best.

Martin O'Neill's Celtic teams were unfairly described as Leicester City North or Nottingham Forest North plus Larsson, and I suppose there's a degree of truth – but not the entire truth – in the charge. Henrik Larsson was one player who made Celtic a European power during those great O'Neill seasons. I have never seen a striker work so hard as Larsson, tirelessly foraging and giving defenders no respite. How often did Larsson manage to ease the pressure on Celtic's defence by gaining a throw-in or a corner out of unlikely situations? Even more critically, how often did Larsson's goals – and so often late ones – mean the difference between defeat and victory?

And he started so discouragingly too by giving the ball away at Easter Road in August 1997 a few minutes after coming on as a substitute against Hibernian and seeing Chic Charnley netting the winner from his misplaced ball. His first great game for Celtic also started poorly when he netted an own-goal for Tirol Innsbruck at Celtic Park on August 26th 1997 just before halftime. Nonetheless, the real Henrik delivered in the second half and he terrorised the Austrian defenders by marauding up and down the left wing inspiring Celtic to a memorable 6-3 win and qualification to the next round.

I would have to say that his greatest goalscoring was against Hearts at Tynecastle on February 4th 2001 when he netted a memorable hat-trick as snow flurries shrouded the Edinburgh ground. If memory serves me correctly, all were prime examples of the predator's art, half-chances clinically finished off and with his left foot, his right foot and his head: a predator, as sleek as a leopard. Courage too in coming back so well and so soon from a broken leg sustained against Olympique Lyon in 1999: add to that a broken jaw against Livingston in 2003 only a few months before his two-goal heroics in Seville against Porto in a gallant losing cause.

Larsson rarely played to the gallery, never kissing the Celtic badge on his jersey and only occasionally – if it was late in the game and Celtic leading comfortably – waving in response to the songs about him. In temperament, he was cool and we rarely saw or heard Larsson giving interviews, there was no media intrusion into his family life, there was no hint of scandal. He may have frustrated some of us by not saying very much at all, by not using his position to take sides on some of the big issues in life, to speak out, to distinguish right from wrong, to promote a worthwhile – even if controversial – cause. However, he was a footballer after all, and like any man, he is entitled to choose to keep his counsel or to brave the forces of wrong as befits his humanity, faith and persona. We must all account for our lives in a similar way.

At his final league match at Celtic Park and at his testimonial

Henrik Larsson –
leading the line
1997–2004

game, when he was given the most prolonged and emotional farewell possible before a packed stadium, at last there were tears – on the pitch and in the stands. I have the distinct feeling that, when Henrik Larsson finally retires, he will recall his career as Henrik Larsson of Celtic and not of Feyenoord or Barcelona.

I watched the film Spartacus recently, and I noted the words delivered by the grizzled gladiator-master to his new recruits: 'I was the best because the crowd loved me. Win the crowd, and you win your freedom.' It reminded me of the true Celtic legends who did exactly that – but unconsciously. Only a few people in life become legends: some we hear about and most never. Much is required to become a 'Celtic legend' – as with life itself, that's the way it should be.

The Glasgow Celtic Way: Valuing the Ethos

ROISIN COLL AND ROBERT A. DAVIS

Recognition that sport and ethics are intimately linked is a perception as old as sport itself. In important respects, the connection emerges from the nature of sport and the way in which sporting activity is conducted. As rule-governed experiences, individual sports lay moral obligations on their participants, often accompanied by strict enforcement regulations and punishments for transgressors. These are essential to the operation of the sport.[1] More positively, however, in the development of the regulatory systems that guarantee the effective functioning of the game or activity, individual sports almost always lean towards the promotion of certain positive virtues among participants and spectators that radiate beyond the sporting occasion itself.

Hence our long-standing acquaintance with concepts such a 'the Corinthian spirit', the 'healthy body healthy mind' mentality or, the ideals of fairness and honest competitiveness that sport is routinely intended to foster.[2] Today people often view some of these ideals with scepticism, given what we now know of their misuse in the past and their frequent betrayal by the 'industrialised' and highly 'capitalised' sporting systems of the present era. Nevertheless, popular enthusiasm for sports of all kinds, and particularly for the involvement of young people in sport through their education and leisure, necessarily retains much of this idealism.

Association football as a pastime inextricably bound up with the culture and experience of the urban working class has deep and tangled roots in the notion of the ethical education and formation of its participants, players and supporters. In the nineteenth century, football brought discipline to the young men of working class communities, dissipating aggression and

(1) S. Loland Fair Play in Sport: A Moral Norm System, London: Routledge, 2002.

(2) R. Gough Character is everything: promoting ethical excellence in sports, Orlando: Harcourt Brace, 1997.

channelling energy, and was frequently directed and promoted by the moral guardians of these communities in churches, trade unions and civic associations. However, we might now evaluate these underlying motives. Historically football brought to marginal and materially impoverished groups, sporting ideals previously regarded as the preserve of the middle classes. Modern football is heir to this Victorian endeavour and the paradoxes attached to it.[3] The traditions of association football can be seen as expressions of social control or, equally, as incentives to forms of virtuous behaviour that bring esteem, purpose and structure to the lives of those attached to them.[4]

These paradoxes deepen in the context of the modern game, where the mass appeal of football can be legitimately interpreted as a fertile context for the moral development of its participants, but where the rich repository of ethical principle on which football can justly claim to draw runs up against realities that prompt serious misgivings about football's continuing moral relevance to society at large. Issues such as the materialism of contemporary soccer, the disparities of wealth and poverty it so habitually exposes – between clubs themselves and often between clubs and their supporters – and the sometimes less than uplifting lifestyles of players in the 'footballers wives' era of personal conduct, are difficult to reconcile with concepts of a moral community. The tragic and iconic figure of George Best perhaps typifies this ambivalence: a player whose personal moral failings were part of his image, yet whose story – particularly in its earliest phases – rehearsed many of the uplifting features of the beautiful game.

At their best, major football clubs can be seen to exhibit their own distinctive inflection of the moral ethos of football. This is to say no more (and no less) than that football clubs have the potential to generate and sustain moral communities, from out of the rich reserves of their collective memory, their narratives, their networks, the conduct of their affairs and their expression of values indigenous to the corporate experience of the club and its 'family' of fans.

The extent to which Celtic Football Club and its supporters can lay claim to certain values is an issue that Celtic has itself

(3) S. Tischler, Footballers and Businessmen: The Origins of Professional Soccer in England, New York: Holmes and Meier, 1981.

(4) J. A. Mangan, 'Soccer as Moral Training: Missionary Intentions and Imperial Legacies', Soccer and Society, 2.2, Summer 2001, 41-56.

publicly debated and discussed. The most obvious manifestation of this is the Celtic Social Charter that in its construction purports to articulate the core values of the club in a local and national setting. The Charter records a series of aspirations for the club and its support that invoke the clearly sport-derived language of 'being the best':

> The best that Celtic stands for is supporting the charitable principles of its founder.
>
> The best that Celtic stands for is promoting health and well-being, understanding and positive social integration.
>
> The best that Celtic stands for is as an inclusive organisation being open to all regardless of age, sex, race, religion or disability.
>
> The best that Celtic stands for is upholding a shared set of positive values including success, fair play, and appreciation of skills.
>
> The best that Celtic stands for is building on the renowned qualities of our supporters.[5]

The Charter is more than a managerial mission statement. Attached to each of the aspirations is a commitment to action, and a set of dispositions, and the key to these actions and dispositions is the club's relationship with its supporters. To require supporters 'to ensure that they live up to best that Celtic stands for', assumes shared ownership of what the Charter elsewhere describes as 'the ideals associated with the founding of the Club.' Such ideals are the characteristics of moral communities and arise out of features of the club's identity. They are ideals shaped by a unique history, by shared memories, by a narrative interwoven with the cultural experience of a specific social and ethnic group, by a gallery of inspirational figures and episodes seen as emblematic of the club and its traditions. Above all, they are the grammar of an international, diverse yet unified network of fans, which both reflects and renews these ideals in the spirit of the club as its story goes on.

(5) http://www.celticfc.net/socialcharter/celtic_charity_fund.asp (last accessed 290106)

All of these features may well be discerned, of course, in the language and posture of other football clubs. Indeed, they may well be, in important respects, signifiers of greatness in the projection of teams such as Liverpool, Manchester United, Barcelona, Juventus and Celtic (to name only a sample). If they are, in fact, essential to the stature and presence of these clubs on the stage of global football, it is worth enquiring how a club like Celtic actually understands them and how its fanbase actually encounters and experiences them. What might be the distinctive *moral* salience of Celtic football club and what kind of moral principles are definitively a part of the fabric of the institution, and why?

An obvious starting point for addressing these questions lies in the charitable foundations of the club.[6] As the Charter testifies, these foundations are not simply an historical legacy to be sentimentally curated by contemporary followers. The strength of feeling that surrounded the unveiling of the statue of Brother Walfrid in 2005, with its open invocation of Celtic's original purposes, underlined the continuing investments of the fans in at least the charitable actions of the club. This is expressed also in the partnership of fans and players, as evidenced in occasions such as Neil Lennon's tribute night, Stan Petrov's involvement with orphanages and the fulsome support of a range of local good causes associated with children and the sick. Resounding public endorsements of what might be termed the culture of charity, such as the award of the FIFA Fair Play accolade to the fans are to be welcomed, but behind these lie deeper expressions of supporter solidarity and goodwill disclosed in episodes such as the many 'Good Samaritan' stories recounted about the journey to Seville, and the many examples of Celtic fans in Spain resisting the ticket touts and reselling tickets at cost price to fellow Celts.[7] The anecdotes convey something of the way in which a club is understood by and relates to its community.

In its origins, Celtic was a paternalistic venture, entirely appropriate for the period, designed to reflect the values of and also to inject values into, an Irish Catholic community suffering the disorientating traumas of immigration, industrialisation and prejudice. Now, in the era of global soccer, the relationship between Celtic and its supporters is more reciprocal, where the fans themselves help inspire the club to live up to its

(6) Frank O'Hagan, 'Celtic and Charity'. Celtic Minded: Essays on Religion, Politics, Identity and. . . Football. Ed. Joseph M. Bradley. Glendaruel: Argyll Publishing, 2004. 93-99.

(7) A. Smith and S. Houston. Ed. Over and Over: The Story of Seville. Daily Record Publications, 2003. 97-98.

own ideals, even within the tensions of the modern game and the marketisation of sport.

The modernisation of football is not just about commercialisation. It is about the transformation from the organic to the cosmopolitan, and we know from many other spheres of human activity that this transformation is often accompanied by the breakdown of values and connections. Unity of purpose among the Celtic fanbase is about the continual reassertion of hope, recapitulating one of the key motivations of the founders. This hope is adherence to the belief that things can get better and that lives can be lived by higher standards than those dictated by circumstance. Attachment to these versions of hope is part of the character of Celtic. It is what empowers the conscientious majority of fans to moderate fraternally but robustly the excesses in language and behaviour of the wayward minority, particularly in the stands of Celtic Park, in the confident assertion that 'Celtic are not about this'. The ethical import of these interventions lies in the fact that they are not simply about how 'the other' is seen and treated, but about the self-respect of the fans who inherit or who sign up to Celtic's values.

The partnership of players and supporters is crucial here and Celtic have been fortunate over the generations in producing role models widely admired for the example they set. Billy McNeil, as player and manager, conveyed loyalty and integrity to spectators and earned a national reputation for dignity in victory and defeat. Tommy Burns communicated to a rising generation of younger fans a football personality in which religious commitment reinforced a vision of footballing excellence and social responsibility. Danny McGrain embodied the virtues of determination, unswerving solidarity with team-mates and open, honest engagements with fans.

In more recent times, the character of two men from quite contrasting points of origin has exemplified the moral fibre of Celtic, at home and abroad, and the values by which the club aspires to live even in the ambiguous climate of the modern game. Henrik Larsson was to Celtic fans the total footballer, at the heart of whose self-projection lay a clear ethical conception of the modern player professional. If virtue is indeed a kind of habit of being. Larsson demonstrated that none of these characteristics needed to be paraded before a cynical media, but would convince simply by the authority of their own quiet demonstration, in word and action, on and off the pitch. From almost the opposite end of the personality spectrum, Martin O'Neill's obvious passion for Celtic illustrated how idealistic commitment and the insistence on hope could galvanise the Celtic community. O'Neill's enthusiasm for the club and its traditions was purified of any suggestion of tribalism by his own declared principles and the values base from which they sprang – values embedded in proper ambition, dynamic self-belief and resilience in the face of adversity. His rekindling of the European dream at Celtic Park was driven by an unfailing optimism that quite deliberately encouraged younger fans and younger players to reconnect with the memory of Lisbon and therefore deepen their appreciation of the club and its core values.[8]

O'Neill's tenure as manager undoubtedly worked a renewal not only of footballing fortune but also of the moral principles for which Celtic has stood. O'Neill's appetite for success drove fans to a better understanding of an experience vital to the ethos of Celtic: 'belonging'. The nature of belonging to Celtic is inextricably bound up with a network of other investments and affiliations to which the Celtic fanbase is implicitly bound: Irishness and Catholicism being the two most prominent ones and which also distinguish the club and its supporters. The attempts to create a taboo on booing players and the insistence on staying for ninety minutes, even when facing defeat or disappointment, frequently differentiate Celtic from other teams (dissatisfaction among the Liverpool fans with the small minority who left the 2005 European Champions League final at half-time illustrates this).[9]

Renewed efforts in the area of anti-sectarianism in the O'Neill era stemmed from a similar confidence in the values base and heritage of the club – values that can be mobilised in the outreach to foreign players new to the club and its ways and in the welcome extended to both players and fans from the giants of European football such as Bayern Munich and AC Milan.

(8) A. Montgomery, Martin O'Neill: The Biography. London: Virgin Books, 2003.

(9) http://football.guardian.co.uk/comment/story 0,9753,1669906,00.html (last accessed 280105)

Belonging is a frequently misunderstood and mistrusted value in football. Yet Celtic's exemplary record on anti-sectarianism, even from its very first days when the club refused to go the same way as other more limited clubs and signed players from numerous faith backgrounds, arises out of its sense of belonging rather than from any externally-imposed or even cosmopolitan ethic. Easily misrepresented as narrowness and exclusivity, the belonging for which Celtic stands affirms legitimate claims on heritage, recollection and identity, but only because these wellsprings are held – especially by many of the supporters – in themselves to be virtuous sources of moral awareness, underpinning the welcome to the stranger, the conviviality of shared sporting passions and the hospitality to all people of goodwill.

Belonging, hope and charity are sometimes portrayed as outdated qualities in the contemporary world. But they form part of a rich moral lexicon, the vocabulary of which derives from a moral *theology* to which Celtic Football Club and those who follow it are also inescapably attached: Faith, Hope and Love. And the greatest of these is love. Behind the ethical principles for which Celtic stands, underpinning the value system to which the club and its supporters make reference lies religious conviction. This fact is acknowledged less and less readily in the modern secular age. Indeed, it is almost perceived as archaic or politically incorrect to discuss something that has religious conviction at its roots and, when it does occasionally become visible, it is usually subject to the withering gaze of a cynical media. Hence when the Church issued advice on personal conduct and sexual morality to Celtic fans travelling to Seville, the guidance was scornfully portrayed as infantile and anachronistic by the Scottish national press.[10]

Even though the advice might have fallen on many deaf ears as well as upon the more morally virtuous and conscientious amongst the large Celtic support, the fact that the Church could actually invoke the ideas and language of virtuous conduct, fidelity and self-respect in its communication to the supporters, underlined the continuing moral purchase of this language on the attention of Celtic fans in a generally post-religious culture.

(10) Daily Record, Monday 12 May 2003, p1.

It may, indeed, have been met with some amusement by many of the people at whom it was aimed, but its seriousness of purpose was recognised by Celtic fans whose religious beliefs – however we might construct these – continue to be part of the ambience of moral life and 'doing the right thing' as they move through the orbit of the club. The discourse of the Church still had relevance to them despite living in a society that is rapidly secularising and has long been anti-Catholic to a greater or lesser degree. That a football club in the twenty first century has sustained this level of engagement with its supporters points to something special in its community: perhaps nothing less than the charisma of Celtic Football Club.

Section 2
Contemplated Fandom

Never been there but still sharing the love

Joe Horgan

It is the absence of Celtic that I have experienced most: a gap where the club and its supporters' culture should have been. I have stood on the terraces and sang. I have stood on the terraces and jumped with joy. Cried. Felt football as a fantastic, wonderful piece of theatre. Understood something of what community and identity mean through following a football team. But the fault line that was always there, one that I thought was to do with age and distance and the game, now being played by money-soaked mercenaries, was one widened by something else too: by an absence of Celtic. I have stood in the rain and the sun for a team I thought was mine. And they were mine. They were. But they weren't mine the way Celtic are yours.

I grew up in England of Irish-born parents, within hearing distance of a football ground. On match nights I could see the glow of the lights and hear the roar of the crowd. When I was about five my father took me there and I was hooked. I fell for it and my Irish-born father indulged my love and brought me back again and again. Of course, looking back now I see things that at the time were only the most vague shadows of thoughts, understandings and articulations. In my innocent love I could barely make them out, but there was always something tangible that despite our love for the game, kept my father and I apart from soccer and, ironically in turn, kept him and I together: the Irishman and his son.

You Celtic fans won't know what I'm talking about because at Celtic it wouldn't arise. But this wasn't Celtic you see: Celtic was only there by its absence. These were the terraces of England and he was Irish and I was his son and the team we loved and followed and the fans we were part of, well, they weren't Irish. Not even nearly, not at all in fact; not in terms of community, family, background, heritage, identity, songs, culture, colours or social or political preferences. We stood out, maybe only in our heads, but we stood out: actually, not maybe only in our heads, but truly in our heads, in our minds and in our hearts. As life was made up of Mass, the Catholic school and our Irish house on our English street and, the odd time we went to an Irish bar or an Irish club, I see now that this was the only time my Irish father and I ever stood together in England: on those terraces there. And we cheered and celebrated. But we didn't sing when they sang for England and we didn't stand by those who carried union jacks. There were other social and cultural customs that we didn't share but they were largely unspoken, unexplored and sometimes intangible – but they were there – and we were here. We were different.

> Celtic truly is a club that exists outside of its own geography, beyond the boundaries of its own national league.

Difference was fine and we all lived with it. These things happen when you are of a family and community that has moved from one country to live in another. However, that wasn't the point as I discovered in later life reflections. No one ever said anything and no one suggested it was more their club than ours but it was. It was England there on those terraces and they were all English. Not that I want to give the wrong impression about this, I loved that club and I was as much a fan as anyone else and nobody ever suggested otherwise. It's just that those things that somehow gave me a slither of distance became magnified as the years went by. As it became harder and harder to relate to a club where millionaire players just seemed to pass through, I began to search for something in vain that would tie me to the club. I couldn't. I can't, though I keep looking. I keep hanging on. My family and my community's distinctiveness is not matched by the club I supported. There is no obvious reflection, no similarity of experience, no coming together of aspirations and goals: no imagination or vision of a people on the march.

Of course I could be a Celtic fan, for in the age of globalisation, with football clubs franchised throughout continents and marketing strategies beginning to dominate, with players who sell replica shirts being viewed just as importantly as a player with a trusty right foot or a sweet left one, Celtic is unique. Celtic truly is a club that exists outside of its own geography, beyond the boundaries of its own national league. Real Madrid, Manchester United, Chelsea – they are football clubs as an arm of business. Far Eastern tours are undertaken in order to maximise commercial potential, planned as a part of financial strategy. People thousands of miles away from Manchester are sold red shirts and an image of sport, of being a supporter in the same way that we are sold images and ideas through movies or music. They purchase a sense of belonging. It is football as virtual reality, stadium as theme park, match day as a trip to Disneyland. Celtic is different.

Not that I want to give the impression that I believe Celtic to be above all that. Nowadays many people see business as business after all. No, Celtic, rightly or wrongly, also has those dimensions to its identity and culture. What I mean is, that as a club founded by and for Irish immigrants in the west of Scotland Celtic really does have a genuine appeal beyond the streets of Glasgow. In fact an integral part of the club is that very appeal, that part of it that is in some way a reflection of the immigrant experience that is in some way recognisable to all of those within the Irish diaspora. Celtic is a part of the identity of the Irish outside of Ireland. I never think there is anything strange about meeting someone in England or Ireland who supports Celtic yet when it is Manchester United or Liverpool and you are far away from either of those cities I can't help but wonder where the allegiance has come from or how artificial and commercially constructed it is. Celtic though is different, so different in fact that the Glasgow bit doesn't even have to be used. Celtic is ours even if we are not fans. Celtic is Ireland's creation and from Ireland has developed a sense of belonging. Not a narrow vision of Ireland but an Ireland that extends beyond the island and out to and within the diaspora. It is also an Irishness that like St Patrick's Day across the globe can be shared and celebrated by people of any national and religious background: thus, along with the inherent Catholic identities of the club and its support, accounting partly for Celtic's openness as a football club.

I remember one time that I worked in a pub and came in one evening and the function room was booked. Inside a Celtic Supporters group was having a bash and although there were

> Celtic is a part of the identity of the Irish outside of Ireland.

one or two Glasgow accents they were mostly accents like mine. Lads walked in and out in the green and white hoops. They sang the Irish songs we'd all grown up with. They waved the tri-colour: and all this in Birmingham in the middle of England. It was like St. Patrick's Day on an ordinary Saturday night. And St. Patrick's Day and the Celtic tops were always one and the same too. They were saying something about us. Even those of us who supported other clubs found something we felt about ourselves and our Irish Catholic lives in Britain in the form of Celtic. So on Paddy's day and many other days I could find myself standing next to my brother in a pub, a brother who followed the same English football club as me, and he'd be wearing a Celtic top. It never seemed to occur to anyone to point out that he had never been to see them.

So who am I to write about Celtic? I've never been to Glasgow. Apart from the TV experience I have never seen Celtic play. I remember one time in a pub in England by chance coming across a Celtic match live on the box and suddenly really wanting them to win. I recall at the time thinking it was odd that this club, this team that I didn't really follow should mean anything to me at all. But of course it did. For I support Celtic as an Irish team, as an immigrant team, as a diaspora team. I look out for their scores solely on that basis. I am enough of a football fan to know that any true Celtic fan would soon know I wasn't one and I would never try to pretend I was. Instead I have found myself wishing wistfully that we had a Celtic of our own in England when I was growing up. A club that whatever the vagaries of fate, that whatever the distortions of the game, I would have belonged to because they would have been what I was – and they would have belonged to me. Not partially what I was, not temporarily what I was but representative of me and my Irish experience in Britain. A football club in Britain that was not only considered Irish but specifically immigrant Irish. A club to remind you of who you were, not who you weren't. So all I can write about Celtic is their absence. And where there was no Celtic there is a vacuum between me and the game, me and my assertion of who I am me and my right to my diasporic Irishness and, as the years press on, the vacuum grows.

Ah, if we only had old Celtic down here.

Being Celtic Minded

ANDREW MILNE

When Celtic record memorable victories, I feel that the endless miles on the pilgrimage to and from Glasgow is well worth it. When results don't go our way, we're frustrated and we'll have a good moan, but within hours of returning home we'll have our names down for the next trip and gradually we'll come around to looking forward to supporting the bhoys once more.

Many people I meet find it strange that fifty odd men and women from around my home town and surrounding villages in Ireland get up in the early hours of the morning every second week during the football season and jump on a bus to make the journey to Celtic Park. Sometimes I often question it myself, but ultimately, I always end up realising that the positives far outweigh the negatives. Celtic Football Club has become a major part of my adult life. Originally I did not come from a Celtic family. I have no links with Glasgow, none of my relations in the past to my knowledge emigrated to Scotland. My cousin traced back the family tree and found that my father's family had actually come to Ireland from Dundee and had no Irish blood, while for my mother's family, the Flanagan's, that history is firmly based in Ireland.

My mother and father emigrated to London in the 1950s in search of work. My mother returned homesick while my father stayed on and sent money home to support his young family. My father may not have brought us up following Celtic but he always taught us to respect other people from other cultures and religions. He had witnessed at first hand how the Irish and other emigrants from past and present British colonies were faced with racist discrimination just like the early Irish settlers in Glasgow and its surrounding towns after they were forced to flee their homeland during the Great Irish Famine and the decades thereafter.

What I have learned from my father over the years, I have

taught my young son, Conor, who has likewise been brought up to respect people of all colours, creeds and nationalities. This isn't unconnected to support for a football team. When you follow a club like Celtic it is important that you are educated in the Celtic way and I don't just mean knowing who the greatest goal scorer ever was, the greatest goalkeeper, being able to name the Lisbon Lions or to buy the club magazine every week.

Celtic is much more than just a football team it could not be special to so many people otherwise. It is part of a way of life, it is an important part of the history of the Irish in Ireland and of the immigrant diaspora in Scotland, it is part of humanity's history of survival, of raising itself up and prospering, but ever mindful of where it came from and ever willing to reach out and help others in a position once experienced at first hand. It is the history of people once forced en mass to live in slum conditions facing exploitation, discrimination, sectarianism and racism. These people were faced with many difficulties but gave birth to a club that made them proud of their Irishness in a country where the very concept of Irishness was portrayed as negative and bad in virtually everyway possible. However, as history tells us, there is nothing second-class about Celtic Football Club and those who support the club.

The memory of our most significant founding father, Brother Walfrid, lives with us in the monument that now stands outside Celtic Park. It should be a reminder of why Celtic was formed and why we are so distinctive. For many Irish people in Ireland who do not support Celtic, they fail to see just why so many from the Emerald Isle are so passionate about a club that plays in another country.

Celtic is the football club of the people: an Irish Football Club and a Scottish institution and like all people and institutions of any diaspora, it's hybrid in nature. It is also true that the majority of fans come from a Catholic background and the club can be proud of its connections with Ireland as well as Scotland and its connections with the Catholic Church. Although these things define Celtic and give it its uniqueness, the club also holds a wider appeal, an appeal that would make Brother Walfrid very proud.

As a club that's now a multi million pound business and a far cry from its humble beginnings, Brother Walfrid would struggle to recognise Celtic now. However, he was a man of his times and times have changed. He may not have much in common with the current business men who run football or the millionaires that play at the highest levels but he would find much solidarity with the Celtic support: they would still be his people. Many of their troubles haven't changed that much – they've just been recycled. It would also bring a smile to his face to see those people from different nationalities and religions passing his monument on match days, to play a part in the Celtic story. Walfrid's monument is a fitting tribute to him while it is also fitting that all the money raised for that particular project came from ordinary supporters – not those wealthy or celebrity supporters that many like to focus upon.

I have met supporters from many backgrounds in Glasgow and on trips to Europe and even in the Las Vegas heat at the North American Celtic Supporters conventions. Although most supporters I have met are Catholic, Irish-born or of Irish extraction, I have also met supporters from other religious backgrounds and none, all of them with a passion for Celtic. In addition, what other club can boast supporters clubs in such far flung destinations around the world. The key to the spreading of the faith and identity that is Celtic lies not with any sophisticated marketing or promotion techniques on the part of the club, this has spread, developed and grown through the very people who have the club at heart: the supporters of Celtic have always been the clubs best ambassadors. Irishness, the Catholic faith, a welcoming embrace for people not from an Irish or Catholic background, support for liberation struggles across the globe, a preference for the poor and the marginalised, a rich history and tradition and a romantic and stunning experience: these are what make us what we are.

Until people experience the Celtic supporting culture they will never fully understand why Celtic is such a unique institution. Reading some crass books about our great club will not tell the story, especially when so many are made-up and contrived to suit commercial purposes. A focus on celebrity players as opposed to the culture and history that is Celtic will not help develop understanding either. You can watch all the videos, documentaries and DVDs of goals and cup wins you want – that's part of the great game of football and of every football club – but you really have to invest understanding and to experience supporting Celtic at first hand to fully appreciate what the club is really all about.

Standing at Celtic Park on a big European night and joining with 60,000 other like-minded people singing 'Walk On' is something special. It can be an emotional experience for supporters, so it must be wonderful for the players to run onto the field of dreams and witness a sea of green, white and orange singing with such passion. When they go into the huddle the roar from the stadium can be heard for miles around. Nonetheless, such events and rituals are just a part of what being a Celtic fan means. It is the people, the history, the culture and the songs that really make this club special. It is from these sources that passion grows and gets such a hold that never lets you go.

The build-up to games, the atmosphere in pubs before and after games, the stories from older Celtic fans who recall many great stories. I don't care if some of the stories they tell are only half true, I never get bored of hearing them. I have heard stories of great players, great games, great victories against Rangers, but the ones I love to hear about are of the antics that supporters have got up to over the years from stealing push bikes to get to Portugal before getting arrested only miles from Lisbon and arriving the day after the game or the one about the bus load of supporters who went to Hungry for a European game and it took them so long to get back to Glasgow that they missed the second leg. Classics!

It is the camaraderie between the fans that counts, and often from different towns, cities and countries and of course, even from different backgrounds. I have met some of my closest friends through following Celtic and can't imagine what life would be like if my older brother Eamon had not introduced me to Celtic. Like my father and mother before them, my brothers were forced to emigrate to find work in London, they settled just outside the capital in Reading and Eamon travelled up by train from his new home to Glasgow for a Rangers game.

A week or so after the game, the match programme and a copy of a Celtic fanzine arrived in the post. The following Christmas he arrived home with a book on Celtic and a video telling the history of the club. I won't say I was hooked but I became interested, especially in the Irish connection and a few weeks after I was lucky enough to see Celtic for the first time in January 1989. If memory serves me right I paid £2 at the turnstiles and sat in the family section. We beat Dumbarton 2-0 in the Scottish Cup, I went back to Ireland that night a happy young man and even managed to get Mick McCarthy's autograph. Little did I know that night on my way home how many times I would repeat that journey.

The Celtic culture has also helped shape my political and social opinions. Unlike my father and my brothers, I have been lucky enough to have found work in my home town and I have never had to emigrate. In recent years Ireland has gone through an economic boom. Thankfully the Celtic Tiger has seen an increase in Irish workers returning home and settling in Dublin and surrounding satellite towns but unfortunately the capital still has homeless people sleeping on its streets and often people lie waiting for a bed on trolleys up and down the country in our hospitals.

As the country gets richer and prospers, just like in Scotland, we still witness children going hungry and immigrants to our shores treated with the prejudice many experienced as Irish men and women who left their homeland in search of a better life for themselves and their families. Due to the economic growth in the country many immigrants have entered the country in search of employment and a decent standard of living. Some have come as refugees from war-torn countries in Africa and others from former Eastern Bloc countries along with western Europeans.

As Ireland was the last white outpost in Western Europe it is understandable that people, especially elderly ones, are sceptical of all the change around and suspicious of the new arrivals. Like many other western societies Ireland is a concern as it now seems to be becoming a country where many people are more worried about materialistic things than about issues that involve community, humanity and the spiritual things of life. The new car, the American fridge and the gold credit card are the must-haves of even some of the working classes today.

Unfortunately for most Irish immigrants in the past the streets of New York, London and Glasgow were rarely paved with gold and the Irish emigrants were exploited and used for cheap labour or to enlist in armies and fight for a foreign government in a foreign land. Most never returned to the land they yearned for. The exploitation of the Irish in Glasgow is well known to the Celtic family. Those who were forced to flee Ireland were met with, high unemployment and low paid jobs in Scotland. Emigrants lived in slum conditions. The Catholic Church must have been a sanctuary for the Irish in Glasgow as was the formation of Celtic Football Club. Not only did the new club give them an outlet to express their Irishness, it gave them a new found pride. The club was also used by founding father Brother Walfrid to raise much-needed funds to feed the hungry Catholic Irish children of the city.

For many immigrants to Ireland today many of these conditions don't apply. Many new refugees have been housed and fed while immigrants coming to work have found employment. However just like the Irish in Glasgow, new arrivals have met numerous obstacles. Many are being exploited by greedy landlords and are working for similarly greedy employers for below the minimum wage. The average working week is thirty-nine hours and anything over that is overtime. Many of Ireland's new foreign workforce are only being paid a flat and often paltry rate for sixty hour weeks. Thankfully some politicians do care and have taken on the job of seeking fair and just working conditions for these workers. This is why as Celtic supporters, in Ireland, Scotland and elsewhere, we recognise that it is important that we never forget our own roots and ensure we educate those willing to learn about the problems that our own forebears faced both at home and abroad. We must never become people who discriminate unfairly and unjustly. We must always look after our fellow man – whoever he or she is.

I never thought that supporting a club like to Celtic would shape how I lived my life, but just like how my father has taught me to respect others no matter what religion, colour or creed, Celtic, its fans and its great history, have taught me that my father was right and his wisdom prepared me to follow in the footsteps of so many of my fellow countrymen and women, both at home and among the diaspora, on the road to Paradise.

Being Number One and Working to Stay There

Eddie Toner

I would like to start this chapter by making two bold claims: firstly, I believe Celtic is the most meaningful football club in the world. Secondly, we have supporters who share an exceptional culture, identity and history.

The first of those two claims would undoubtedly initiate heated debate in bars and clubs from Buenos Aires to Barcelona, from Parkhead to Peterhead, Manchester to Milan and just about everywhere in between. The fact is that many football fans the world over will argue that their club is the greatest – and they all have their own very good reasons. Their club means so much to them. I wouldn't disagree with this last part but I would disagree with the conception of what constitutes meaning. For example, success and greatness can be measured in many different ways and for that reason many justifiable reasons will be put forward to support each fan's claim. I believe this is what helps to make the game of football so special, one that is enjoyed by millions around the world. I will therefore stand by my first claim but be happy to concede that there are many others who would wish to dispute it.

I give no ground whatsoever though on my second claim. Celtic supporters are the greatest. I have known this from a very early age. I have spent my Celtic-supporting lifetime emphasising that belief to friends old and new. Some were happy to accept my testimony; others disagreed. It was then to my great delight, when in 2003 the governing bodies of firstly European then World football came to the same conclusion as myself. Celtic does have the greatest supporters in the world and we now have awards from both UEFA and FIFA to prove it.

These awards are not normally given to football supporters but usually to clubs. Seville brought Celtic supporters to the attention of the European football public and the award winning norms were changed because of Celtic's supporters. One of the proudest moments in my life came when I was given the honour to travel to Basle in Switzerland and collect the FIFA 2003 fair play award on behalf of the Celtic supporters. Earlier in that year we were also awarded a special accolade by UEFA.

So, what is it that separates the fans of Celtic from those of other clubs around the world? I think you need to go back to November 6th 1887 to start to find the answer to that question. It was on this day at a meeting in St Mary's RC Church Hall, Calton, in Glasgow's East End, that saw the formation of Celtic as a football club. Brother Walfrid, John Glass, Pat Welsh, John O'Hara, John McLaughlin *et al*, having witnessed the suffering and starvation of their fellow countrymen and women who had settled in Glasgow's impoverished East End, and with a passion for their Irishness, their culture and their politics, came together to form a football club whose principal aim was to help combat and alleviate that poverty. It was also intended that Celtic was to become something the community could become proud of. It would provide a sense of identity and esteem.

Walfrid and his compatriots gave us a vision that was Christian and therefore charitable. The vision of the founders of our club was that they would create an institution that would reflect our culture and encourage our forebears, the powerless and marginalised, not to lose hope, but to be proud of where they came from and be proud of what they were. As with any Christian who lived out their faith, the vision was also about showing respect for others and being able to welcome our fellow man and woman as equals, even if they wanted to play for or support this Irish Catholic football club. Accordingly, from its very inception, Celtic has been an open and inclusive club. We have never closed our doors to anyone on the basis of their religious faith, their nationality, colour or class.

The Celtic support for over 110 years has been mindful of the club's unique and humble origins. I believe it has been an ongoing adherence to these fundamental principles, laid down by Walfrid, which sets the Celtic supporters apart and makes them the unique.

> The vision of the founders of our club was that they would create an institution that would reflect our culture and encourage our forebears, the powerless and marginalised, not to lose hope, but to be proud of where they came from and be proud of what they were.

Nonetheless, to be unique and to be recognised elsewhere as special, entails responsibilities: it also entails an active memory of the vision and philosophy of Brother Walfrid and his compatriots. It is incumbent upon the support to ensure that the standards and dreams set by our predecessors are maintained and even enhanced. The continued growth of the Irish diaspora, either directly from Ireland or via a couple of generations' stop-off in Scotland, has ensured that the Celtic support has now spread beyond the west of Scotland all over the globe.

You only need to look back to Seville in May 2003 to find the most public example of the uniqueness and special bond that draws the Celtic family together. Seville was not just about the UEFA Cup Final and trying to win a football match. For the Celtic family it was about much more. This event provided the opportunity for a community that has stood in concert for over 100 years, to come together in a very public fashion and show the world what supporting this football club and being part of a special community is all about.

No other club in the world could expect the tens of thousands of people who travelled hundreds, or in most cases thousands, of miles to follow their team to the south of Spain for a football game. The days leading up to the game saw Seville being transformed into a sea of green, white and orange as the Celtic fans descended from every continent in the world. Every train, plane, car, bus, taxi or even bike seemed to arrive with fans wearing the hoops or flying their tricolours with great pride. By the day of the match the estimates were that more than 80,000 had arrived, more than half of these without match tickets: but that didn't matter. Our fans were there to celebrate their club. This was their opportunity to show the world how much their football club meant to them and how special it was to be a part of the community it represented.

If the civic authorities or indeed the residents of Seville were in any way anxious about this invasion of their city then their fears were soon proved to be without foundation: Celtic fans quickly won their way into the hearts of the local Sevillians. The bars were soon bursting at the seams and the beer was flowing. The air was full of Celtic and Irish songs and the atmosphere was so welcoming that it didn't take the locals long to join in. In fact, even the fans of FC Porto, Celtic's opponents in the forthcoming football game, were so overwhelmed by the camaraderie and exuberance of the Celtic support that they didn't have any problem joining the general football festival and celebrations. It was a sight to behold watching rival football fans celebrate together in a manner that was a credit to both sets of supporters and an experience that will never be forgotten by anyone who witnessed it.

That week Celtic fans carried on a tradition for which they had become famous when travelling at home and abroad. They represented themselves in a way that showed that they had a genuine pride in their club and a real belief in what it meant to them. The travelling support in many ways had become self-policing! Seville was to be a fine example of the celebration of the game of football. It rightly earned the supporters of Celtic the title of being the greatest.

Maybe one of the things that caught the eye of those who made the UEFA and FIFA awards was that this kind of behaviour was in many ways in great contrast to an age of a sharp decline in moral standards. One would only require to walk into a newsagents shop and witness this decline as the tabloid headlines scream out about perverse notions of sexual activity and conduct, violence, game shows and the cult of celebrity. It would also appear that the editors and writers of our national newspapers now believe that people's personal lives are more newsworthy than the major issues that affect our world. More often than not reporting on real events like war (especially its causes), poverty (especially its causes), famine (especially its causes) and corporate stealing and corruption is consigned to the inside pages whilst we are treated to the latest gossip regarding some so-called Hollywood or Big Brother celebrity. Is it any wonder that many struggle to get a grip on what is and isn't important these days, all the while suiting the capitalist monsters that continue to exploit our basest tastes and mores (and ones that are often created and manipulated by the very forces that thrive on them)?

> (Celtic fans) represented themselves in a way that showed that they had a genuine pride in their club and a real belief in what it meant to them.

Whether we like to admit it or not both the written and the broadcast media are important today. They help to influence people's opinions and shape their values while they are undoubtedly partly to blame for the shortcomings of the world in which we live: but only partly, because ultimately everyone has to take responsibility for their own behaviour and how they treat their fellow human beings.

Football hasn't escaped this drop in values and standards. Over the last two decades football, described by the legendary Pele as 'the beautiful game', has been hi-jacked by commercialism, greed and money. We now have billionaire investors running clubs across the world while the media seems to determine so much in relation to the game. In many cases these investors, although hugely successful in the business world, have no understanding or appreciation of the game of football. Often such people treat supporters in a discourteous and dismissive manner: ultimately as meat that walks and talks and is only important in monetary terms. It seems to me that people with this view have a primary motivation governed by a philosophy of raising their own profiles and promoting their own business interests through their involvement in the game. What can the fans offer these people? The fans are expected to turn up, pay their money then go home until the next week – or, simply watch at home in the comfort of their armchairs. Is it any wonder that recent times has seen a marked drop in the attendances of some of the world's top clubs? Clubs no longer seem mindful or supportive of the communities from which they have come. Pessimistically, are we witnessing the end of football and the development of some of the worst social and cultural excesses that we see in much sport in North America?

> We also have a situation where many top players earn more in a week than many of us can earn in a year and where some players are now paid more in a year than the ordinary working person will earn in a lifetime.

We also have a situation where many top players earn more in a week than many of us can earn in a year and where some players are now paid more in a year than the ordinary working person will earn in a lifetime. Some players on the European stage have weekly salaries that are more than the average price of a house in the west of Scotland. The television and media coverage has seen these players elevated to a position previously only ever enjoyed by film star celebrities. Their superstar status and earning potential has resulted in there being a huge gap between the players and the followers of the game. It was normal in the past for players to mix freely with the supporters at social events etc, but now there is an unwillingness to do so. It would seem that even the simplest of tasks like accepting a presentation and signing an autograph for a kid, a kid who might have waited outside the ground for hours in hope of catching a glimpse of their heroes, seems too onerous for some of our prima donna footballers and their minders in suits at our football clubs. The behaviour of some players too, both off and on the pitch, leaves a lot to be desired and they need to be reminded that their public celebrity status carries with it a responsibility to set an example to the young supporters who hold them in awe.

Nonetheless, as football is increasingly challenged by many hostile forces we must not also forget that some supporters cannot be exempt from criticism either. Many supporters complain of a seeming increase in the numbers of fans who turn up simply to scream and shout personal abuse at players, referees, the opposition supporters or indeed, anyone who happens to incur their wrath. In some cases, this abuse can be racist, sectarian or just downright insulting and disrespectful. These morons also believe that having paid their way into a match they are free to indulge in behaviour that most would consider offensive on the street outside. Examples of this appalling behaviour are well documented. High profile examples like the supporters of the Spanish national team racially abusing black players in the England side and, closer to home, the disrespect, shown by a significant number of Hearts fans during a minute's (24 seconds actually) silence to mark the death of the Holy Father, Pope John Paul II prior to the 2005 Scottish Cup semi-final. We also need only consider the nauseating treatment meted out to Neil Lennon at almost every ground he visits in Scotland. Celtic supporters know that this abuse is nothing less than racist and sectarian.

We recognise the football environment is one where people can shout, be aggressive, get angry, celebrate and even swear, and generally, be a different character from their usual selves. But that doesn't mean it is an environment without controls or a sense of responsibility. How many people sit in the stands

> These morons also believe that having paid their way into a match they are free to indulge in a behaviour that most would consider offensive on the street outside.

watching other so-called supporters indulge in loutish behaviour and feel unwilling, or perhaps unable, to challenge it? What does the future hold for the game if the clubs and the fans cannot work closely together to help eradicate it? Not just remove it, but encourage people to see that such behaviour is simply wrong.

Celtic supporters cannot rest on their laurels. Many true supporters claim that Celtic is not exempt from such manifest-ations and our supporters' culture can occasionally be threatened by small minorities among our own number who claim to be Celtic supporters but by their inappropriate and wrongful actions display an attitude that shows they have little or no knowledge of the club's proud history and culture. They have little or no awareness of the principles laid down by Brother Walfrid, the history of our community in Scotland and of the very fact of 'our' supporters, past and present, being the victims of poverty, marginalisation, racism and sectarianism. Of course, many of us may have made social and economic progress in recent decades but we can't ignore the fact that many more from our community of Irish immigrant descent still live in most of Scotland's poorest and most socially deprived areas.

I experienced a personal example of some Celtic supporters' ignorance and crass behaviour in December 2005 during an away match at Aberdeen. On leaving the ground I was appalled to hear at least one person, claiming to be a Celtic fan, trying to encourage others in a clearly racist chant of 'Hamed Namouchi (the Glasgow Rangers footballer) is a fucking refugee'. I confronted this guy who more or less told me where to go before also becoming very aggressive towards me. I pointed out to him that not only was his chanting racist it was totally unacceptable for it to be sung by a follower of Celtic. Here was a guy claiming to support Celtic, a team born from the Irish, Scotland's largest immigrant community (I'm afraid the irony was lost on this particular moron), who was making derogatory remarks towards Namouchi because of the colour of his skin, his recent immigrant status and the fact he played for our biggest rivals, Rangers. I felt threatened after confronting the guy but, fortunately, my fellow supporters around me let him know in no uncertain terms that he was out

> Celtic supporters cannot rest on their laurels. . . our supporters' culture can occasionally be threatened by small minorities among our own number who, by their inappropriate and wrongful actions display an attitude that shows they have little or no knowledge of the club's proud history and culture.

of order and he disappeared with his tail between his legs.

I would like to say that this was an isolated incident, among the Celtic support but sadly, this is not the case. Although I can cite countless examples of generosity, good manners and Christian outlook and behaviour amongst the fans, by far the dominant characteristic of the Celtic support, I can also cite other examples of times when I have cringed at the antics of my fellow fans. I hate to hear Celtic fans indulge in the singing of certain songs. I have heard tiny groups singing songs mocking the Ibrox disaster (when 66 fans of Rangers lost their lives when leaving the ground after the 1971 New Year Celtic v Rangers game), I have also heard chants 'celebrating' the unfortunate premature death of the late Davie Cooper, just because he played for Rangers? I also dislike the way some traditional songs have been bastardised to include unthinking but undoubtedly sectarian lines like 'soon there will be no Protestants at all'. I know very few fans who sing this and it hasn't been heard for many years – but it still exists as a chant for small groups of ignorant and crass Celtic supporters.

I do not take the arguments on board of those anti-Celtic people who like to have a go at our away support in particular. I believe that the away Celtic support is very special and amongst the most committed of all. My beef is with anyone, home, away, pub or armchair, who demeans our Irish and Catholic background and who gives a bad image to our club culture and identity – and I mean by our own standards and judgements – not those of a superficial, sectarian and racist kind that originate from elsewhere.

As a community which originates from Ireland our songs are always going to be different to those that dominate in Scotland/Britain. Isn't that what living in a multi-cultural society reflects? I have attended many Celtic functions where songs of Irish struggle have dominated. This is a significant part of our supporter culture and identity. So long as we reflect our history, culture and identity through 'the lullabies, and battle cries and songs of hope and joy', and not the chants that contain foul and abusive language and make you want to cover your ears, then we'll be doing fine.

> So long as we reflect our history, culture and identity through 'the lullabies, and battle cries and songs of hope and joy', and not the chants that contain foul and abusive language and make you want to cover your ears, then we'll be doing fine.

Originating from Ireland, and being shaped by two, three, four and five generations of living in Scotland, the Celtic support has a rich culture and huge repertoire of songs that demonstrate pride in our history and identity. Do we really need to put up with the small groups who want to bring shame on the vast majority of us? Is it not time for the real fans to stand up against this type of behaviour in an attempt to educate those who discredit not only themselves but also our history, our culture and our club – not to say the religious faith of the majority of our support?

I still believe we are a very special club with very special supporters. The evidence for this is manifest on a regular basis. The dominant part of our supporters' culture has always been characterised by charity, the celebration of our roots and identity, the wearing of our symbols and the singing of our Irish songs in the face of bigotry, racism and hostility. These are some of the things that form part of our history and make us distinctive. Despite the efforts of many from outwith our community and even occasionally some from within, I have every confidence that we will maintain the Irish and Catholic identities of our club and support while also remaining open to those not from these backgrounds but who wish to join us and celebrate our journey as a football club.

Nonetheless, as the inheritors of Walfrid's vision we must be on our guard as defenders of this great club and its surrounding culture. Those who wish to change our identity are often clearly identifiable: they are many in Scottish society and we are forever resisting them. Those who would demean us by claiming to be Celtic supporters but whose behaviour and attitudes run contrary and oppositional to that claim and to our very being are sometimes more difficult to resist. But resist we must, if we are to defend the values, morals and identity of our club and true supporters. We are distinctive and we wish to remain so. But such things are not written in stone and even the Roman Empire fell. Resistance has a special meaning in Celtic supporter's culture. So let us stand up and resist those who would demean us from within as well as those from outwith.

Making sense of the Celtic experience

MICHAEL KELLY

In 2005, I flew to New York for a short break and to see U2 play a concert at Madison Square Garden as part of their immensely successful *Vertigo* tour. Naturally, I had been looking forward to the occasion for some months and, of course, had a great time. However, I must admit that, as the plane eased into the Irish skies and onwards toward the vast Atlantic, the incongruity of the situation struck me very forcefully.

Here I was, an Irishman going to quite substantial lengths to see an Irish group play in a city thousands of miles from my home. What's more, I had already seen them a couple of times already during the summer. The thought occurred, did I need to visit the psychiatrist's couch? That would be a step too far, an exaggeration, but my journey certainly set me thinking.

I had occasion to draw parallels between this experience and that of being a Celtic supporter who lived in Ireland. The distances may not be comparable, but the principle is quite similar in that, at least every two weeks during the season, thousands sail (or, increasingly these days, fly) from Ireland to Glasgow to watch a team in green and white hoops battle it out, to cheer their efforts to the rooftops, to support them in their efforts and to partake in what is as much a celebration of a heritage and a community as it is a sporting occasion.

Why endure a journey of twelve hours (or more) for ninety minutes of football? Why partake in this celebration of Irishness miles away from Ireland itself? Touching also on my original question, why does one leave the island of Ireland (or elsewhere) to go and celebrate Irishness through musical endeavour or through the medium of its most successful sporting export, Celtic?

As it has been for many generations of the Irish diaspora in

Scotland of course, Celtic quite simply represents a rallying point and a means by which the offspring of the Irish in Scotland can express their Irishness in a country that can be hostile to such expressions, and in a way that stands in stark contrast to the way Irishness is positively looked upon and embraced in many other countries. By way of illustration, I listened recently to a Chicago lawyer who, because Irish-sounding names are apparently very popular in the States, was actually in the process of changing his name by deed poll to 'Patrick O'Brien' in the hope of securing election as judge from an electorate who liked the sound of his name! Call me cynical if you will, but I cannot envisage an analogous state of affairs arising in Scotland. In fact, it would appear that the very opposite – for example, witness the inactivity and silence of many Irish descended Scottish Labour politicians during the Northern Irish 'troubles' – has all too often been the case.

Equally (and ironically), supporting Celtic also provides a means by which many in Ireland can express and celebrate their nationality, whether it be those living in the northern counties for whom the wearing of the colours can still lead to threats and, indeed, acts of physical violence or, on the other hand, those in the 'Celtic Tiger' society of 'the Republic' that is moving further and further away from traditional values towards an individualistic culture where loyalty can often be towards the self and one's own well-being rather than family, community or the country's people.

In many ways, attending Celtic matches and Celtic supporters' functions and mixing with like-minded people has served to reawaken and reinvigorate pride in Irishness for many on this side of the water. Indeed, many who have been unacquainted with the rich heritage of patriotic ballads and songs of Ireland or who held 'officially' sanctioned, sanitised or dominant views of Ireland's periods of 'troubles', thoroughly enjoy their experiences within the Irish-Celtic culture of the west of Scotland. In many locations there, the music and songs of Ireland, Irishness and Irish history fill the air and supporters from Ireland find a living breathing part of their culture thriving amidst those of Irish descent in the west of Scotland. In doing so, they are almost 'born again' in their love for their country when they see that love mirrored in the thousands who fill Celtic Park.

Obviously, there has always been a great well of support and good will for Celtic in Ireland. How could it be any other way after all? We recognise the Irish symbolism that distinguishes our great club and its support. What country in the world could be the harbinger of such an institution in Scotland and fail to be proud of its creation? The accounts of Irish men and women being driven from their homeland through hunger, poverty and other by-products of a foreign occupation and proceeding to rise again and make great contributions to their adopted homelands is one that can be and has been told many times over. Up until the birth of the 'Celtic Tiger', emigration was one of the seeming constants of life in Ireland and, like parents taking pride in the achievements of their children, we have always taken great pleasure in the feats of the sons and daughters of Ireland whether it be the work of missionaries throughout the Third World or as artists, musicians, sportsmen, sportswomen and politicians.

Equally, the story of Brother Walfrid and the club he helped establish to offer pride and esteem and to raise funds to feed immigrant Irish Catholic youngsters in the environs around the east end of Glasgow and, which went on to conquer Europe at football, has captured the imagination of many in Ireland as well as amongst the offspring of those whom the club was created for originally. A deep affection for the club has been passed down from generation to generation by those Irish and their offspring who lived and worked in the west of Scotland and who have followed the Celts over the past century.

However, back in Ireland, for many years (and, indeed, this continues today) those carrying the torch for Celtic struggled in the face of the constant exposure of English football and English/British culture in general and had to make do with the meagre rations of the odd newspaper report and the weekly exercise in translating the static from the weak medium wave signal of Radio Scotland – which, incidentally, included manoeuvring one's radio to get the best signal in ways that would challenge the most dedicated yoga master! Nevertheless, with the advent of satellite television coverage and the internet, that flame has been re-kindled and one only has to look at the numbers of supporters' clubs cropping up all over Ireland or take a walk down any street and see the Celtic colours sported by young and old alike to see that the 'grand old team' is at the height of its popularity in its land of origin.

That isn't to say that affection for Celtic and its supporters within Ireland dominates totally. Indeed, one is sometimes struck by the impression that, while it is common to have a 'soft spot' for Celtic, to actually go further and actively support the team with fervour, sometimes surprisingly takes people aback – they seem sometimes almost unused to such fervour for a soccer side, especially on the other side of the water.

There are a number of elements to this phenomenon. Although gaelic sport is number one in Ireland soccer remains significant. However, importantly in terms of analysis, at one level Ireland is mainly a country of soccer–'armchair supporters' whose 'support' for English clubs often extends merely to sitting in front of the television or the big screen down at the local. On the other hand, Celtic supporters will generally have actually been to Celtic Park at least a few times in their lives and know what it is like to go and support their club with a passion that is lost on those whose enthusiasm dissipates as the jersey leaves their back when they get in from the pub. At a different level, support for Celtic is often intrinsically linked with expressions of Irish culture, identity and patriotism and this does not often sit well with certain elements of the 'Celtic Tiger' society who reject some of these notions as passé and outmoded. In itself not only does this say something about the effects of 'the Troubles' of the past thirty years but also how many people in Irish society have adjusted to their newly found wealth as well as the overpowering effects of British cultural influences and agencies in Ireland.

Despite such common observations, the passion for Celtic among its supporters in Ireland remains vigorous and vibrant and it is growing stronger all the time. So, what are the implications of the strength of the Celtic support in Ireland today for Celtic FC and its future?

The Association of Irish Celtic Supporters Clubs (A.I.C.S.C.) was established in 1998 at the same time as the rejuvenation of Celtic in the aftermath of the removal of the regime of the Kellys *et al*. The increasing amount of televised Scottish football available in Ireland had also once more boosted interest in Celtic. In addition, a need was also identified to band together in order to protect various interests in the face of Celtic majority shareholder Fergus McCann's commercial media-led and much-trumpeted 'Bhoys against Bigotry' campaign, which many had seen – rightly or wrongly – as an attack on Celtic's and its supporters' Irish and Catholic backgrounds.

Although like all football clubs, Celtic's support contains a few negative and 'off the wall' characters, it always seemed strange to most knowledgeable people connected with Celtic supporters (and indeed many within the club itself) that those who had largely been the victims of 'bigotry' had now placed the spotlight on themselves. The causes or most significant and powerful manifestations of sectarianism, bigotry and prejudice in Scotland were left unchallenged.

One of the motivations in the founding of the A.I.C.S.C. was the feeling that some employees and others connected to the 'new Celtic' were slowly but inexorably squeezing out the 'Irishness' of the club. Infamous remarks attributed to Fergus McCann around that time regarding 'Irish bigots' did nothing to assuage these sentiments and, feeling that we had to stand on our own feet to combat this rather than rely on the supporters' regimes in situ at the time, the Association was founded with one of its main principles to protect Celtic's Irish heritage and also to help protect Celtic from racism, bigotry and prejudice, even from those who may draw profit or wages from the club itself.

Through a process of challenging ignorance and even sectarianism itself we have let people know that sectarianism has many faces and that this is a problem rooted in history. We feel that we can help in the fight against sectarianism and racism in Scottish football.

Nevertheless, interestingly, the formation of the A.I.C.S.C. came also at a time when the actual Irish-born influence within the football part of Celtic itself was arguably at its strongest for a number of years, as very soon both the largest shareholder and manager of the club hailed from Ireland together with the team's midfield general and future captain. These circumstances have arguably helped to increase the club's profile in Ireland and to a degree aid our cause.

The A.I.C.S.C. was also set up to promote Celtic within Ireland. To this end, each year members of the first team squad along with directors and officials from the club attend our Annual Charity Dinner and celebrate along with over one thousand supporters in one of Dublin's more prestigious hotels, where significant amounts are handed over to Irish charities. We have also been in a position to assist many clubs get off the ground, organise trips and bring folk over to Celtic Park who may otherwise not get a chance to do so, including, most importantly, young boys and girls who will hopefully go on to be the lifeblood of the club's Irish-based support long into the future.

We have also played our part in chartering trips to away matches in Scotland and Europe, securing favourable ticketing arrangements for supporters and attending regular meetings with decision-makers at the club. Significantly, we have also been at the table in talks with the Scottish Executive together with the other supporters' bodies in relation to the on-going drive to combat sectarianism in Scottish society. Many of us in Ireland know the blight of sectarianism all too well and the Irish descended in Scotland have also suffered their fair share of it. What role can those of us from Ireland (along with those Irish offspring in Scotland) play in standing up to this problem?

It is equally clear that, when we travel to Scotland and mingle with Hoops fans at Paradise and at other grounds up and down Scotland, we are meeting with people who, despite their Scottish accents, see their Irishness as their foremost cultural and community identity. In the same way that many in Canada, America and Australia, who are often fully settled in the country of their birth, celebrate the country of their heritage, culture and identity, the Irish in Scotland also do this through a unique expression of their passionate support for Celtic.

So, what does the future hold? Hopefully the Association in Ireland will ensure that support for Celtic not only endures but is also strengthened in Ireland. Recent developments such as the Celtic Summer School beginning to establish itself in Ireland and several Irish-born or Irish-minded Scots-born youngsters gracing the youth team and first team bode well for more Irish-born players featuring in the Hoops in the years ahead.

This is something tangible the club can continue to work on that can only serve to assist us in our efforts to promote the club in Ireland – a trick, incidentally, that Arsenal, Liverpool and Manchester United mastered some time ago courtesy of the likes of Brady, Stapleton, O'Leary, Moran, Whelan and McGrath. With this aspect of Celtic's Irish identity in mind the signing of Roy Keane was a masterstroke.

We will also stand fast with our fellow Scots-born Irishmen and women in the west of Scotland in ensuring that the club remains true to its Irish heritage and, indeed, embraces that in meaningful ways that ensure that it leads from the front as a beacon for the Irish in Scotland and never shirks – despite the slings and arrows that will often come from elements of society – from holding its head up to be proud of its Irishness. In doing so, we must, of course, remain true to the spirit of Walfrid and continue the good work being done for charitable concerns by the communities from which our various supporters' clubs spring. In addition, and reflecting our strong and significant political and social roots and identities, we must always be respectful and mindful of those not of our community but who share our history of marginalisation and oppression. We must also reach out to them and become an example and beacon to such communities. We must strive to maintain that ethos as part of our great football club's character and our supporters' practice.

With this last thought in mind (and bearing in mind my own long-distance journey of faith and devotion), a more recent trend has seen immigrants from eastern Europe, who have made their home in Ireland, travelling to Glasgow with Irish supporters' clubs to cheer on the Celts. The club founded for immigrants fleeing poverty in Ireland is now attracting thousands from that same land to come over and watch, bringing with them other immigrants who have come to Ireland to find their fortune. Now, there's a turn of events for you – Poles coming to work in Ireland, travelling to Celtic Park to cheer on their fellow Poles playing for the Irish football club in Scotland. Incongrous? Bizarre? No, that's just Celtic and diaspora in the modern world.

On further reflection I can see now more clearly what was always in my mind when that journey to see U2 in the USA was being planned. Being Irish has more parts to it than simply being 'from' the island of Ireland. Being 'of' the island of Ireland and being proud of this is a much more appropriate way to see and understand our diaspora, Celtic and that identity we esteem and share. At Celtic, our Irishness is at the heart of our togetherness, our charity, our social and political conscience, our reaching out to people who need and our capacity to celebrate life to the full. Life may not be about football, but the very existence of Celtic Football Club and the community of supporters that gather around it is one of those gifts that enhance our lives.

Keeping or selling your Heart and Soul

KAREN GILES

As we raised our glasses at the start of 2006, our host and a friend danced a little jig round the kitchen table. 'That's the beauty of a siesta,' said a wife through gritted teeth. 'While we were preparing the food and entertaining the kids, they were sleeping though the second half at Stamford Bridge.' It was that bad. Chelsea versus Birmingham City, midday, New Year's Eve. One of those occasions when, had it not been for your £3,500 season ticket, peeling potatoes would have made more sense. Hernan Crespo scored in the 25th minute. Game over. To add insult to tedium, Jose Mourinho ticked the crowd off for not showing the opposition enough respect and then dragged Joe Cole over the hot stuff for a spot of show boating.

'I had to tell him, that one more match like that, playing for himself and the public and not the team, and he would be out,' explained the Chelsea manager, seething with indignation. 'At times it was like watching the old Joe Cole out there – too many tricks and stuff,' he added. And to those who fought the urge to snooze with some good old terrace buffoonery. 'I told the crowd to stop all that ole, ole stuff,' said Mourinho.

From the mouth of the best paid manager in Britain, confirmation that our beloved game has taken a chilling turn for the worse. Entertaining the masses is no longer a priority. Thrilling those who pay a small fortune to watch the shaven-chested Frank Lampard and Co is now a sackable offence. Very soon the bicycle kick will be outlawed, high kicks deemed worthy of a yellow card and a goal scorer's celebration restricted to a humble tug of the forelock.

I blame Rom's roubles, all £440 million worth, which have stripped the game of its essential ingredient – unpredictability – and turned an already uneven playing field into a slippery precipice, impossible to scale without an equally obscene pile of cash. The day Roman Abramovich chose Chelsea FC as his personal plaything, an executive toy with frills, one of the most compelling leagues in world football started to lose its competitive edge. Money has always been a prime factor in determining success. Now, thanks to a young Russian, with a vacant smile and limitless resources, it is the only factor.

In one calendar year, Chelsea amassed 101 league points from a possible 114. By Christmas, the 2005/6 Championship had been decided. By January 7, we were looking for our thrills elsewhere. The third round of the FA Cup has never enjoyed such rapt attention and thunderous applause. Never mind Mourinho's all-conquering squad, plundered at a vastly inflated cost of £240 million, it was non-league Burton Wanderers who got the competitive juices flowing by forcing Manchester United to a replay and Luton Town for showing European champions Liverpool not an ounce of respect. That is how we like our football, raw, passionate, unpredictable and caked in sweat.

Sadly, we don't get enough of it. Greed and subterfuge play too significant a role in today's game to allow the likes of Burton keeper Saul Deeney, Brentford's DJ Campbell and Gez Murphy of Nuneaton more than their designated fifteen minutes of fame. World Cup year had scarcely dawned and the Premiership's latest sugar daddy, Alexandre Gaydamak, was shifting his belongings into Fratton Park, Mike Newell was attempting to blow the whistle on bung and Sven Goran Eriksson was exchanging indiscreet tittle-tattle with a 'fake sheikh' in Dubai. A more sordid, undignified, disquieting start to 2006 you could not have wished for. Only nobody batted an eyelid. We have become immune to the crap.

'Twas the season to be merry and optimistic yet the festive headlines read as follows. Ron Atkinson announces his return to football. Lee Bowyer appeals against a red card. Harry Redknapp toys with the idea of bringing back Paulo Di Canio to the Premiership. And Eriksson confesses he is the luckiest man alive. As a Portsmouth diehard admitted, after learning about Redknapp's shock return to Fratton Park earlier in the season, you couldn't make the stories up if you tried. One week he was burning effigies of traitor Harry, the next he was celebrating his reappointment.

It is a fickle business. Two years after his public misdemeanor, it was inconceivable to think Atkinson would ever work in the media again after being caught on tape calling Chelsea defender Marcel Desailly 'a ****ing lazy thick ******'. But then he was back, seemingly repentant, re-launching his career with a six-part fly-on-the-wall documentary for Sky One. Atkinson acted as a football adviser to the black Swindon manager Iffy Onuora. As publicity stunts go, it could hardly be more contrived or objectionable. If racism is to be stamped out of the game, people like Atkinson, with their ingrained bigotry, should be dispatched to Coventry, not handed a platform from which to broadcast their prejudice. At this point, one wonders how people truly understand matters such as racism and sectarianism?

Bowyer claimed he was being picked upon, that his reputation went before him. Now this is a player, remember, who during his formative years at Charlton trashed a McDonalds restaurant because the man who served him was Asian and who was then found not guilty of causing Asian student Sarfraz Najeib grievous bodily harm outside a Leeds nightclub, only to later pay the victim £170,000 in an out-of-court settlement. On the pitch, he is no less of a thug, fighting with his own team-mates and stamping on the head of an opponent in Europe. Perhaps he has a point. Perhaps we do judge him harshly. But a more deserving recipient of our contempt I defy you to name. With the exception, perhaps, of Di Canio, another of football's low life characters who continues to make a comfortable living whilst dragging his occupation through the mire. What does it say about Redknapp, that the Portsmouth manager seriously considered employing a player who flaunts his perceived fascist beliefs on a regular basis in Serie A. If the tattoos on his body aren't repulsive enough, the Nazi salutes as he leaves the pitch are particularly heinous. No manager with a conscience would touch Di Canio with a barge pole. Which probably explains Redknapp's interest.

Not for our Harry, sleepless nights fretting over the Italian striker's suspect leanings or for that matter, the business credentials of Portsmouth's new co-owner. With a cheery smile and a rub of the hands, Redknapp set about spending Gaydamak's cash even before the authorities had a chance to verify the benefactor's complex passport. There are real fears that the dashing Sasha, with his engaging smile and enigmatic personality, is investing father Arcadi's ill-begotten gains into Portsmouth FC. However, proving it is another matter.

Sports Minister Richard Caborn demanded greater transparency where foreign investment is concerned. Portsmouth owner Milan Mandaric could not give a monkeys. There is an international arrest warrant out for Gaydamak Snr concerning the Israeli-based Russian's alleged arms-for-oil deals in Angola in the 1990s. Within days of the billionaire's son depositing £12 million into Portsmouth's coffers, the club was conducting a search of its own. Despite pledging his allegiance to the club and its 'unique supporters', Gaydamak Jnr did not show up for Portsmouth's first game under new ownership. He had made other arrangements.

So who can you believe in this business? 'I know I am very lucky with the job I have. I'm proud to be England manager,' said Eriksson, in an interview to mark his fifth year in charge of the national side. Within forty-eight hours of the comments going to print, the Swede was caught red handed, discussing his future with an under cover *News of the World* reporter posing as a wealthy Arab sheikh.

'Five and a half years,' explained the affable Eriksson to his host, 'it's a long time to be England manager.' Anyway, if I win the World Cup, I will leave, goodbye.' It was left to Eriksson's agent Atholle Still to provide the final *coup de grace* the moment the story was broken. 'Sven said to me quite recently, perhaps I've got used to this job, despite the annoyances of it. Perhaps you should have a word with Brian Barwick and see if the FA would be interested in me staying until 2010.'

It would be laughable if it were not so galling, the greed, hypocrisy and sheer conceit of the man. As Eriksson admitted to his new best friend, the Football Association paid him £3 million a year after tax to select an England team that picks itself. Yet still he fancied a return to club management. Aston

Villa was a nice possibility at one stage. The chairman was old and sick. Opportunity knocks: especially if David Beckham can be persuaded to trade Madrid for Birmingham. Because he's unhappy in Spain, you know: a bit like Michael Owen at Newcastle!

Of course Eriksson should have been sacked, the moment the pages devoted to his indiscretions hit the streets: Still called it a 'disgraceful entrapment'. Others would call it a fair kop. If the England coach had been sitting in the pub at the end of his road, engaging the locals in a spot of playful banter, it would have been different. But Eriksson had caught a plane to Dubai with his agent, with the specific intention of exploiting his position for all it was worth.

Not that the FA had any intention of getting rid of Eriksson, even after the first embarrassing expose. That would have involved a certain amount of principle. Indeed, had it not been for the Premier League kicking up a stink about the follow-up story, in which Eriksson claimed bung culture was rife in the Premiership, Barwick, the chief executive would almost certainly have drawn a veil over the whole shoddy business.

Unfortunately for Eriksson, it is the Premier League who wear the trousers in English football and having taken great exception to three of their member clubs being labelled corrupt by the national coach, his contract was terminated in a matter of days. While no action was taken against Championship manager Newell, who claimed to have been offered 'sweeteners' by agents, Germany '06 was the Swede's England swansong.

Which brings us back to New Year's Day 2006 and the mother of all hangovers and the news that Michael Owen had broken his foot. Just when we were all starting to dream the dream, to plan our crossing, to procure our tickets by fair means or foul, a dose of reality hits us where it hurts. For all the hype and expectation surrounding Eriksson's charges in Germany, the Curse of the Metatarsal continues to jeopardise England's chances in football. Seven casualties in a matter of four years is not just an unfortunate coincidence. It is an absolute scandal.

Once upon a time we did not know our metatarsal from our elbow. Today, thanks to the wonders of modern technology, the bones in the foot are as familiar as the players that break them. David Beckham, Wayne Rooney, Steven Gerrard, Gary Neville, Danny Murphy, Ashley Cole and now Owen, have all snapped metatarsals in recent years. But that's what happens when you wear slippers to work.

If ever there was a symbol to vanity, the modern football boot is it. Never mind protecting the foot against the elements and injury, today's lightweight boots, made of the softest, most pliable kangaroo hide, are more glamour accessory than battle necessity. Frozen pitches and strapping centre halves are not a priority when it comes to fulfilling the requirements of the modern pro. Style comes first, freedom of movement a close second and comfort third. Guarding the most vulnerable part of the foot against an impact injury is not a concern, either for the player who has a lucrative boot sponsorship and does not want to jeopardise the deal with complaints, or the manufacturer, whose priority is the high street.

After Liverpool baulked at the asking price, Newcastle United coughed up £17 million to bring Owen back to the Premiership to kick start their miserable season in 2005/06. Then someone treads on his foot and the only thing Owen was capable of kicking for three months was a balloon. And did Umbro, the suppliers of Owen's boots, pay United compensation? Did they heck. Despite the extra publicity doing wonders for their sales, an apology was not forthcoming never mind a cheque.

These are only a tiny sample of important undercurrents now affecting the 'beautiful game'. Such matters in football are of concern to all those who consider themselves 'real' football supporters. When a club like Celtic has a history and identity that fuses so profoundly with its fanbase, where the history and identity is bottom up rather than driven from the top down, it takes character and principle to maintain a semblance of heart and soul. It also takes 'good' people.

But that's football for you. Morally corrupt, invariably flawed, the game we love has always been able to enthral and frustrate in equal, baffling measures. Only a word of caution for those that believe it was ever thus. Abramovich.

'Playing in the Hoops – living for the Hoops'

REFLECTIONS ON FAMILY, COMMUNITY AND CELTIC

GEORGE MCCLUSKEY

On any occasion when Celtic fans come together they inevitably reminisce about former players and times past. Many of those who have been privileged to have played for Celtic at some time during their careers are no different from supporters when it comes to discussing the relative merits and abilities of those who graced the hoops. Put two or more former Celtic players in the same room and they end up reflecting back on the past and comparing it to the present.

Of course such comparisons – though interesting – are ultimately futile given the changes that transform the game from one decade to the next. It is also an unfair exercise since the physical demands of today's game, new innovations in training methods, team strategies, diet and sport psychology, the enhanced role of the player's agent and developments in competition structure, all ensure that we are not comparing like with like. Perhaps the best we can say is that the small group of footballers of genuine genius such as Pele, Cruyff, Maradona, Best and our own Jimmy Johnstone, would have expressed their skill in any era.

Clearly the game has changed, especially over the past fifteen years or so – and not always for the better. The days when a player would line up for the team which he has supported from childhood and which connected with his family, friends and community would appear to be under threat from the commercial interests and powerful identity shapers which increasingly dominate professional football. While one cannot condemn or label all professional footballers today as mercenaries whose sole interest is to get huge amounts of money out of the game, who have no love for the shirt they wear and who do not know the history and values of the club they represent, nevertheless, there seems to me to be an almost irreversible trend away from a deeply shared identity between player, club and supporters: an identity which I was privileged, both as a player and supporter, to experience through my involvement with Celtic. This identity is also one that I see being passed to my own children.

Kissing the jersey to deceive the support was not invented by Paolo Di Canio and Mark Viduka!

This is not to say that there was a golden era during which every single player – Celtic or otherwise – simply 'played for the shirt'. My involvement with Celtic – as well as with football in general – has given me enough insight to conclude that among the ranks of so-called 'Celtic greats' (or 'greats' belonging to any football club), there have always been those who, while publicly claiming undying loyalty to the club, its supporters and everything it stood for, simply use it as a platform for an increased contract or a lucrative transfer deal. Kissing the jersey to deceive the support was not invented by Paolo Di Canio and Mark Viduka!

If comparing players from different eras is difficult we might consider that it is more important that those who follow football identify the values that make a footballer truly great. In many ways these can be the values that underpin the ethos of the club and which are lived out by our sporting icons in their conduct as a player and, more importantly, in their everyday life. What values we look to from our professional footballers and what value we gain from our club says much about us as individuals, as a community and as a society. This is particularly important to those of us amongst the Celtic support who remain within the Catholic (and Christian) community that Brother Walfrid founded the club for. As far as professional footballers are concerned – whether they like it or not – they have acquired the status of being prominent role models, especially for young people.

It is interesting to look at the actions and attitudes of players and clubs to see what sort of example they offer. Of course, we are all examples, good and bad, to each other, but professional footballers have an elevated and very public place in modern society and their role as examples, good and bad, are there for all to see. Due mainly to the influence of the modern media the position of 'successful' footballers today is now one of great responsibility. Therefore, it is timely and important to ask what do we – the Celtic Football Club, players, employees and supporters – stand for? What are the values and attitudes we have inherited, how do we live these out and what do we seek to pass on?

We live in an age where tradition and history can be distorted, abolished, bought and sold. Likewise this is an era where millionaires who often know nothing and care less about fans (or even their fellow human beings in general?) and the game itself, can take over and transform a club beyond recognition. In effect, some of these people appear to seek to create a new club, more often than not one that bears no resemblance to the club established and envisaged by its original founders. In other words, a re-created club in the image of its new owners safely distanced from the so-called 'old baggage'.

> We live in an age where tradition and history can be distorted, abolished, bought and sold.

It is important, therefore, that the whole Celtic network – what we often call 'the Celtic family' – identifies and recognises what we have been given by our forebears and what values have revolved around our club since its foundation, what makes it unique and what it represents in order that it isn't simply taken over by the values and forces that have come to control much of modern football and society generally.

Celtic was given birth in the spirit of resistance to bigotry, racism, sectarianism and poverty. It seems to me that these are some of the pillars we have to defend if our club is to remain true to itself, its founders and its supporting community.

Although necessary in many respects, ability and achievement on the pitch are not – nor should they be – sufficient to gain the genuine affection and respect of Celtic's supporters. To be held in the highest regard by the fans of this great club requires, in my view, that a player should have a love and passion for the club as well as a knowledge, understanding and appreciation of what it represents. In other words, as well as having played *in* the hoops a true Celtic player must also have played *for* the hoops and *for* the community that this club has been built upon. There are numerous examples of players who graced the green and white who did exactly that.

I was lucky enough to play with some of them as well as know many others for whom playing for Celtic was much more than simply playing for a football club. The term 'Celtic-Minded' for me expresses this connection between the supporters and the community on the one hand, and the player and club on the other. This is the only description one needs to be connected to Celtic and it can come from family and community or it can come from the experience one acquires in life.

My experience, as one brought up in the Celtic tradition and who witnesses my family growing up in the same tradition, is that this is an inclusive identity. The fact that many of those who came to be Celtic greats – John Thompson, Ronnie Simpson, Tommy Gemmell, Bertie Auld, Kenny Dalglish and Danny McGrain, to list but a few – came from backgrounds removed from that traditionally associated with Celtic, is a clear demonstration of the fact that Celtic Football Club – while representing an essentially Irish Catholic immigrant community and their offspring – is about inclusion, openness and, of course, joyful celebration.[1] Like the Christianity of Brother Walfrid himself, Celtic's identity is open to those who wish to share it, experience it or support it, regardless of background: just be or become 'Celtic Minded', that's all you need.

Anyone who was fortunate enough to follow Celtic to Seville in 2003 will fully understand these sentiments. Some 80,000 fans in Seville and, literally millions throughout the world who, while watching on television, transformed a football match into a celebration of pride, identity and community: another mark in our proud history. In many ways, by our simple joyful behaviour, we challenged some of the triumphalism which is associated with the modern game and perhaps, reminded people what sport – at its best – is about: the celebration of being part of or simply supportive of a community.[2]

The term 'Celtic-Minded' for me expresses this connection between the supporters and the community on the one hand, and the player and club on the other.

(1) See, for example, Tommy Gemmell's revealing chapter in the forerunner of this book 'Celtic minded, a Protestant view' in Celtic Minded, Joe Bradley (ed.), 2004.

(2) In recognition of the Celtic supporters' behaviour – especially at the EUFA Final in Seville in 2003 both FIFA and EUFA awarded them the accolade 'Best Supporters' for 2003.

'NOT MORE IMPORTANT THAN LIFE AND DEATH – SIMPLY PART OF LIVING'

Bill Shankly was born in Glenbuck in Ayrshire not far from where I was born and grew up. The village, like so many in the west/central belt of Scotland, was based around the local mine and for the generation of Shankly and, indeed my own father, living conditions were harsh. Unlike many of his contemporaries in Glenbuck Shankly escaped having to go down the mine. In his case – as in countless of others' lives (and possibly that of my own) – this was made possible through football. After a distinguished playing career that brought seven caps for Scotland, in December 1959 Shankly was appointed manager of Liverpool FC, a team languishing in the English Second Division. The rest is, as they say, history. Like his contemporaries, Matt Busby and our own Jock Stein, Shankly poured passion, honesty and commitment into football.

I think that people like Busby, Shankly and Stein were able to connect with the people on the terraces because they came from communities that they could identify with and who could identify with them, and from which they were not removed. I wonder how some of modern managers and players (never mind fans of many major clubs) today might consider the words and values underpinning 'and if you know the history'. Yet, for some in the popular media, Shankly is best remembered for his comment about football that 'it's not a matter of life and death – it's much more important than that!'[3]

Given Shankly's commitment to social justice and the quality of lives of ordinary people – as well as his renowned ability to produce classical sound bites – I'm not sure that he really believed that or that he meant it to be taken literally. It's unfortunate that many people have taken it thus since it grants a false status to the sport and blinds us to the very positive role which it can play in society. For me football is not a matter of life and death; rather it is very much part of life. It has been a huge part of my own life, my community's life and my family's life. It is no exaggeration to say that following Celtic is a central part not just of my own life and my wife Ann's but it also plays an essential and integral part in the lives of my children. Indeed, the rituals enacted out in the homes of my parents, aunts, uncles and family friends when I was growing up and going to Celtic matches, are currently replayed in my own home by my own children as they prepare for matches each week. Perhaps that is what makes Celtic unique.

> Busby, Shankly and Stein were able to connect with the people on the terraces because they came from communities that they could identify with and who could identify with them.

(3) The exact quote reads as follows: 'Some people believe football is a matter of life and death. I'm very disappointed with that attitude. I can assure you it is much, much more important than that.'

Whereas, for many followers of football today, especially impressionable youngsters, loyalty and tradition can be swapped or sold according to the images presented by the media and advertising industries. For Celtic, love of the club is passed on from one generation to the next through the telling and sharing of stories. In this way a certain faith is preserved and nurtured.

> I was extremely fortunate to play for the club that I supported as a boy, and one which also played an important part in the life of my entire extended family and the community to which I belonged.

GROWING UP IN THE CELTIC TRADITION

I was fortunate to grow up in a tight-knit community in which – although material possessions were not in abundance – people pulled together and shared what they had. I suppose in many ways, the people in the community I grew up with shared common hardships and difficulties. There was a distinct lack of jealousy since we were all 'in the same boat' and this produced a sense of communal self-reliance and bonds of trust and mutual care. Unlike today's society in which more and more people seem to 'need' to get the latest luxury goods – be it the latest mobile phones, ipods, mp3s, designer labelled clothes, garden decking or replica football shirts for that matter – growing up in Lanarkshire taught me different values – ones which I hope shape my own children's outlook. Despite the lack of money in those days my experience of growing up was a very rich one. Without idealising the past or the conditions then, I feel that people had a greater sense of community and identity, an identity not shaped by the mass media but a much deeper identity formed from the bottom up by the community and people who brought you up and to whom you looked to as role-models.

I was extremely fortunate to play for the club that I supported as a boy, and one which also played an important part in the life of my entire extended family and the community to which I belonged. My earliest memory of going to Parkhead was going there along with my father and brother John when I was about seven. I was born in Hamilton where my father was from and moved to Birkenshaw where my mother was from when I was four. Most of the villages and towns in this part of Lanarkshire were built around coalmines – in which my father worked for a few years before going to the steel works in Ravenscraig. I think that the close-knit nature of mining communities added to the sense of belonging in Birkenshaw and Uddingston.

Another aspect of this idea of community was the shared sense of common identity and knowledge and awareness that many communities in places like Coatbridge, Viewpark, Clelland and Carfin and around parts of Glasgow had about their cultural identity that owed much to Ireland as the country of our forebears. It was not that someone set you down and gave you a lesson about the history of Ireland or your grandparents or great grandparents. It was more a growing awareness that, in a sense, you were different from other people in Scotland, that we had our own story about where we came from, what shaped and influenced us, and what view we had on life: these are the things that have made us what we are.

And you never did anything on your own. Even going to Celtic Park was an event that seemed to involve the whole community. The next match would be all the talk in the aunts' and uncles' houses, in school and on the streets, the week before the event. You would hitch a lift with one of the supporters clubs and everyone's mood the following week would be dependent upon the outcome of the previous match!

However, going to Parkhead was not the only activity carried out as part of a community. It seems to me that most social activities involved going in company, be it going to St. John the Baptist's Church in Birkenshaw or making your way to school. One incident I remember from those times that helped shape my sense of community revolved around the struggle we had to get a school bus. I went to St. John the Baptist's Primary School in Uddingston around a mile and a half from Birkenshaw. In order to get to school we had to cross a number of major roads that even then were dangerous. The authorities wouldn't give us a school bus – even though they provided one for the non-Catholic school at Tannockside. We suspected strongly that our status as a Catholic School made them look unfavourably towards us. Such things were not particularly unusual at that time.

So in 1965 the mothers decided that they had enough and

> Another aspect of this idea of community was the shared sense of common identity . . . that owed much to Ireland as the country of our forebears.

that we would go on strike until the education authorities provided one! Every morning we would put on our school uniforms and go with our mothers to Birkenshaw Circle where the main bus stop was and wait for the bus which, of course, didn't come. Then at around 9.15am we'd head back home, change out of our uniforms and go out to play football. This daily ritual lasted around three months until the authorities gave in and provided transport for us: a small victory but one that was won by the efforts of our community.[4]

My earliest playing days were not spent in the green and white of Celtic Boys; rather, my first competitive games were in the colours of Coltness for which I played for the under-12s. My father was working in Ravenscraig at the time and was approached by one of the coaches who asked him if I would play for Coltness. He agreed and off I went. The fact that, because of the area from which the team drew most of its players it was predominantly Protestant was never an issue for my father or me. Indeed, my father encouraged me at every twist and turn and delighted every time I scored for Coltness . . . except on one occasion, I suspect. It was in 1969 when Coltness met the Blantyre Red Rockets in the final of an under-12 competition. Unfortunately the Rockets had been formed the year before by one John McCluskey – my own father and, to his horror, one junior George McCluskey scored a hat-trick as his team ran out 4-1 winners.[5]

I joined Celtic the next year and went through the ranks breaking into the first team in season 1976/77. I have fantastic memories playing for Celtic (none better than scoring the winning goal in the 1980 Cup Final against Rangers). But I was always conscious that I was not simply playing for a football team. My wife, Ann, along with many cousins, aunts, uncles and friends, would be at all the games watching very much 'one of their own' playing for the team we all adored and that was in turn, 'our own'. There is no doubt that playing for Celtic gave a great sense of pride to my parents and entire family circle. Indeed, when I reflect on just how much Celtic meant (and means) to my family I was humbled to find out about the sacrifices made by my parents that I might have the chance to play for 'our' club.

(4) The pupils of St. John the Baptist Primary School in Uddingston are still benefiting from this campaign – the education authorities, as is their duty, still provide transport to the school.

(5) It is also interesting that for the final Coltness coaches laid out orange towels for the players, perhaps giving a subtle message of how they viewed the contest.

In 1970 John and I were both playing for Celtic Boys and we needed suits to be bought for a youth tour. They duly appeared and we thought nothing more of it until my mother let slip just a few years ago that, in order to purchase the suits, she pawned her gold bracelet and my father worked every hour of overtime at Ravenscraig to get it back. I'm sure that my mother, being the woman she is, would have done the same if we had been playing for someone else but, of course it wasn't just someone else: this was an opportunity to pursue a dream, to represent a people on the field of play.

Often people outside of the Celtic-supporting community fail to understand or appreciate just how important Celtic is for the community that supports it. It is not simply that Celtic's success provides an escape from social living: rather, for a community which has endured economic and social hardships and being looked down upon by others in the wider community, Celtic gave pride and identity to its supporters. For many from an Irish background Celtic is a vehicle through which that identity is remembered and celebrated.

> For a community which has endured economic and social hardships and being looked down upon by others, Celtic gave pride and identity to its supporters.

LINKS WITH IRELAND

Over the past years – both in my role as a player and more recently as a youth development coach and a representative of Celtic – I have visited Ireland on numerous occasions. I love these visits and feel a natural affinity with people in Ireland. Donegal is a place that is close to the hearts of many Celtic fans – especially those whose families emigrated from that part of Ireland and settled in the West of Scotland.[6] I was delighted to receive the *Celtic Player of the Year* in 1981 from the Donegal Celtic Supporters' Association in Rathmullin.

On my visits to Donegal I am struck by the familiar ring to the names of the people I meet – Gallagher, Sweeney, O'Hara, McCormack, Finn etc. Just like the school register at Holy Cross in Hamilton. My own name 'McCluskey' is common in Donegal and Derry and although I'm not too informed regarding my own family history I'm sure my people came from that particular part of Ireland.[7]

My three daughters have all been involved in Irish dancing

(6) The Irish Famine of the late 1840s and the human disaster which followed led to a huge emigration of the population. It is estimated that at least one million died and another million emigrated with 100,000 arriving in Scotland. See C. Kinealy, A Death-Dealing Famine, the Great Hunger in Ireland, 1997.

(7) McCluskey comes from the Gaelic mac Bloscaidhe which refers to a branch or extension of the O'Cathain clan which had ownership of much of Donegal and Derry up to the seventeenth century.

from a young age and have benefited from the social and cultural contacts this involved. I am also a frequent visitor to Belfast and have very close links with the Celtic supporters there as President of the *Beann Mhadaghain* Celtic Supporters Club and a close friend of *an Brathair Bhailfrid* CSC (Brother Walfrid CSC) – named after the main founder of Celtic. Through these encounters I have learned much about the difficulties the people have had to endure there and how, despite all of this, they have, in the main, kept their dignity and humanity. I am also delighted to have met (in Barcelona of all places) with Fr. Aidan Troy who became known throughout the world during the infamous Holy Cross dispute of a few years back.[8] He struck me as a man of enormous courage, wisdom, warmth and vision – as one whose presence during that awful episode can only be considered prophetic. I was deeply moved by the images of the children of Holy Cross having to endure such shameful treatment and I share an interest on the situation there today.

My friendships with Celtic people in Ireland has led me to become involved in the work of Project Zambia – a charity set up by St. Mary's Christian Brothers' School in Belfast through which people in Ireland help some of the poorest people in the developing world to help themselves. I am very moved by the plight of the orphans, AIDS victims and those who are struggling against all odds to improve their conditions and I'm delighted to promote the work of this charity whenever possible. It is a disgrace, a crime and a sin that in a world in which so much wealth is flaunted – and in the modern football game as well – that people are still struggling to exist from day to day and are dying literally every second from the lack of clean water, food and basic medicines.

It strikes me that this type of work is precisely what Brother Walfrid carried out in the east end of Glasgow when he sought to alleviate the conditions the Irish Catholic community experienced at the end of the nineteenth century. Indeed, it seems only natural that those associated with the values that established Celtic Football Club should reach out and continue to help those of Irish Catholic descent in the west of Scotland, as well as others from outside of this community, and who

(8) On these events see A. Cadwallader, Holy Cross – the Untold Story, 2004.

currently suffer from poverty, deprivation and degradation.

It is this sense of social conscience, of being aware that you are responsible for others – especially those in need – of knowing your history and the values which formed you, your family and your community, that makes the 'Celtic family' unique and gives us an identity worth having. Perhaps that is what it means to be truly 'Celtic-Minded'? Perhaps that is the core of the criteria we should bring to bear when we consider those who are Celtic footballers, employees, trustees and supporters.

'You're in my Heart and in my Soul'

TOM P DONNELLY

I was born at Abbotsford Place, Gorbals, Glasgow in 1946. According to my late father, I went to my first Celtic game when I was about two or three years old. I believe that ever since then I have been a diehard Celtic supporter. Celtic has become part of my very being. When Glasgow City Council decided to tear down the Gorbals my family moved to Castlemilk. Subsequently I left Glasgow at the age of twenty-five and emigrated to Canada with my wife Cathy, also a Gorbals girl. Through yet another stage of community emigration, like my family before me, I was becoming displaced from that which I loved and cherished.

I had a hard time when I first came to Canada as Saturdays had been my day for going to the game to see my beloved hoops, and this was not to be anymore. It used to destroy me not knowing a score or what kind of game it had been. I had to wait until the following Sunday and hope the newspaper contained the score. But this was not always the case and often I had to phone around other Celtic Supporters who I knew owned short wave radios. Sometimes the games would not come through on the radio but there was usually one way or another you could get knowledge of the score. Other times I would say to hell with the cost and just call home to one of my family and ask quickly 'what was the score today'? That was the start of a conversation that cost a lot of money to find out how 'the tic' had played. My brother Michael would sit down every week and send me a nine or ten page letter about games with little drawings of the goals scored. I loved those letters but it would be a week after the match was played that I would receive them. It was often emotional torture: just waiting, waiting.

Around this time there was a couple Celtic clubs in the

Toronto region but none close enough to me so that I could get the score. However, sometimes I did visit them and they were often a place for supporters to gather and talk about Celtic and get news of the team from people who came on holiday. These proved a real lifeline over the early years of my migration to Canada. Those of us who met on a regular or semi-regular basis began to feel like a re-formed community despite being thousands of miles away, as well as a world away, from our beloved Celtic. I took years to settle in Canada as I truly missed my family and Celtic very much.

It was not until the 1980s and the changes in technology that Celtic supporters started to collectively address their problems and began to think about receiving games via satellite. There were a few clubs in North America but they were well spread out; Kearney and New Jersey in the USA and Toronto Celtic Supporters Club in Canada, and a few others in small places where 'ghuys' met but nothing was formally organised.

Then it all began: the Genesis of Celtic supporters organising themselves on another continent. The Bramalea Celtic Supporters Club just outside of Toronto had sixty-five members at the time. The members decided to move out of a basement and began encouraging their own members to go into their pockets to build a real club. Subsequently, these lads rented a large unit in an industrial area in 1985, and by the turn of the new millennium, we had over 300 members

In or around 1994 a bunch of Celtic Supporters also had a meeting with various supporters from the Bramalea, Durham, St Catherine's, Toronto and Burlington Celtic supporters clubs. At this meeting it was decided we would start a Canadian Federation of Celtic Supporters clubs.

Within a few days I had received calls from Los Angeles, Kearney, New York and San Francisco based Celtic supporters. The word was out we were going to try and get games via satellite and the bhoys who phoned all said without any hesitation, 'count us in'. In less than a week the North American Federation of Celtic Supporters was born. This has now grown to seventy-two clubs based all over North America.

My current job as Vice President of the Federation takes me all over North America and as I go to each town where there is a club I am always met by the President or one of the relevant Committee. Every single club will make sure I'm catered for if I need anything or if there is anything they can do for me I've just to let them know. The hospitality that is shown to me, and I believe to any travelling Celtic supporter, is amazing. This always makes me feel very proud especially when I get e-mails from people or when I return to Glasgow people stop me and say they were at this club or that club and they were treated unbelievably well. It makes it all worthwhile. It is always great when you meet other Celtic supporters who maybe do not have any family in the States or in Canada but they're on business. When you meet these people he/she will talk about how good it is to be among their own in a strange land.

Haven't we grown in recent years? The NAFCSC Convention held every two years has grown from a celebration held by three hundred and fifty people attending the first one to three thousand Celtic supporters attending annually. This is a 'Celtic Family' gathering of gatherings.

I still miss going to Celtic Park to this day and when I do go the tears stream down my face as the team runs down the tunnel and onto the field. The hairs on the back of my neck stand when the supporters hold up their scarves to sing 'You'll never walk alone'. I join in but I can never get through it as I choke up with emotion and I don't feel the least bit worried about saying that because I love my club and the family of supporters that has always been around it. The original Celtic community is still there in spirit at this great club and it comes alive whenever and wherever we play.

Before I left for Canada I used to go to see Scotland play at Hampden. That was until the night I went to a match and the Scotland fans booed Jimmy Johnstone. Like many Celtic supporters I knew the stories of how unwelcome Celtic people were at Scotland games and although I had heard utterances on numerous occasions, this was the worst I'd experienced and I vowed never to go back. That night the Scotland supporters showed us what they felt about Catholics, Irishness and Celtic

> The NAFCSC Convention held every two years has grown from a celebration held by three hundred and fifty people attending the first one to three thousand Celtic supporters attending annually.

footballers in Scottish society: worse for me was the newspapers in Scotland either staying silent in the face of this bigotry or making excuses and defending the Scotland fans behaviour. That night I was blatantly confronted with something many other Celtic supporters had long recognised. That night I realised more than ever who and what I was and how unwelcome my community was in Scotland.

Like many Celtic supporters I had actually grown up in an Irish household. The influence of my Irish-born granny had been important in my early years. The Gorbals of course was a very Irish community, certainly up until the 1960s at least. My granny taught me all the Irish songs; Forty Shades of Green, Danny Boy, The Soldiers Song and Sean South I remember in particular. Her words came back to haunt me that night I witnessed Jimmy receive that sectarian and racist abuse at Hampden Park. She used to say to me, 'why are you going up to Hampden to watch that mob full of bluenoses?' I would always wind her up by saying, 'Granny they are my country and you have to support them.' Granny always saw her offspring as Irish like herself even though we all had Glasgow accents by this time. Granny was a wise woman.

The Irish had it rough in Scotland when they went there and Granny and Granda were only a tiny sample of those who had to put up with being called names and treated like dirt. However, I am proud of them for the way they stuck it out and would not be put down by anyone.

That heritage has always resonated with me and I have taken it to Canada. I'm one of the many Irish-Scots in North America who have a Scottish accent but an Irish name and Irish origins. I also stick with the religious faith handed down to me by people who had to fight tooth and nail to keep it. This heritage and identity is something I share with many other Celtic supporters in this vast continent and when we come together to support the club or simply celebrate who and what we are, this is when the real meaning of Celtic begins to shine through. This is when the idea of 'family' takes on a whole new significance. 'Celtic Football Club', icon of the Irish diaspora wherever they settled.

Section 3
Culture and Identity

Playing the same tune, singing the same song?

JAMES MACMILLAN

An unexpected and delightful request came my way recently. On 5th November 2005 a brand new statue of Brother Walfrid was unveiled outside the main entrance to Celtic Park. Otherwise known as Andrew Kerins he was the Marist brother from Sligo who was principal founder of Celtic Football Club in 1887/88. The sculpture was constructed by one of Scotland's leading artists, Kate Robinson. The organising committee of supporters invited me to write some music to commemorate the event. A group of young musicians from the Coatbridge St. Patrick's Branch of Comhaltas Ceoltoiri Eireann performed the new piece.

This turned out to be a welcome, but well-overdue return to some of my musical roots. When I was younger I used to play and sing the traditional music of Ireland and Scotland in the folk-clubs and pubs in the West. I'm not the only 'Art' composer to be seduced by folk music. Classical music is infused with vernacular forms through the centuries, and modern Scottish classical music is no different. Eddie McGuire, composer of ballets, operas and orchestral scores is a member of The Whistlebinkies; James Dillon, one of the leading post-Darmstadt modernists, was a piper as a boy. He is a huge Celtic supporter and even when he was featured composer at Musica Nova in 1981 he chose to miss one of his performances so he could attend the Celtic-Juventus game at Celtic Park. I once watched Gordon McPherson, Professor of Composition at the RSAMD, lead a ceilidh session with his accordion in Orkney. Lyell Cresswell, William Sweeney and Judith Weir have all dabbled in the deep and fruitful reservoir of the Scottish tradition.

Soaking up these influences were vital experiences for them, but the practical involvement could be fairly hazardous at times. During the 1980s' miners' strike some old school friends and I were invited to perform at a benefit event for victimized strikers in a working men's club in Ayrshire. The act before us was a bizarre banshee of a crone, crooning and whooping through a maudlin, drunken lament. We were convinced she was some undiscovered avant-garde comic genius, and were doubled up under the table in appreciative hysterics. We were informed, icily, that the song was about the Ibrox Disaster and *deadly* serious.

We tried to make amends by presenting a series of defiant workers' songs, but the atmosphere was by now severely poisoned, our misinterpretation of the singer being further misinterpreted by the assembled Ayrshiremen. Desperately we launched into Bandiera Rossa – an even bigger mistake. Half of the audience thought it was an Irish Republican anthem, the other half thought we were singing in Latin, neither a good idea down in Ayrshire. The PA plug was ripped from the wall, and like a pack of hounds, they chased us out.

We were astonished that our repertoire of fraternal, socialist solidarity had so enraged the comrades. It was as if the sound of the music itself had provoked an instinctive fury. I have seen something of this rage in recent years in relation to Celtic. Much irritation has been expressed in the Scottish media about Celtic supporters' Irishness – and Irish music and song feature prominently in the abuse – the 'Have a Potato style of hokey Irishness', as referred to by a *Herald* sports columnist, and their penchant for 'deedly-deedly music' as expressed by a *Sun* 'writer'.[1] In fact, this not-solely-neanderthal hostility to Irish culture in Scotland is usually expressed by those clamouring for people of Irish decent to abandon their Irishness and 'assimilate': to become more acceptable. This is in stark contrast to the Scottish Executive's enthusiasm for 'One Scotland Many Cultures' where, it is suggested, people of different origins and cultures can live side by side, recognising that difference need not be a cause of social strife.

(1) E Grahame, The Herald, Sport, 8/4/02 & B Leckie, The Sun, 8/4/02

Those pushing for the 'assimilation' option, liberal and conservative, should be aware of the cultural devastation that would result from a one-size-suits-all Scottish identity. I was reminded of this when writing the Walfrid composition and began researching *Comhaltas Ceoltoiri Eireann* (Association of Irish Musicians). This is a worldwide phenomenon rooted in Ireland and dedicated to nurturing Irish traditional instrumental music, song, dance and language. The first branch to be established outside Ireland was in Glasgow in 1957. Today there are four branches (two in Glasgow, one in Coatbridge and one in Newarthill) and their activities have blossomed spectacularly and confidently in the current generation. The vibrant culture of Scotland's first and largest modern immigrant group is flourishing because of CCE.

A central figure is Frank McArdle, a Maths teacher in St. Roch's Secondary School in Glasgow's east end. Since the 1970s he has been organising classes for the Irish Minstrels branch of CCE. It has been an amazing success story. Most of Glasgow's Irish ceili bands have their roots in the activities of the Irish Minstrels. The standard of musicianship is very high – the branch has produced countless all-Irish (ie, world) champions and the Scottish folk scene is peppered with his 'graduates'. In recognition of their contribution to the traditional arts they received their first ever invitation to the Celtic Connections Festival in 2005.

I visited the branch on one of their Tuesday evening meetings and it proved an inspiring and jaw-dropping encounter. Going from one classroom to the next one sees the operation in full flow – beginners, intermediate and advanced classes in violin, flute, whistle, piano accordion, button accordion, clarsach, and uillean pipes. Scores of kids and adults were taking part. There was even a class in set-dancing, where I saw a number of Albanian asylum seekers from nearby Sighthill.

At one point I had to scoop a child, no more than a toddler, penny-whistle in hand, up off the floor, and redirect him back to his class, full of pre-schoolers learning melodies by number. Unlike their counterparts in Ireland, their tutors are unpaid, all sharing McArdle's motivation and love of their mother culture. This scene is replicated in the other branches week after week.

Apart from a small Lottery grant for instruments and something from the Irish diaspora-funding body, Dion, they receive no official support, and yet this is a model for how music and the arts can operate at the core of a community. Their quiet, stoical determination to build upon their traditional roots seems somewhat at odds with the ineffectual belligerence of Sheena Wellington and others in the Scottish Traditional Folk lobby. The Scottish folkies' unseemly over-eagerness to attack the 'high arts', and Scottish Opera in particular, has allowed some politicians to divide, rule, control and damage the united campaign to defend Scottish culture. CCE seem a million light years away from the grubby politicking of Scotland's culture wars, and are better off for it.

However, they give the impression of working cheerfully and fruitfully in the face of an unspoken nervousness about their raison d'etre. Perhaps there is a narrow and ungenerous view out there that might see their burgeoning enthusiasm as 'divisive': the old question of hostility being an ever-present part of the Irish diaspora mind-set in Scotland. Who is looking at us? What will they say? Are we doing anything that will offend them? Keep it to yourself. Keep the head down.

Even among older Irish descendents there is a well-meaning, bent-over-backwards, over-eager-to-please desire to be seen to disconnect from their Irish roots and be sufficiently Scottish to pass 'the test'. For example, Irish-born Cardinal Keith Patrick O'Brien seems to see it as part of his ecumenical duty to play down the Irishness of his flock in Scotland. In a recent interview with *The Tablet* he said that Catholics in Scotland whose families came from Ireland 'no longer see themselves as part of an Irish diaspora'. I imagine this must come as news to thousands, not just those involved with CCE, but countless GAA people in Scotland, Irish language enthusiasts, many Celtic supporters and others who we never hear about, forging, enjoying and celebrating their Irishness or the other complex identities of a contemporary Irish-Scottish existence. What is so reprehensible about Irishness that compels the great and the good (as well as the not-so-great-and-good) to advise, indeed promote, wholesale abandonment? Was Norman Tebbit just the most obvious of a whole strata of society's identity forgers?

There is also a more gangrenous, self-loathing version of this, expounded by self-appointed pronouncers on Irish-Scottish matters, which is pitiful to behold. According to Edinburgh historian Owen Dudley Edwards the working-class, west-of-Scotland, 'Paddyer-than-thou' Hiberno-Scot is responsible for 'the sickness of modern Scottish Catholic culture'. Such a person is also a 'Cro-Magnon Catholic' with neo-fascist tendencies who gives succour to the IRA.[2] Of course, the same bilious ranter has not been known to engage in any kind of research of the Irish in the west of Scotland, and one wonders by what his pronouncements are motivated, and why they should be published as though of great value and insight. Nonetheless, apart from anything else we might say about this crass ignorance and unqualified and unknowing commentary, trying to square this odious caricature of grunting cavemen, jack-boots and balaclavas with the gentle children at St Roch's, stroking tenderly at harp and string, with their parents in the next room dancing arm-in-arm with refugees, takes a huge and delirious leap of imagination.

Such is the demon that Catholics of Irish descent in Scotland have endured, even from those who share much of their own background. Such is the power that creeps below the surface of much of Scottish society. A part of that society will not be happy until these people who have come to Scotland over the past one hundred and fifty years stop being 'different': stop expressing their distinctiveness in music, song, dance, their choice of football team, their choice of schooling, sometimes even their politics, etc, etc.

It might be better that McArdle and his CCE volunteers remain oblivious of Dudley Edwards' fatuous rage, otherwise I can't imagine them ever wanting to venture out again, never mind putting their heads above parapets. Maybe that's the choice many of Irish descent in Scotland have made over their period of time here.

Notwithstanding Dudley Edwards' hideous snobbery, modern Catholic culture in Scotland is demonstrably not sick. Neither has it been solely shaped by the immigrant Irish presence: which is in fact acknowledged by virtually all of its knowledgeable writers despite some of them choosing to focus on this community as their subject of study. But what is not

(2) Edwards, Owen D (2005),–Scottish Affairs, review article: Who's British Now? Spring, No 51, pp113-127

usually acknowledged by wider society, in positive terms, is how modern Scotland has been textured and tinged by this community over the years, and the pride that this engenders within the offspring of that community. One only has to seriously reflect upon the many artists in Scotland who are second, third and fourth generation Irish to see this impact and to feel a sense of pride and achievement.

For some though, this pride has curdled to a scorn that is heaped contemptuously on this community's legitimate anxieties over sectarianism and prejudice. Dudley Edwards has occasionally used the political journal *Scottish Affairs* to vent the incoherent apoplexies discussed above. He has recapitulated his tedious theme in a more recent issue.[3] Here we can observe the extraordinary contortions in his review of the periodical, *The Drouth,* which took as its special theme for one number: 'Bigotry'. Ironically Dudley Edwards is on the editorial board of the said periodical but, in breach of the usual scholarly protocol, he also felt entitled to review this particular issue. This is not only strange but in fact demonstrates superbly his pretensions of power, and his attempt to render powerless those who have a varying perspective on the Irish-descended and Catholics in Scotland. His targets often have a more well-tested and researched perspective on these issues than he does. One can't help but wonder at his attempts (and possibly *Scottish Affairs'* attempts?) to silence those who deviate from his conforming discourses.

No doubt much to his annoyance, the 'Bigotry' issue of *The Drouth* has been by far the best selling of nearly twenty issues of the magazine, and the editors (and Dudley Edwards' colleagues on the editorial board) clearly felt they were dealing with a pertinent issue. Dudley Edwards accuses some of its contributors of peddling 'ancient but lucrative martyrdoms'.[4] One might respond that this is a bit rich from a man who is party to the production of a publication and then proffers a review of same. If not perhaps 'lucrative', how very rewarding for Edwards!

Music is an activity and part of culture with a range of meanings, connections and links to many parts of society.

(3) Ibid

(4) The Drouth, issue 12, 'Bigotry' edition by G Calder, Summer 2004

Beyond the simplicity of the football field itself, football is the same. Celtic is ours. Everyone who is enthralled by the Celtic story sees the social, historical, political, cultural and religious perspectives that give this great institution meaning. With all this in mind, as a Celtic supporter I am proud of Brother Walfrid's lasting legacy of compassion, hope and the preferential option for the poor. I was delighted that my fellow supporters thought it important to mark his memory with works of art such as sculptures and specially written music from a so-called 'Art' composer. The unveiling drew these things into alignment with traditional musical contexts from the land of our forebears brought to life at the hands of vibrant young working-class people of Irish descent. The Arts clearly matter to the Celtic family, just as much as the culture of charity that has so shaped Ireland's reputation for generations, and which finds its source in the politics of the Gospel.

This is our culture. It is complex, paradoxical and good. It is alive, well and being nurtured lovingly by, amongst others, Frank McArdle and his colleagues in CCE. My encounters with them in Coatbridge and the east end of Glasgow allowed me to rediscover a musical world that had been so vital for my growth as a musician when I was younger. At the end of the particular evening spent in his company, he handed me a whistle and invited me to play along. I felt inexplicably and profoundly moved – in various ways I was coming home.

Irish music and song

Brian Warfield

BEGINNINGS

The very first awareness I had of a football club called Celtic was on my uncle Leo's knee singing, 'Hail Hail, the Celts are here': he was a big Celtic fan. I remember him by two songs. As well as 'Hail Hail' there was the 'Wearing of the Green': because of him, ever since I was aged about three of four, I've been a fan. He was a generous happy man and I loved his company. These were two great songs and moments that I will cherish and I know that they will live in my memory forever. He promised he would take me to Glasgow to see Celtic play, but we never did make it together.

Singing a Political Ballad – produced from a drawing by Jack B. Yeats in *Life in the West of Ireland*

Throughout the years we watched the progress of Celtic and we were ecstatic when they reached the European Final in Lisbon. We watched that game on the BBC at the time and I remember the commentator saying that Celtic were the first British side to win the European Cup. The commentator had a point, but he was only partly correct. Celtic were hardly British the way that Arsenal, Manchester United, Glasgow Rangers or Hearts were British. This is a bit like saying Amir Khan is British but nothing else.

This convolution was particularly evidenced by the fans singing at the top of their voices at the game, 'Sean South from Garryowen': hardly a very British song. This was also a song that was unlikely to be sung by any other 'British' football support. However, the singing of this and other Irish songs was one of those things that made Celtic fans stand out, unique, and provide an attraction and romance that few even in the global game of soccer could match. That song is still sung by Celtic supporters. For forty years wherever Celtic supporters have met and socialised, they have continued to sing this great Irish song.

Coincidently, the Wolfe Tones are forty odd years on the

road, although it's only in the last twenty odd years that we have developed a close relationship with Celtic's army of supporters. We are probably the last of the great Irish ballad groups still performing together since the beginning of the ballad boom in the sixties. We formed in 1964 in an era when change, justice and equality were sought in many places, particularly in the USA and Ireland. We brewed a unique blend of music and song that was a product of the context of our times: our songs reflected upon older days of rebellion and reflected newer days of social and political revolution, and of hope and peace.

The ballad singing tradition goes back a long time in Ireland. Songs and ballads have been passed from one generation to the next. The original balladeers were story tellers and news carriers but they had to be entertainers too in order to hold their audience and earn a living from their profession. The old balladeers sang and performed their ballads in pubs, at markets, patterns, fairs, sports occasions, race meetings or wherever there was a gathering: they were a part of the atmosphere of all Irish festive occasions.

In the beginning, the Wolfe Tones repertoire consisted of all kinds of folk songs; American, English, Scottish, Irish, emigration, work songs, industrial and sea shanties. These songs opened a window into the lives, situations and the conditions of the people of past generations and helped relay their stories and experiences to other generations. 'Official' histories rarely did this: in a winners-take-all situation it is frequently left to the common people themselves to retain and sustain their community memories and the histories that reflect their own experiences. In their own way ballad songs in Ireland told the history of our land and our people: the history of our country.

The Wolfe Tones brand of music became very popular in Ireland and England, so much so, that in 1964, a record contract was signed, with a debut release of 'The Foggy Dew' on the international Fontana label. As the popularity of the Tones grew, the sixties began to erupt with civil rights issues, the Vietnam War and peace protests. Side by side with this change in social and political perceptions and of course civil unrest in the USA,

> These songs opened a window into the lives, situations and the conditions of the people of past generations and helped relay their stories and experiences to other generations.

was a growing tide for freedom and equality in the six counties of Northern Ireland. The Nationalist population in the North were unwilling to except any longer the status quo and a situation where they'd been treated as second-class citizens since the partition of the island. They were unwilling to accept blatant religious, social and political oppression and discrimination for any longer, so the spirit of the sixties erupted in Ireland and the people sought change. The songs of the Wolfe Tones reflected at first this demand for change and then sought to record the events and stories of the history of Irish-British relations that led to this development and eruption, and also, to reflect the living history of the people who demanded change and recognition.

> In times of cleavage and conflict, what are commonly sung as songs of reflection, history and aspiration, have the potential to be considered 'something else',

However, in times of cleavage and conflict, what are commonly sung as songs of reflection, history and aspiration, have the potential to be considered 'something else', even more sinister and subversive, by those whose interests are best served by silence, misinformation, lies, distortion and false propaganda. Well, there's nothing sinister about Irish ballads, but there is something subversive. The stories of any oppressed people are subversive when they break the silence and propaganda of the ruling classes, the dominant, and often colonial and imperialistic, power.

Like other people of the Irish diaspora in Scotland along with dance and other cultural mores, Irish music and song have been important to people of Irish decent; in Garngad, Gorbals, Toryglen, Carfin, Coatbridge, Greenock, Port Glasgow and Dumbarton. As elsewhere, the history of the Irish people on the island of Ireland as well as amongst those who have been born elsewhere of Irish descent, is enshrined in our songs and ballads: a story that could not be freely got from other sources. These great hardships suffered by the Irish people over the centuries – wars, invasions, famine, plague, evictions, despotic governments and oppression, as well as the rebellions and the brave men who fought against oppression – are all remembered in Irish song: the one thing that in the past has kept spirits alive.

Even when battles were lost, consolation was taken in musical expression. When our lands were confiscated, the oppressor was marked out in our songs or in sorrowful ballads of eviction and emigration. How else could we announce their evil deeds, how else could we remember what they had done? When silence was demanded, song became the Irish means of communication. The Irish scattered all over the world but no matter where they made their home there is one thing that continues to emerge, that is, their great love of Irish music and song. The Irish emigrants who have made their way to Scotland have been no different to their fellow diaspora travellers to England, North America and Australia.

Often it has been song and music that has kept the Irish and their offspring in touch with their home and culture. It was said that all their wars were merry and all their songs were sad – I don't know who said it but it's not true. The songs and music of the Irish are full of expressions of joy, wit, sorrow, anger, pain outrage and could be either inspiring or soothing. Nonetheless, very often the musicians who told these stories were hunted down, tortured or even hung for treason. Music was the universal language and the soul of Ireland, said Thomas Davis.

Irish people, particularly Irish priests and monks helped keep Europe's intellectual rigour alive during the Middle Ages. However, in the early years of colonised Ireland and during the reigns of Henry and Elizabeth the books held in the great Monasteries, the written history of the Irish people were burned and destroyed in the great game of colonisation. The Bards who carried the story of the Clans were outlawed or killed. Every generation faced invasion and turmoil, religious persecution and discrimination. The Penal laws imposed after the Treaty of Limerick denied the Irish education or the right to obtain education abroad: even young men wishing to serve their faith as Catholic priests had to leave their own country to learn in colleges abroad. During these times the people were brought to a state of illiteracy and found it difficult amongst other things, to obtain knowledge of their own past history. Those lucky ones sent their children to hedge schools where the hedge school master passed on knowledge to those who could afford it. In many places the teachers were also the story tellers and ballad singers in the area.

> The songs and music of the Irish are full of expressions of joy, wit, sorrow, anger, pain outrage and could be either inspiring or soothing.

When educated Irish-minded Protestants joined the fight for freedom in the late eighteenth and nineteenth centuries the newspapers of their political movements were closed down, their presses confiscated and their writers and publishers imprisoned. The policy of censorship of all things Irish continued through every reign and against all who sought liberty whether Protestant or Catholic. The British objective in each generation was to destroy the subject of Irish history and deny the people knowledge and ownership of their own past. Forthwith, Irish song was always a nuisance to the British for it reminded everyone what they did to Ireland and its people. To destroy Irish music and song was to destroy Irish identity and to justify conquest, destruction and oppression. The legacy of this is still witnessed today for many Celtic supporters in Scotland.

> The British objective in each generation was to destroy the subject of Irish history and deny the people knowledge and ownership of their own past.

The ruling classes of Ireland believed these songs incited people to rebel against their rule, so they passed laws and legislation outlawing poets, rhymers, musicians, and their songs and ballads. An act was passed in 1533 to suppress foolish books, ballads and rhymes in the English tongue. This was to encompass the seditious songs in Irish language in 1537. In that year a musician called John Hogan was arrested in London for singing a political song. In 1541 another act stated, 'no musician or poet shall make a verse or *abhrain* (Irish for song) in praise of any person other than the king'.

Although Elizabeth I passed enactments against minstrels she herself had many Irish musicians in her court including an Irish Harper called Donogh. Irish music and dance became highly popular during her reign. Nonetheless, she banned Irish bards playing and reciting for the Irish themselves.

> no idle person Vagabond or masterless man, Bard, Rymeror any other notorious or detected malefactor doe haunte remayne or abide within the Bounds of your authority

At the period of the Confederation of Kilkenny from 1642 to 1648, Irish minstrelsy was much in evidence. Laments were written for the departed heroes Maelmuire O'Reilly slain on the bridge of Fenagh in 1642 and a glorious lament was composed for Owen Roe O'Neill on his death in 1649. In 1654 the Cromwellians, while sending the Irish to hell or Connaught ordered:

All harpers pipers and wandering musicians must obtain
letters from the Magistrate before being allowed to
travel across the country and all musical instruments
savouring of popery were to be destroyed.

After the Treaty of Limerick street ballad singers began to replace the harpers, pipers and bards. Many of the traditional musicians had gone with their lords and leaders to the armies of the enemies of Britain in Europe. When it became treasonable to mention their country in song, many of Irish poets and bards of this time used allegorical names for Ireland; *Roisin dubh* and *Caitilin ni h-Uallachain* being amongst the most well-known and names still with us today reminding us of those times.

In the eighteenth and nineteenth centuries the poverty and living conditions of Irish peasants is recorded as being amongst the worst in Europe. The Irish had little to look forward to: they had lost their struggle for the land and emigration developed to become a way of life for many generations of Irish people. The 1803 period of rebellion is remembered in ballads about Robert Emmet. Michael Dwyer the great hero of 1798 and 1803 was one of the last to hold out against superior forces but was conned into surrender and promised free passage to America. His enemies reneged on their promises and instead transported Dwyer to Australia as a political prisoner. While there he was given fifty lashes for 'singing a rebel song' by Captain Bligh of Mutiny on the Bounty fame, then Governor of the colony.

SONGS OF THE PEOPLE

Due to British colonialism, by 1840 Ireland had become one of the most impoverished countries in the western world. Housing conditions for the Irish were wretched beyond words. The census in 1841 graded 'houses' in Ireland into four classes: the fourth and lowest class consisted of windowless mud cabins of a single room, in which nearly half of the rural population of Ireland lived. In parts of the west of Ireland more than three fifths of the 'houses' were windowless, one-roomed mud cabins. Furniture was a luxury; the inhabitants of a town land in

Donegal, numbering about 9,000 had in 1837 only 10 beds, 93 chairs and 243 stools between them. Pigs slept with their owners for heat and to keep everything alive. The evicted and unemployed put roofs over ditches burrowed into banks in fields and existed in bog holes. By 1841 when a census was taken, the population had reached 8,175,124, but when the famine came in 1845 the population might well have been above ten million. The great Famine holocaust visited Ireland between 1845-51, devastating the country and forcing millions to flee the land and seek relief all over the world. In addition, over the next few decades, the ensuing evictions and land clearances by ruthless landlords in their quest to rid their lands of 'excess population' resulted in the further slaughter and scattering of millions.

Colonialism meant that most people depended on the land for a living and the small holder in most cases had no security of tenure and were tenants at will and could be evicted at any time: the people depended on the will and whim of their historical oppressor. Most of the people evicted from small holdings – many actually lived in hovels in the ground – did not have the money to go far and many of those forced out of the country at that time settled in the West of Scotland amongst several other destinations. From the period of the Famine, and as a direct product of the consequences of British-Irish historical relations, emerged Celtic Football Club.

The Irish in Scotland are a product of this history. Many Irish travelled and settled in Scotland due to the Great Famine while the many years of oppression thereafter caused further waves of Irish migration. Among those to choose Scotland was Andrew Kerins in the 1870s, the Catholic Marist Brother Walfrid from County Sligo. Along with his fellow Irish Catholic compatriots, he made a huge contribution to the cultural, charitable and sporting history of the Irish in Glasgow by founding Celtic in 1887/88. The legacy of Brother Walfrid and his fellow founders of Celtic has meant so much to the Irish communities and their descendants in Scotland. Land and the cruelty of landlords were very much in the minds of the founding fathers when they invited Michael Davitt the founder of the

Land and the cruelty of landlords were very much in the minds of the founding fathers (of Celtic) when they invited Michael Davitt the founder of the Irish Land League to place a sod brought over from Ireland in the field (at Celtic Park).

Irish Land League to place a sod brought over from Ireland in the field to mark the connection between the homeland and the new sporting and spiritual home for the Irish Diaspora in Scotland, Celtic Park in Glasgow.

SILENCING THE STORY

These are just some of the historic milestones that make up the subject matter of the songs and ballads of Ireland that are also the songs and ballads of the great Celtic support. It is the story and history of our country, of our heritage, our background, our heroes, our oppressions and our joys and celebrations: we have the right to tell these stories, to teach them and to sing about them. It is oppressive of anyone to hinder people from singing about themselves, their home-land or their history: it is also further evidence of a long established prejudice and attempt at controlling and shaping our Irish culture and identities.

It is oppressive of anyone to hinder people from singing about themselves, their home-land or their history.

The Wolfe Tones have carried the story of Ireland and the Irish to the world for forty odd years and have been acclaimed and honored in many countries. We have gold discs, been number one in a variety of countries, been voted top folk act in Ireland on around a dozen occasions and in one year recently even outsold U2 record sales in Ireland. We have received the keys of cities and were given many civic receptions: we have citations from assemblies and parliaments and are welcomed and sought after everywhere. We have played in almost every major concert hall in the world, from Carnegie Hall New York, to the famous Paris Olympia, the Albert Hall London to the Victoria Hall Melbourne.

One question remains: why do we encounter a problem in Glasgow? Why are the Wolfe Tones, Irish song and music insulted and made a scapegoat for what is a prejudiced, racist and sectarian society: a society which is the product of its own history. A society that requires to learn some history and find out a little more about its greatest single ethnic group that lives in its midst: the Irish descended in Scotland. Maybe if it learned even about its own past then matters might improve.

The Wolfe Tones have played a small part in the recent

history of Ireland and in reminding others of the troubles visited upon us by our neighbouring colonial power. The Wolfe Tones have been about for forty years but Celtic is going on one hundred and twenty. Through Celtic, part of the story of Ireland and of the Irish-descended in Scotland continues to evolve. In the face of bigotry, racism and sectarianism, song and music is a way to challenge these destructive social and cultural forces: so the cry is 'let the people sing, their stories and their songs'.

Why do we encounter a problem in Glasgow? Why are the Wolfe Tones, Irish song and music insulted and made a scapegoat for what is a prejudiced, racist and sectarian society: a society which is the product of its own history?

Something about us

Richard Purden

While doing a series of interviews about Celtic fans in the media, I was fascinated to discover a melting pot of faith, politics and ethnicity in the minds of the musicians, politicians and artists that I spoke to. However, it was once taboo for anyone in the public eye to nail their Celtic colours to the mast.

It's not just been perceived as ill-advised for those in the public eye not to let people know they support Celtic: there are countless situations in everyday Scottish life where bringing Celtic into the conversation, even by the most confident of people at the top of their trade, is avoided or met with a deafeningly quiet distain. Chris Geddis of Belle and Sebastian explained to me that his first piece of television work for the band brought about that same kind of experience.

> There's definitely a perception that it's something you should keep quiet or not mention. One of our first TV slots was on an STV arts programme, I worked at Celtic Park at the time selling pies in catering, I took them to Celtic Park talked about working there and supporting the team and a few people were a bit like. . . oh!

There's probably not one Celtic supporter who hasn't experienced that kind of discomfort. Although having no Catholic or Irish roots, Chris has become immersed in Celtic 'ideology'.

> It's a fairly big part of who I am. It kind of fits with the way I think about other things, life in general, how I approach art and politics. I suppose there is a kind of Celtic minded way of looking at things and the world, an idealised way of looking at. It's an inclusive thing: the ethos is that it's a community club.

In doing a series of interviews, some of which appeared in *The Irish Post* and *Celtic View*, my aim was to celebrate the vast contributions Celtic fans have made to life and society not just in Scotland but beyond in their applicable field of either the arts or politics. I wanted to discover what Celtic meant to them and why they supported the club. Within all that celebration there was also another consciousness, a struggle to assert Celtic identity, an identity that is played out in a variety of discourses and social situations giving many a confidence and window onto the world.

Recently I decided to revisit some of those original interviews. My first interview was with Mani of The Stone Roses and Primal Scream. The Stone Roses meteoric rise in 1989 was the last chance of a musical version of working class revolution, and one that invariably was vehemently anti-monarchy. They had one foot in the future and one in the past with blissful Aeolian melodies, anti-Thatcherite politics, scriptural lyrics and an image that blended all the best of street cool since the 1960s. Their debut album still regularly tops popularity polls. Mani explained his growing up in an Irish community in north Manchester and how support for Celtic was commonplace there.

> I think Manchester and Glasgow are very similar, the cities should be twinned, the people in the East End of Glasgow are exactly the same kind of people I grew up with, it was also the East side of North Manchester, they are both Irish Catholic communities. It's the only other city I would live in outside of Manchester. Like the cities, the clubs are very similar. Celtic as a club means truth and honesty more than anything else.
> You're born a Hoop and you die a Hoop, it's as staunch as you will get and you're there till you're boxed up and shipped out. Not only that, its absolute entertainment.

Left wing politics has always had a platform in popular music culture and especially for The Stone Roses and Primal Scream. It could be argued politics in Scotland has acquired a sense of rock n'roll since the birth of the Scottish Socialist Party (SSP). Some aspects of socialism in Scotland have undergone re-birth with people like second generation Irish politician Rosie Kane being at the forefront of these changes. As a new MSP it was a visually arresting pop moment when she refused to swear an oath to the queen and raised her hand to reveal the words 'My oath is to the people' in red ink: the kind of politician, never mind person, that Thatcher tried to destroy. Kane proved you didn't have to be middle class and Anglican to better yourself while mixing modern sass and front with Scotland's rich trade unionist past. Progressive politics was once again being spoken in a working class Glaswegian tongue. Her formative years were spent growing up in a staunch Celtic home with an Irish-born father. The experiences of her formative years were essential in shaping her views and success as a politician.

> My mother was a true and absolute diehard Celtic fan, it was her greatest love. From the age of 6 she was taking me to meet the team and she would write letters to the players and Jock Stein, we'd watch for things like Bobby Lennox's car. . . I was kicked out the Brownies because I wouldn't swear allegiance to the crown. My father said 'You don't dae that!' Looking back it was practically Masonic. I didn't know what it meant; I was eight years old. I didn't get to graduate into the Guides but I joined the Irish dancing instead.

IRA activity and reactions towards it (particularly via the media) in the 1970s and 80s helped make life very difficult for many Irish and their descendents throughout Britain. For many it was a terrifying experience just to be Irish or to have a different perspective of the Northern 'Troubles' from those that dominated. 'There was a lot of suspicion,' says Kane.

> You had the hunger strikers, the McGuires on bomb making charges and Bloody Sunday all on TV: there was a suspicion of all that was Irish. I didn't want my dad to speak in front of my friends: he's got a very strong Irish accent to this day. The image was that the Irish were stupid, daft and uneducated. I knew my father wasn't educated because he fled poverty at 14. My father didn't have a formal education but he was very smart and quick minded. There was a negative attitude and bullying towards anything Irish and it was reinforced by the newspapers.

Another side of the hostility that those of Irish descent have faced in Scotland is one of the most frustrating popular misconceptions: one often reinforced by some football pundits: often it is the opposite of the 'get back to Ireland if you like it that much' remark. This concerns those Celtic supporters who have lost contact with their original families in Ireland and who lack the direct family link that has been broken by social, educational, political or economic dislocation. Sometimes this even extends to an accusation that for some of those of Irish descent in Scotland and who are Celtic supporters that they have little experience of the country or awareness of Irish history. Not only is this accusation fundamentally flawed, but it fails to take into account that for all immigrant groupings to Scotland and elsewhere, Indian, Pakistani, Polish, there will always be change: a change that results in a re-formation of identity combining heritage and new experience and resulting in an identity that cannot ever be the same as the one left behind – whatever that may be anyway. Nonetheless, this does not mean that pride, a sense of belonging, celebration, a look to history, a sense of community and esteeming one's family and community background cannot be prioritised. Indeed, isn't this one dimension of so called multi-culturalism?

This kind of narrow drivel is frequently spouted by columnists in the Scottish tabloids that questions their credentials when it comes to sectarianism and racism never mind education and knowledge. Kane's relationship to Ireland is one common among Catholics of Irish descent in Scotland.

> There was a bus that left the bottom of our road that would take us over to Ireland. Every summer we'd go to Monaghan where my dad grew up. Every time I came back with an Irish accent, it came easily because it was my dad's tongue. We'd go via Belfast with the barricades, searches and troops at the turnstile. There were search points where the army would get on your bus with guns. We were exposed to that regularly to such a point where it became the norm. We were like celebrities, it was such a tiny place; they loved the wee Scottish accent. In Scotland it was the opposite with the Irish accent. It was so much easier to be me there: I knew I was safe in Ireland.

Although the vast majority of the Celtic support is Catholic of Irish descent, I have always taken an interest in interviewing people who do not come from this background but who support our club. This experience has given me the impression that when it came to Glasgow Rangers, the idea of linking that club's associated identities to other worthwhile facets of life is more problematic: they just don't translate well. So many things about the Celtic support are about causes relating to the marginalised and oppressed and about ideas of fighting back against something seen as wrong. Many symbols of the Celtic support also reflect this. I'm sure this has much to do with the religious background of many of the support as well as their history as Irish driven from their own land and having to face adversity in another.

SSP politician Carolyn Leckie comes from the opposite background to Kane but shares virtually the same politics.

> It was embarrassing to come from an Orange background but I'm not embarrassed anymore. For a large part of my adult life I've been embarrassed. I never really wanted to talk about it; I was mortified. I think now I have right to have my background and talk about it because your birth is an accident; nobody should be made to feel ashamed: if I still espoused those kind of views then people would have a right to question them and challenge me about those views. I loved the football when I was younger but politics became much more important. The associations with Rangers in terms of racism and bigotry: I just couldn't stomach it anymore. I think achieving understanding is half the battle in terms of trying to get agreement. We've got to respect the other's experiences and backgrounds, meet them where they are and then move on. If you have no understanding then it's a recipe for really negative conflict.

Bobby Gillespie of Primal Scream is one of the last truly great working class rock n' roll stars. Glaswegian and political to the core, his father was a trade unionist with no interest in football. Gillespie went to a non-denominational school were everyone supported Rangers. Nonetheless, Gillespie feels that due to the politics of the Celtic support his instinct is to support Celtic, even if he has no familial or Catholic link to the club and most of its supporting community. The ethos he developed growing up as a teenager is something he carried through to Primal Scream, libertarian rock n' roll outlaws, who, like The Stone Roses, were about uniting like-minded people. They brought rock audiences and clubbers together with their masterpiece Screamadelica in 1991. The cultural impact of that album was phenomenal due its blend of gospel, house, soul, rock n'roll and dub. It remains one of the most important albums of the era.

> I grew up in Springburn in the 60s, all the mates went to Catholic schools. I went to a non-denominational school. I supported Celtic: Celtic was non-denominational, I remember

asking my dad 'how come Catholics can't play for Rangers?' and he explained it to me. I thought Pele can't play for Rangers, he's black and he's a Catholic. Because of the school I went to you would hear 'If you fight for Londonderry clap your hands'. I didn't sing it, I didn't know what that meant, there was a very anti-Catholic feeling but I grew up in a street full of Catholics and all my friends were Catholics, all the guys I hung out with Catholics. I was like 'what's this about'; what's wrong with Catholics? You see through it all, I'd think I like this guy who's a Catholic but I don't like you, apart from that I thought the football with Rangers was ugly; just a big boot up the pitch. Celtic's was more stylish and more aesthetically pleasing. With Stein in control the vision was beautiful and I still find it inspiring to this day.

What fans of Celtic feel for the club is beyond football. While many clubs around the world have a fanatical support, there is a depth of feeling at Celtic that runs deeper than that which normally dominates. The way Gillespie feels about the club partly demonstrates this mindset.

Jock Stein was certainly a socialist and so was McNeil. I think the values they had came though in their attitude to the game. The way they played, they were a real team and they were in it together. Today everybody is a mercenary, everybody is a prostitute. People like Bill Shankly and Stein had the same thing because they grew up in mining villages. They were miners, socialists and left wing. The way they lived their lives came through in their work. In Hugh McIlvanney's book on football there is a chapter about Celtic, it's incredible what Stein said in that. He said it's not important that we win the game, its important how we win the game. It was beautiful attractive, interesting football. He said it's got to be glorious. He wanted to win with intent so that people watching think, this is how football should be played because this is a beautiful sport. Lisbon was like the meeting of two ideologies. It's an amazing moment when Shankly comes in the dressing room and says, 'John, you're immortal'. These guys had heart, they were really soulful men. There's no one like that in football anymore, I don't even know if guys like that exist in the world anymore. For me it's really poetic.

Through music and politics these artists and politicians have in some form, been shaped by a Celtic minded ethos. Sometimes just the visual power of the green and white hoops is enough to bring people to the club. However, the history, the Catholic,

Irish immigrant, Irish political, rising from poverty and, socialist aspects to the support, has ensured the Celtic ethos has reached the deepest darkest corners of the world and attracted many to the cause of 'the hoops'. The Celtic support has long been the Club's most significant asset.

Supporting Celtic is part of the way of life for some bands and none more so than Mogwai. Their drummer Martin Bullock explained how the tired, splitting the audience line has no credence, the chances are if you are a Celtic fan, you're going to get a bigger international support irrespective of what happens in Glasgow when people don't like you if you support either Celtic or Rangers.

> We've played some really weird places where people turn up with the Hoops on because we've mentioned that we are into Celtic, there's loads of wee guys down the front with the Hoops on. There was one guy at a Fuji rock festival that had been to a few of our gigs in Japan. He turned up with an old Hoops top and at the end of the show I jumped of the stage and gave him my Hoops. As I was taking my top off there was a massive surge to the front and people were trying to grab it. I was like 'Naw it's for him there', he had this mad worried look on his face, like he wasn't going to get it. When he got it he was jumping about mad in the top going nuts.

That's the Celtic family, that's being 'Celtic Minded'.

Football memorabilia: memory, heritage and meaning

Edward Grady

For many years the hobby of collecting football memorabilia has been associated with 'geeks' or 'anoraks'. Despite this specialised hobby being an integral part of some people's lives for decades such descriptions of memorabilia collectors persists.

Yet being a dedicated collector of the memorabilia of a club one can technically become an historian who proudly identifies himself or herself with the club and fanbase in a deeply meaningful way. In themselves, such people can also become important sources of memory via the collecting of such items.

Collecting football memorabilia has been defined as a dynamic factor of culture but generally, each collection is unique to its collector, who in the main is termed as being an avid collector on the basis of being dedicated to a single club or specialisation. It is probably realistic to assume that the main motive or objective of the avid collector is to pass the collection on to a younger generation. Although the collection may have a considerable financial value it is the retaining of memory and heritage that can prove of greater value. The monetary side of things is often secondary.

For example, if evidence of an event like Cetlltic winning the European Champions Cup in 1967 is produced in a company of people in an appropriate age group, it is likely that one, more, or all in the company would be able to provide dialogue that connects the event or reference to either themselves or their family in general. In this way such a tangible item becomes a prompt in the stimulation of memory and the telling of stories.

The title *Programme Monthly* is perhaps misleading as it caters for the buying and selling of all sporting memorabilia. The actual publication has been in the public domain for twenty-four years. Edited by John Lister of Kirkcaldy, it is an informative read split into two sections. The main section is focused on collector related articles and provides details of future programme fairs. The second section allows for the buying and selling of memorabilia. However, the main advantage that *Programme Monthly* has over the traditional dealer catalogue is that it enables collectors to advertise their 'swaps', 'wants lists' or 'to sell' items. Therefore, from a collector's perspective, the added value is the opportunity to add to their collection.

The programme fair is the result of an organised event that consists of several dealers who have agreed to market their items of memorabilia in the format of a 'stall'. Traditionally this avenue has been considered important to the serious collector or deemed as an alternative source for a dealer to purchase a collection or individual item that could then be sold on to a customer.

Since the arrival of the internet, the availability of football memorabilia has increased ten fold, as opposed to the traditional format of the dealer's catalogue or the more prestigious *Football Monthly*. A recent academic article suggests that according to www.forrester.com more than 80% of global trade will soon be conducted via the Internet with auctions accounting for 25% of all auction sales.

Although in hindsight, as eBay is a global twenty-four hour operation, it has made it easier for foreign collectors and ex-pat Celtic supporters around the world to add to their collections. This most certainly is a factor in determining the going rate of each programme or item of memorabilia. From an ex-pat's perspective, being able to hold onto Celtic football/cultural roots enables a sense of belonging and identification with the club and its culture.

Of course, many Irish and Irish Scots who emigrated to North America, Canada, Australia, New Zealand and South Africa have tended to hold onto their alliance with the club they supported before leaving for their new homeland. The evidence of this can be measured in the growth of the formation of Celtic Supporters Clubs over the years. The North American

Federation of Celtic Supporters clubs (founded in 1996) proudly boasts that it has affiliated club members in Africa, Asia, Australia, New Zealand, Canada and in the USA although clubs in Canada and USA outstrip all others. Within the US there are forty-nine reported registered clubs whilst there are thirty in Canada.

The tendency to form the supporters clubs that over the past decade or so have been watching Celtic matches via many of the Irish bars around the globe has become very strong and indicative of the culture of the Celtic support. Hence the roots of Celtic FC, as a club of the Irish diaspora in Scotland, remains key in not only understanding the club but also in maintaining and sustaining the culture of Celtic fandom. In addition to Celtic Supporters Clubs throughout Britain, Ireland and Europe, there are supporters links spanning Bermuda, Hong Kong, Japan and Brazil.

In keeping with the tradition and heritage of the club and in maintaining a sense of community over the generations, the descendents of the ex-pats also become associated with the club that was a focus for their mothers, fathers, grandmothers and grandfathers. When applying this theory to Celtic, the passing of memory, heritage and meaningfulness through generations has been the norm especially with Irish-Scot and direct Irish immigrants who were supporters of Celtic before leaving their homes for pastures new.

As a native Glaswegian, Johnny Moore (President of San Francisco CSC) has experienced the association of Celtic whilst being an immigrant in the USA. His club is headquartered in an Irish bar in Millbrae, twenty miles south of San Francisco. Johnny and other 'exiled Celts' support the club via Celtic Pools, and in holding season books and shares. Many of these members of the Celtic family have lived in the USA for more than thirty years with many of their kids having been born there. Most of their kids have inherited the passion to support Celtic. Importantly for Celts such as Johnny, such supporters operate in the 'Celtic way' with regards charity and have donated much to the same throughout the years.

EUROPEAN CUP FINAL VICTORY IN 1967

The European Cup Final victory in Lisbon (1967) will go down in history as the greatest accolade in the history of Celtic Football Club. Celtic was the first club from Britain and from outside of Latin European countries to have qualified even for the final when Billy McNeill lifted the cup. To have tangible items relating to this victory reflects much about the meaningfulness of the win.

In 1992 Billy McNeill was interviewed during the production of a special video to celebrate the Lisbon Lions twenty fifth anniversary in which he referred to the victory in Lisbon as being very special although he and the other members of the team had not quite realised the magnitude of actual victory and how it meant so much to the supporters. McNeil stated that he 'honestly believed that the association towards Celtic Football Club and the winning of the European Cup to be incredible' and it was the supporters who first recognised how significant this achievement was. Suffice to say that such an occasion will always exist as part of the Celtic collective memory.

Collecting from this period is certainly an aspect of football fandom but the significance of a club winning Europe's greatest football prize can only be fully comprehended in the context of the story of the Irish in Scotland. After all, it was the club that represents this community who had won football's greatest prize. That alone makes one reflect on the hopes and dreams of those who founded and first supported our great institution.

CENTENARY YEAR 1988

In the year leading into the club's centenary, the most significant thing that occurred was the replacement of the traditional shamrock and the introduction of 'Celtic Cross' being displayed on the team jersey as the main feature of the club's crest. Not only was the 'Celtic Cross' a powerful emblem, it reiterated the origin and values in which the club was founded in terms of the strong association of Irish and Catholic identity in Scotland. Strange though it might have been, the Centenary of Celtic Football Club produced a romantic feeling and sense of belongingness for all supporters associated with the club's history and culture.

Collecting memorabilia from this period does not solely relate to the success of the club during the season of 1987/88, it was a celebration of 100 years of the existence of an Irish institution in Scotland. Celtic fans were reminded of the foundation of the club, what it meant in terms of its establishment along with the memories of the club's achievements on and off the field of play.

UEFA CUP FINAL IN SEVILLE 2003

Qualifying for the first European final since 1970 created a worldwide scramble not only for the prized gold dust in the form of match tickets but also flights and accommodation.

Although the match ticket allocation was not known until a couple of weeks prior to having qualified for the final, getting to the destination of Seville soon became the priority for all Celtic supporters. Those younger generations of supporters who had been bred on memories of Lisbon 1967 (rather than Milan in 1970) developed an urge to travel and witness for themselves, a European final. An estimated 80,000 fans descended on the city of Seville.

In those few years after the final the memories can easily be retrieved by someone referring to any keepsakes collected, such as the match programme, match ticket or flight ticket or photographs.

The passing of memories and the maintaining of heritage and traditions are important aspects of football memorabilia collecting, such tangible items having a strong association with the club. Celtic is famous not only for the uniqueness of its history and the nature of its support but in collecting memorabilia, the younger members of Celtic supporting families have the privilege of having the more senior members remind them of the foundations and history of the club, significant eras and famous stars, victories or even defeats of yesteryear.

Having collected historical items related to Celtic for a number of years from a personal perspective, for me this provides a very special association with our club and allows contact with legends who were part of the club during those epic periods around the 1966/67 season, the Centenary season of 1988 and more recently the UEFA Cup Final in Seville in 2003. These are extraordinary periods in the history of Celtic, but it is their meaning that really elevates Celtic Football Club and its supporters to a special and unique place in the history of world football.

Celtic memorabilia

Section 4

Against false witness about us

How can you be 'anti-sectarian' when you don't even know what 'sectarianism' is?

GERRY COYLE

Seventeen years on I can still vividly recall the sense of disbelief I felt as I sat looking at the newspaper in front of me. Staring back from its pages was a picture of my former Celtic hero standing shoulder to shoulder with Rangers manager Graeme Souness under the headline 'Mo signs for Gers'. The fact that I was at the time sitting in a dimly lit Pamplona apartment recovering from the excesses of the previous night's wine fuelled celebrations (San Fermin was in full swing) and in the company of two Spaniards, for whom the whole Celtic-Rangers 'thing' and the magnitude of what Mr Johnston had just done meant precious little, only added to the surrealism of the occasion.

It is hard to believe that was in 1989. Even harder to think now, in our present PC 'anti-sectarian' climate, that we were then almost into the final decade of the twentieth century and a Scottish football club had yet to sign a Catholic player – in actual fact, some other teams have had a conspicuously poor record when it comes to having Catholics at their clubs. More to the point, such a policy had continued unchallenged by the nation's football authorities, by many voices in the rest of society and, for the most part, by the Scottish media for one hundred years: indeed it was only on rare occasions prior to the 1970s that Rangers policy was even referred to by anyone within the media. It was clearly thought acceptable that a football club should be allowed to exclude part of the population on the basis of its ethnic background and religion – probably the most flagrant public act of institutionalised anti-Catholic discrimination in Britain outwith the Act of Settlement. It was that acceptance which tells us much, not only about our national sport, but also Scotland.

Some will of course argue that that was then this is now and it is true times have changed. Rangers Football Club has now signed several Scottish-born Catholic players,[1] an Italian Catholic has in recent years captained the team and the club has appointed its first manager from a French Catholic background. However, any prophesies that the dawning of such an era would bring with it a change in the mindset of the supporters and their long entrenched anti-Catholic culture has sadly proved wide of the mark.[2]

Many of the 50,000 who pack into Ibrox stadium still chorus gleefully about being up to their knees in Fenian blood on a regular basis.[3] Equally revealing is the chant of 'you only sing in the chapel' that is usually reserved for encounters with Celtic. In the minds of many Rangers followers, Catholicism clearly remains synonymous with their ethnic and historical football enemy. While outsiders may have frowned at their actions, for the thugs who attacked St. Marks Catholic Church in Motherwell as part of their celebration of Rangers winning the 2002/03 SPL title – and for many sharing such a cultural prejudice it was the natural thing to do. Victory over Celtic is never merely about victory on the football field: it is about defeating and – even subjugating – an alien culture and identity of which Celtic FC, its support and the Catholic Church are the most visible symbols. There is no escaping the fact that by practising its shameful and longstanding policy of not signing Catholics, Scotland's establishment club, the biggest and most successful sporting institution, at least in terms of winning trophies within the country, has contributed significantly to this kind of sectarian mindset.

However, to focus simply on Rangers when discussing anti-Catholic/Irish bigotry or sectarianism in would be to rigorously avoid the true nature and extent of this phenomenon – a mistake commonly and maybe conveniently made by too many people in Scotland. The fact is the sectarianism associated with Rangers Football Club and its fanbase is only a small vocal and expressive part of a greater picture. In order to understand that picture

(1) Although widely acclaimed as such the Johnston signing was no Damascus like conversion on the part of the Ibrox hierarchy. One suspects that a desire to get one over on rivals Celtic – who had only days previously paraded their prodigal son as a close season signing – and the fact that FIFA and UEFA were making threatening noises were the real motivating factors.

(2) G. McNee , Sunday Mail, 11/2/96

(3) It is notable how match commentators choose to ignore this, usually referring to such singing as 'the atmosphere inside Ibrox' or the Rangers support 'getting behind their team'.

we must first recognise the elements that have gone into creating it.

It is essential to remember that the chief sport of any nation is a product of its cultural and historical past and therefore reflects much of that past – as well as the present. Given this premise and the fact that, since the Reformation, Scottish society has been imbued with anti-Catholic prejudice then it would be unrealistic not to expect that phenomenon to be reflected to some degree in the national game. How we perceive its existence however is influenced by the manner in which it is presented to us: what we accept as 'normal' or 'deviant'- therefore deserving of censure – a kind of consensual perception of life if you like, is largely perpetuated by, and reflected in, specific groups or institutions within our society, most notably the media. It is only by acknowledging these truisms that we are able to make sense of some of the bizarre (from an outsider's perspective) incidents that occur in Scottish football – incidents which invariably reveal that anti-Catholic prejudice permeates not just the sport itself, but Scottish society as a whole – and the equally bizarre manner in which these incidents and that prejudice are depicted by numerous sections of the national media.

In Season 1995-6 Partick Thistle's Rod McDonald was red carded in a match against Rangers, after previously being cautioned for having the audacity to – as media publications like to call it – 'cross himself' on the field of play.[4] At half time the player was summoned along with his manager Murdo Mcleod to referee Jim McGilvary's office and told that he would be reported to the SFA for 'inciting the crowd'.[5] Whether Mr. McGilvary actually believed this to be true is a matter for conjecture. What is almost certain is that he was responding to what he perceived to be the accepted wisdom, the 'common sense' perspective of the sporting and therefore social/cultural environment in which he was operating.

While, Partick Thistle, as one would expect, voiced their displeasure at their player being ordered off in such circum-stances, it was significant that the expressions of disbelief came largely from the country's legion of foreign players, many of

(4) It is notable how even journalists with a Catholic background succumb to the use of this terminology. See for example G. McNee 'Old Firm Get Wires Crossed', Sunday Mail 11/2/96. 'Making the sign of the Cross' is the more accurate term.

(5) Daily Record, 5/2/96

whom were perhaps realising for the first time the nature of the milieu in which they were plying their trade.[6] As always however in such instances it was the response of the sporting media which was the most illuminating.

In a column headlined 'Play Don't Pray' former Celtic player and (at the time) football pundit, Alan McInally, insisted that McDonald should have 'taken a leaf out of Tommy Burns book' by keeping his religion a private matter, ie, well away from the football field. According to 'Rambo' the need to book the player for 'an inflammatory gesture' was simply 'a sad fact of life in the West of Scotland'.[7] Blessing oneself an inflammatory gesture? Prejudice 'a sad fact of life'? Keep your Catholicism out of sight? In other words, we know there are bigots out there, but best to keep the heid down and not annoy them, eh son! Such sentiments, by their extraordinary acceptance of anti-Catholic bigotry as a normal feature of everyday life, merely serve to reinforce the religious intolerance that they profess to condemn.

If this 'sad fact of life' means hiding Catholic faith or disguising Irish origins and identity in public in Scotland has in reality been the dominant reaction amongst Catholics of Irish descent to anti-Catholic and anti-Irish racism and sectarianism over a period of several generations, then the question is raised over the impact that this has had on the practice of the Catholic faith, support for Celtic and esteeming one's Irish roots and identity. How much has this community just kept its head down over the past 150 years? In 'keeping the head down', how many within the Catholic community by self-suppression and even inverted bigotry, carried out the will of those who wish not to be 'offended' by the very presence of such a religion and ethnic group in Scottish society? How many deny their faith and Irishness as a reaction to the bigotry they have faced.

Even when the critique of the McDonald incident appeared informed there was inevitably a sting in the tail – indicative of the familiar 'two sides of the same coin' approach that does little for the cause of anti-sectarianism. Typical of this kind of reaction was an article by Gerry McNee in the Sunday Mail the following day. Mr McNee began his piece promisingly enough

(6) Ibid 5/2/96 p. 46. See also 'Samba Star Joins In The crossing Debate' Daily Record 5/2/96 and The Herald, Letters to the Sports Editor, 12/2/96

(7) Daily Star, 10/2/96, p43

pointing out how the absurdity of what had happened at Firhill would make Scottish football a laughing stock in Europe and questioning why any 'genuine world-class player in his right mind would contemplate coming into an environment so filled with sectarian hate?' Of course, McNee did not label (or recognise?) this for what it was: a public and visible aspect of Scotland's pervasive anti-Irish and anti-Catholic culture. By the final paragraphs the seemingly obligatory need for perceived 'balance' had clearly reasserted itself as McNee turned the focus on Celtic (as the symbol of the 'other' side), commending the club for playing 'good' club songs before the previous week's game against Hibernian – a reference to the fact that 'The Fields of Athenry', which was evidently considered to be on a par with 'crossing yourself' in its potential to incite, had been omitted. However, until Celtic put an end to its supporters 'flaunting the Irish flag' the club's anti-sectarian credentials would – according to McNee's interpretation and representation of 'sectarianism'- remain in doubt. What exactly had a Partick Thistle player making the sign of the cross at Firhill got to do with Celtic and its Irish heritage, one might legitimately ask. If McNee was genuinely going to offer a sociological, theological and philosophical analysis of the legitimate place of faith in everyday life or to argue that history, culture and identity do not have any place in the world of football, it wasn't forthcoming.

Of course, in writing his comments McNee, an experienced journalist and himself ironically a member of the Irish diaspora, was doubtlessly well aware of the unwritten rule of the media in this country, that it is not advisable to highlight bigotry solely in relation to Rangers Football Club[8] or, indeed, to scrutinise too closely the subliminal codes which underlie the mindset of Scotland's football establishment.

This also raises the question about the knowledge, understanding and agendas of those who purport to write about this subject matter in the tabloid press. Would 'writers' who have alternative views be given employment if their writing actually challenged the very industry and the ideologies that dominate mainstream thinking?

(8) Hugh MacDonald, Celtic Minded, 2004, p192

In very recent years there has admittedly been some evidence of a change in climate in relation to the issue of players blessing themselves on the field of play. With an increasing number of foreign players in the Scottish game and the fact that Scottish football has become more available to a world-wide audience on a regular basis, due to its increased coverage on satellite TV, this practice has stopped being demonised. It is questionable if any referee would now have the temerity to book a player for such an action (although celebrating a goal in front of the home support at Ibrox in an Old Firm match can still apparently constitute incitement).[9] It would appear that as our national sport has become less parochial, more globalised and open to public viewing, it has become less reflective (as one might expect) of the prejudice inherent within that parochialism.[10]

Proof of a greater acknowledgement being given to the legitimacy of Catholicism within the Scottish football arena for example came in season 2004/05 when the SFA (albeit after much deliberation and pressure from outside agencies, notably Celtic FC, who themselves had come under pressure from representatives from within its mainly Catholic support) decided to mark the death of Pope John Paul II with a minute's silence before the start of both cup semi-finals. Although this act of respect was replicated in many social, cultural and sporting forums across the globe, such a decision it has to be said was commendable (although one suspects that there was a certain convenience in the fact the country's 'establishment club' would not be participating). It was also 'brave' (some will say foolhardy) given the potential the occasion presented for revealing what in this country is generally thought best to keep hidden from view. In both semi-finals the minute's silence was disrupted to a greater or lesser degree by the supporters of all the clubs involved, with the exception of Celtic – the major offenders being the Hearts fans prior to the match with Celtic.

A natural assumption would be that this behaviour would be roundly condemned by all and sundry, with the country's media leading the onslaught. This was not the case. There was of course condemnation but more often than not it was

(9) In a match against Rangers at Ibrox, in season 2004/05 Stilian Petrov and Craig Bellamy were booked for celebrating their goals even though neither player had left the field of play to do so.

(10) This applies in relation to offialdom (although individual officials, most notably certain linesmen, still seem intent on keeping up tradition by giving inexplicable decisions in Rangers favour in crucial matches) rather than supporters. As examples in this essay illustrate, supporters of many clubs in Scotland still exhibit anti-Catholic/ Irish prejudice.

tempered with questions as to the appropriateness of such tributes within a football environment.[11] For some of the commentators who brought this question into the debate this was a first: they had not raised this issue on previous occasions, most notably on the deaths of members of the British Royal Family.

It is interesting to compare reaction to events at Celtic Park two years previously when prior to the match against Livingston (a match which saw Celtic secure their second successive title under Martin O'Neill) a minute's silence to commemorate the British Queen Mother's death was reduced to 32 seconds (a fact which was well documented in the media) after it was disrupted by a significant number of the home support. Press, radio and television duly united in unanimous condemnation describing those responsible as 'imbeciles' and 'morons' and branding their behaviour as 'shameful' and 'disgusting'. Crucially and indicatively, debating whether such a tribute should have taken place however was omitted from the media agenda.

Ironically it was a debate that would have arguably had more pertinence to events at Celtic Park than Hampden. Given the club's roots and identity in the former British colony of the island of Ireland and its connections with Irish nationalist politics, a tribute to the former King's Consort was never likely to be well received by its support.[12] In the minds of many Celtic fans, the British Royal family remains a symbol of 800 years of colonial oppression in Ireland – the country from where most of the Celtic support originates. Furthermore, the Royal Family's adherence to the discriminatory Act of Settlement has also done little to endear it to a fanbase which is mostly, though by no means exclusively, Catholic.

It is hard to make a similar case for the Hearts support. Quite simply the Pope is a symbol of one thing and one thing only in Scotland: alien and despised Catholicism. We must therefore conclude that, whereas the Celtic support's disruption of the minute's silence for the Queen Mother, was a politically conscious act of defiance against a symbol of their own historical oppression, what took place at Hampden was nothing other than a naked display of anti-Catholic sectarianism that is in itself part of a much wider problem in Scottish culture. The

(11) J. Traynor 2005

(12) J.Bradley, Celtic Minded, 2004, p24-27

fact that there was also disruption, though to a lesser extent, at the other semi-final between Dundee United and Hibernian, ironically two teams with Irish Catholic antecedents, says much – though plainly not enough to be a matter of interest and comment for crusading 'anti-sectarian' sports commentators. Indeed, it would be foolish to think that anti-Catholic sentiment is the preserve of those who sit in the Govan stand. In a forthright insight to this issue, former Celtic player, Tommy Gemmell, himself a non-Catholic, has described how he believes such sentiment to be rife in the Scottish game: a view gained courtesy of his experiences during his playing career with the Celtic.[13]

Nothing illustrates this better in the present day context than the abuse meted out to Celtic's Neil Lennon in football stadia the length and breadth of Scotland. An Irish-born Catholic who makes no secret of what it means for him to play for the jersey, Lennon personifies everything that is anathema to the bigoted element within the Scottish football supporting public – as far as many are concerned he is 'the real McCoy'. No one was more aware of this fact than former Celtic manager Martin O'Neill.

During his time at the club O'Neill found it necessary to speak out against the abuse his fellow countryman was receiving both on and off the park, eventually but unequivocally stating that he believed it to be anti-Irish/Catholic in motive – an unusual step for someone who was normally circumspect on such issues. (Indeed, so perturbed was O'Neill by the anti-Catholic and anti-Irish atmosphere in Scottish football and culture that one might imagine that this experience would be a significant factor in discouraging him from contemplating a return to Celtic). The Celtic manager of course took his support for his player a stage further in the aftermath of the controversial Rangers v Celtic encounter at Ibrox in season 2004/05, a match which Celtic lost 2-0 and one in which Lennon had received a particularly torrid time from the Rangers support.

The image of Martin O'Neill standing in front of the Broomloan Stand, fist clenched, his arm around the shoulders of an almost embarrassed looking Neil Lennon is one that will live long in the memory of Celtic supporters. It was a gesture that

(13) T.Gemmell, Ibid p169

showed O'Neill was well aware of what Lennon represented to his own support, as well as those who had made him the target of their prejudiced outpourings. It was also on a personal level a gesture of solidarity with the man he had brought to the club.

Despite the match having more than its fair of controversy it was on this incident that the post match media spotlight invariably fell – not significantly on the abuse Lennon, or indeed, members of the Catholic faith had received at the game, from a majority of the Rangers support. Pundits and public alike joined in the chorus of incredulity: had O'Neill lost the plot? What was he thinking of? Didn't he realise his actions could have had serious consequences in the powder keg atmosphere of a Rangers/Celtic fixture? Decoded, it was clear that what the Celtic manager had really done was commit the cardinal sin of allegedly inciting the supporters of the establishment club (and those beyond in the wider society). What's more, he had done so on their home territory. It would appear that while the 'common sense' perspective – and the bias (which in reality underlies it) – may come in many guises, certain themes remain constant.

Of course Neil Lennon and Martin O'Neill are not the only ones to have fallen foul of the charge of incitement in recent years. In 2004 they were joined in the dock by 18-year-old Aiden McGeady. The young Celtic star's crime?: exercising his FIFA sanctioned right to choose to play for Ireland, the country of his family, in preference to Scotland, the country of his birth. As a consequence he has been duly punished by opposition fans who boo and jeer whenever he touches the ball.[14]

(14) Aiden's father, John, was so concerned re the abuse his son was likely to receive in his Old Firm debut in season 2004/05 that he made a personal appeal to the Rangers support in advance of the match.

While commentators have tried to obscure the racism directed at Neil Lennon by blaming his 'aggressive' style of play and socially constructed physical attributes for the treatment he receives, in Aiden McGeady's case the racism has simply been ignored, and unrecognised. Ironic, is it not, that we are exhorted (rightly) to 'show racism the red card', yet when that racism is anti-Irish in nature not even a caution is merited. Indeed, by their condemnation of the player for proclaiming allegiance to his diasporic heritage, football pundits have done little to discourage the hatemongers: that is, the hatemongers of a specific expression of modern multi-cultural Scotland. Of course, in some eyes McGeady's crime is even more heinous than either of his co accused: his Irishness is no accident of birth: it has been consciously 'chosen'. McGeady rightly perceives his family and community background i.e. Irishness, as determining his cultural and national identity – in a similar sense to many within the Celtic support itself, who, although Scottish born, consider themselves Irish because that is their diasporic identity: Ireland being the country from where their families originate.

Faced with this overwhelming evidence of anti-Irish/ Catholic[15] prejudice it is perhaps inevitable that a media so obsessed with the mantra of balance should insist in dragging the Celtic support under the sectarian umbrella. The question is, are they justified in doing so?

If we take the literal interpretation of the word, the very act of supporting a football club is in essence a 'sectarian' activity in the sense that it engenders a sense of 'us' and 'them'. To an extent it also incorporates a degree of intolerance and narrow mindedness, two other prerequisites of the term:[16] few football fans in the heat of the game or, even for that matter, in its aftermath, are magnanimous towards their opponents. In these respects most Celtic supporters are no different to those of any other football club in the world (although we might like to pride ourselves on acknowledging the merits of other teams). The problem with the word 'sectarian' arises however in the context in which it is employed by both politicians and media commentariat in Scotland, i.e. in reference to religious bigotry.

It would be naive not to recognise that there are those among the Celtic support who could be deemed to be sectarian in this respect. However, when politicians and media comment-ators in Scotland raise the issue of sectarianism in football invariably the term is applied to Celtic fans in relation to their Catholic/Irish identities or their support for Irish Republicanism (not in relation to religious bigotry). In one sense this is gratifying: the perceived need (given the prerequisite for 'balance' in such matters) to add an extra ingredient to the mix would imply a recognition that there is insufficient religious

(15) Although these terms are not necessarily synonymous (see G.Coyle, Irish Post 2001 p.15) they have for historical reasons become so, particularly in the west of Scotland (see T. Campbell and P. Woods 'The Glory and The Dream', 1986) This is especially true with regard to the prejudiced mindset which classifies them as indistinguishable.

(16) Definition of term sectarian: intolerant, narrow- minded, esp. as a result of rigid adherence to a particular sect or faction, New Collins Dictionary

bigotry present in the Celtic support to justify discussing the issue in those terms. It is also however a source of extreme irritation to those of us who are Celtic-minded and therefore possess a knowledge of the club's political antecedents i.e. are aware that the Irish Nationalist/Republican tradition is a legitimate part of not only our Club's history, but much more significantly, the history of the community from which the club has sprung.

While such a tradition has been a feature of Celtic culture since the club's formation, it has in recent years notably been given fresh impetus by 'the troubles' in the North of Ireland. By the 1980s and 90s the standard favourites of 'the Celtic choir', songs like The Merry Plough Boy (a 1960s number one in the hit parade in Ireland) and Sean South, had been supplemented by a new series of songs and chants of a more obvious pro-Republican nature and which often refer to contemporary events and figures in 'the troubles'. By the same token of course events in the North of Ireland have also injected a more contemporaneous element into the usual sectarian repertoire of the Rangers support.[17] However, unlike their Rangers counterparts, the Celtic support's phase of contemporary politicisation, is not exclusively 'parochial', i.e. it is not confined to an Irish context. Indeed, it acquires a more Catholic context (in both senses of the word) in its looking towards other oppressed and marginalised peoples across the globe.

In 1982 for example, when the Falklands War was at its height, Argentinian football jerseys became a common sight in 'the Jungle' at Celtic Park and graffiti referring to the conflict could be seen on walls in Celtic heartlands throughout the west of Scotland. (on one wall on Royston Road, alongside the usual pro-IRA and Celtic slogans, the words Viva Argentina were painted in large bold letters). Clearly the colonial and capitalist nature of the war and Britain's involvement had provided a natural source of empathy for those who recognised the parallel with Ireland.

However, such a parallel does not require to be part of the equation. There has also been a long-standing tradition among Celtic fans of identifying with what they perceive as 'oppressed

(17) These songs notably still contain a distinct 'anti' element of a sectarian nature, eg, their lyrics are often interspersed with derogatory slogans about the Pope or the late Bobby Sands MP.

peoples' and their 'struggles' in Europe and beyond. Hence the appearance of Basque (these flags could actually be viewed amongst the fans at Celtic Park in the late 1970s) and Palestinian flags at Celtic matches in recent years – a trend which has ignorantly (and perhaps conveniently) been taken in some quarters to signify a support for terrorism.[18]

When you put all this together it becomes evident that many Celtic supporters' political consciousness is in fact a complex phenomenon and one that hardly befits the simplistic and derogatory label of 'sectarianism' that has been attached to it. Indeed if anything its tendency to embrace and empathise with those whom it perceives as the victims of injustice is in fact in keeping with the club's inclusive ethos and its tradition of identifying with the oppressed, which of course was its very raison d'etre.

Does one have to be Celtic minded in order to perceive this? Perhaps. An ignorance of the true nature of the club's identity may well be to blame for the facile use of the 'sectarian' label to describe this manifestation within Celtic culture. One suspects however that in many cases this perception is also characterised by ignorance, prejudice or even, in some instances, self-interest.

Certainly with respect to the media there is undoubted advantage to be gained in perceiving Celtic and Rangers fans to be equally culpable of sectarian behaviour. After all, by focusing on both sides of the divide one can increase the pool of 'newsworthy' material on which to draw. That in itself however does not explain the persistent adherence to 'the balance' mantra and the ingenuity with which it at times appears to be conjured. How often have we seen the true nature of attacks on the Catholic community in Scotland, whether they be verbal or physical, obscured by an obligatory need to introduce material which is perceived as evidence of that community's own transgressions? Furthermore the parallels that are drawn, more often than not, are of a most tenuous nature.[19]

Even when such attacks are reported in isolation there is very little attempt to analyse and therefore expose the context that has given rise to them i.e. the anti-Catholic and anti-Irish

(18) A Scotland Today interview with a senior Strathclyde police officer at the height of the Executive's drive against sectarianism in football in 2005 contained CCTV footage of a young Celtic fan draped in the Basque country's national flag. This image was used by the officer in question to identify an example of support for 'a terrorist organisation' and therefore the kind of 'sectarianism' that was being targeted.

(19) See D. Sewell 'Catholics Britain's largest minority' Viking, London 2001; Leader, Irish Post, 27/10/01 'Bigotry's hidden agenda' Ibid 10/7/99

racism and sectarianism that pervades much of society.[20] All of this is of course symptomatic of 'the denial' malaise which afflicts Scotland, a malaise which is readily reflected in the reporting of a prejudiced, compliant and unquestioning media.

Politicians, despite at times exhibiting a crusading zeal in their approach to the issue, have demonstrated a similar tendency to drag the fingernails along the surface rather than get their hands dirty by digging too deeply. The Executive's constant preoccupation with football when dealing with the issue of sectarianism is itself indicative of this kind of approach, a classic case of dealing with the symptoms rather than the cause. Hauling fans out of their seats and banning them from stadia for singing real 'sectarian' songs may signal intent but it does not cure the bigotry that causes them to behave that way in the first place. The theory of the ninety-minute bigot[21] provides a convenient phenomenon for a society in denial.

Even if we are willing to accept the argument that Scottish football does exhibit bigotry and therefore is deserving of the high profile it has been given in this issue, we must ask ourselves, why now? All the evidence suggests that such bigotry, particularly of an anti-Irish/Catholic nature, has been a problem in the country's national sport, indeed even an endemic feature of its institutional core, for the best part of a century.[22] Yet, throughout that time, it has been allowed to exist unchallenged.

The key to understanding this is that the reality simply reflected the bigger picture. It would appear that, if anything, a combination of self interest (let's make Scotland more presentable as the 'best wee country in the world') and outside pressure (what if these Catholic countries find out what we're really like to their faith cousins) has been responsible for whatever changes that have occurred, rather than any initiative on the part of the country's social and political leaders – certainly not a change of heart. One wonders if the depth of unashamed and taken for granted anti-Catholicism that existed up until very recent decades had still been in existence today, would the Executive be as keen to address it, as it has the football and marching manifestations of 'Scotland's shame'?[23] I think we probably all know the answer to that one.

(20) See 'The Poison which is shaming our society' The Universe 27/6/04

(21) See G. Spiers, Scotland on Sunday, Sport p15, 14/1/96

(22) J.M Bradley Celtic Minded 2004 p.29-30. See also G. Gough S.C.O. 2004 on how this problem was not confined to Celtic.

(23) A phrase initially used by MacMillan to refer to anti-Catholic bigotry in Scotland, subsequently hijacked by the anti-sectarian industry.

The Celtic Minded, Irish Iconography and the Police State

Hugh McLoughlin

I was delighted recently to get a chance to take a stroll down memory lane, but was disappointed when I accidentally came across evidence that for those of us who are Celtic-minded, it is often a case of *plus ça change...*

Kevin McNally, the impossibly youthful looking, Celtic-minded proprietor of the Derby Inn, Mossend in Lanarkshire, asked if I could trace the issue of the *Scottish Daily Express* from the early 1970s which featured the photograph and story of a group of Celtic supporters partying in Budapest with Richard Burton and Liz Taylor. Kevin's late father, Jimmy McNally, was for many years a respected figure in Celtic circles and he featured in the photograph.

In my younger days, in those early '70s, I used to judge and chair the *Scottish Daily Express* sponsored Scottish Schools Debating Competition. (Yes, I was one of Glasgow University Union's master debaters!) Although then as now Tory supporting, the *Scottish Express* was a quality paper. The driving force behind the Schools Debating Competition was the Political Editor/Chief Leader Writer, the late, Charles Graham, arguably the finest Scottish journalist of the twentieth century.

In the late '60s it had been Charlie Graham who had led the *Express* campaign against 'bishops in the Kirk'. Many of today's newspaper columnists would do well to read these articles in order to learn that defence of your own religious heritage need not descend into a bigoted, vituperative attack on another's. Charlie, though against bishops in the Kirk, had no qualms about sitting beside one at Celtic Park. Charlie was ecumenical before the word had entered the Scottish vernacular.

Brought up by relatives after the death of his parents, he had attended both Glasgow High School and St Aloysius College, depending upon which relative was then taking care of him.

I remembered the story about Burton and Taylor for three reasons. Firstly, Charlie Graham had talked to me about it at the time and I remember how he had been cock-a-hoop since not only had it been a genuine scoop for the paper, but also Celtic had gained a remarkable victory. Secondly, friends of mine from Motherwell were there and had been photographed with the world's then most glamorous couple. Thirdly. . . well I'll come back to that in a moment.

When I betook myself to the Mitchell Library in search of Kevin McNally's Holy Grail I had only one small problem. I knew that Celtic had played Ujpest Dozsa twice in Budapest in 1972, but could not remember which one was the game we were interested in. I made the mistake of checking October 1972 first. The correct game was the European Champions Cup Quarter Final first leg on 8 March 1972 (Celtic won 2-1).

My friends who were at the game were all members of one of the biggest Celtic supporters' clubs in the country at that time: Motherwell British Legion, no matter how improbable that name might seem to many. The outing to Hungary had been organised, as were so many foreign trips, by Pat Connelly, the British Legion club master. Pat is currently Provost of North Lanarkshire Council and like his old friend Jimmy McNally is another very well-known figure in Celtic circles.

And that brings me to the third reason why I could remember about the Burton/Taylor-Celtic connection: it had been Pat Connelly who had alerted the neophyte *Scottish Daily Express* sports reporter covering the game of Richard Burton and Liz Taylor's carousing with the Celtic fans in their hotel. (Pat, it must be said in case his much loved wife Nancy reads this, was not carousing!)

My initially looking up the wrong game wasn't a total waste of time for I came across the following headline in the *Scottish Daily Express* of 2 October 1972: *Celtic flag mystery*. The story read in part:

Will the Eire tricolour ever fly again over Celtic Park?
Parkhead fans have been wondering, since Celtic's weekend flag spectacular, if the club is quietly doing away with the controversial flag. Celtic flew their record-breaking seven Championship pennants at Saturday's match with Ayr United. On the tricolour's pole was a special commemorative flag to mark the achievement.
But it was the first time in the living memory of the majority of supporters that the Eire flag was missing at a first team match. Only six weeks ago (ie, during August 1972) Glasgow magistrates asked Celtic to remove the flag – it has flown for decades – as a public gesture to help curb religious bigotry. They also asked Rangers to state that they were not a sectarian club. Celtic refused to lower the flag and Rangers hedged the question. (*sic*)

This was not the first time the city's magistrates had demanded the hauling down of the tricolour. Twenty years earlier, on New Year's Day 1952 Glasgow Rangers and Celtic met at Celtic Park. What happened after Rangers scored their fourth goal was the subject of a report in the following day's *Glasgow Herald*:

> Eleven persons were arrested during the New Year's Day football match yesterday between Celtic and Rangers at Celtic Park, Glasgow, where bottles were thrown and mounted police had to clear spectators from the track.

As a consequence of this incident, the *Glasgow Herald* was able to further report towards the end of the following month on 26 February:

SFA Council Approve Ban on Eire Flag
The much discussed flag of Eire will cease to be flown at Celtic Park on match days – at least that is the decision of the Scottish Football Association Council, who approved by 26 votes to 7 at yesterday's monthly meeting the decision already taken by the Referee's Committee in connection with the disturbance on New Year's Day at Celtic Park.

The only problem for the SFA was that they could not enforce their decision. Glasgow city's magistrates' committee had the same problem when they associated themselves with the SFA's demand for the removal of the tricolour. Happily, for the Celtic-minded, Bob Kelly wasn't prepared to play that particular ball game. Nor, twenty years later was Desmond

White. These Chairmen, and their Boards of Directors, were themselves happy to join with the Celtic minded amongst the supporters in associating their Celtic Football Club with the sentiment expressed by the Puritan divine, the Rev Calybute Dowling, who supporting Parliament in its struggle with King James VII and II, had said:

Many of us refuse to deny our Irish and Catholic, and frequently, nationalist and republican heritage.

That person is no rebel who for the sake of conscience, freedom and life defends himself; and in order to save himself from endless oppression must take up arms.[1]

This goes to the very heart of the problem we who are Celtic minded – and while being happy to acknowledge that this does not include all of the support of Celtic Football Club, it has to be said that it is the overwhelming majority – have in this supposedly modern, multi-cultural Scotland. Many of us refuse to deny our Irish and Catholic, and frequently, nationalist and republican heritage. We will neither turn our backs on all, nor on any of it. And we can discern no sensible reason why anyone should ask us to do so (sensible reasoning does not of course include racist or sectarian attitudes towards us). Even, and perhaps especially, when matters have now gone way beyond demands for the tricolour at Celtic Park to be hauled down as a sop to the bigots and sectarians in our society. They now want to shut Irish and Celtic minded public houses: our 'difference' seemingly to blame for a list of 'problems' long associated with Scotland: problems that in fact existed even before most of our forebears arrived on these shores.

1 The Wurteberg Pietist Pfaff in tones reminiscent of Calybute Downing in England in 1640. See 'Piety, and Politics: Religion and the Rise of Absolutism in England, Wurtemberg and Prussia' Mary Fulbrook, Cambridge University Press, 1983. Ms Fulbrook is Professor of German History and Head of the German Departmen at University College, London.

(2) 'Miscellany-at-Law: 9 Diversions for Lawyers' RE Megarry (see p34: 'Homo Sapiens: Cakes and Ale').

Sir Robert Megarry, the eminent legal scholar and humorist, once astutely observed: 'Thirsty folk want beer, not explanations.'[2] However, when reports from North Lanarkshire of the demise in controversial circumstances of a popular Celtic-minded pub – McCormick's Bar, Bellshill – have been so grossly exaggerated but, sadly, those of the death of another in Motherwell – Tully's – have proved all too true, then perhaps, explanations might be thought necessary, even by the thirstiest of Celtic minded people, the membership of the West of Scotland branch of the Catholic Drooth Society.

Would you believe me if I told you that 60% of those interviewed travelling to or from Ireland at ports and airports in England and Wales who could in one way or another, for one reason or another, be identified as 'Irish', had been stopped and questioned by police officers on at least one occasion? If you wouldn't believe me, would you believe the Commission for Racial Equality? They have also pointed out that of those stopped, three quarters had been detained for less that half an hour and so would not be recorded in any official statistics. Thus, this perceived 'harassment' could and did go unacknow-ledged by the State, and, unreported and un-commented upon by all but the Irish press and broadcasting media. Even at that, by no means by all of them. Of course, the Celtic minded who come over regularly from what was never John Bull's other island will have absolutely no problem at all in believing that.

What if I told you that an eminent academic had been forced to conclude:

> It appears that anti-Irish attitudes are strongly ingrained in the police force and justice system. Irish accents trigger reactions out of all relation to the context in which they are heard. This is particularly serious because the police are in a position of authority and have the power to enforce their prejudices, including the apparently legitimate use of violence.[3]

Would you believe that?

Well, in 1993, Professor Paddy Hillyard of Queen's Univers-ity, Belfast, did so conclude when he published the results of his study into how the working of the Prevention of Terrorism Act (1974) affected those of Irish affiliation living in Great Britain. He found that during the twenty-year period 1974-93, a total of 7,052 persons identifiable as having Irish affiliations were detained under the Prevention of Terrorism Act. In the overwhelming majority of these cases, some 86%, the detention resulted in no further action whatsoever being taken. Professor Hillyard calculated that those involved had spent a total of 33 years in custody.

But, perhaps you might be inclined to think that the good professor's conclusion was maybe just a wee bit too harsh? Or, you might think it is fair enough, but either way this sort of thing could never affect you, or somebody just as ordinary as you. Could it? Well, at about a quarter-to-six in the evening of

3 'Suspect Community: People's experience of the Prevention of Terrorism Act in Britain', Paddy Hillyard, Pluto Press, London. Paddy Hillyard is Professor within the School of Sociology and Social Policy, Queens University, Belfast.

Wednesday, 22 September 1999, on Victoria Park Road, Hackney, East London, Harry Stanley, originally from Bellshill, discovered that the Metropolitan Police had paid no attention whatsoever to Professor Hillyard's warning of six years earlier about the police being *in a position of authority* and having *the power to enforce their prejudices, including the apparently legitimate use of violence.* Harry, an ordinary guy just like you or me, was peremptorily shot dead by armed officers of the Met for merely having been reported to them as sounding Irish (to a London ear).

Eight years later in the summer of 2005, Jean Charles de Menezes was gunned down in London partly because the Met had learned nothing from their killing of Harry Stanley: except of course, as some might argue, in how to manufacture a lie. But, in this case their lies were less successful as Senor de Menezes was not of Ireland. Therefore, the national press and broadcast media would not play the game. And, more importantly, neither would his own Brazilian government.

What about closer to home? Have there been instances here in the heartland of Celtic mindedness of the police exercising anti-Irish, anti-Celtic minded, prejudices? I know it sounds like a rhetorical, even stupid, question, but here is a wee story for you. You can make up your own mind.

Late one September Saturday night in Motherwell following a Motherwell v Celtic match at Fir Park, the proprietor of a Celtic minded pub locked up her premises at half-past midnight. Suddenly, she was attacked by a gang of about a dozen 'evilly disposed persons', to borrow a polite phrase from the legal profession. They were in fact a mixed bag of 'football' supporters, united in their hatred of all things Celtic minded. They had been hiding in the bushes across the street waiting their chance. Fortunately, some of the proprietrix's regular customers waiting nearby for taxis came to her assistance. They held the thugs off and managed to get back into the pub and close, lock and bolt the doors. The baying, besieging mob hurled bottles and cans, as well as insults, abuse and threats, at the premises. Despite three frantic phone calls to the police, and despite the fact that Motherwell police office is only about 100 yards from the pub, it took almost 20 minutes for the police to arrive. It was rumoured that the first demand made by the police was an enquiry as to why there were customers in the pub after hours?

You see, what had originally raised the hostile hackles was the recently repainted frontage of the pub: the shields of the four Irish provinces hand-painted on an emerald green background. To be precise, unlike in almost every other town and city outside of Scotland where this would not even be a cause for negative comment, the sight of the Red Hand of the O'Neill's used in its correct Irish setting had proved too much for anti-Irish, anti-Catholic and anti-Celtic persons in Scotland. Like Tam O'Shanter's wife, they nursed their wrath to keep it warm.

A few days after the incident outlined above, the police informed the proprietrix that a complaint had been received from a local organisation. The licensing police had sought legal advice as to whether or not the frontage could be deemed 'sectarian'. They were told that it could not – as it was not. Nonetheless, they ordered her to remove it!

Faced with her refusal, their illegal demand was repeated over the next couple of weeks with increasingly dire warnings of the likely outcome of her continuing refusal to co-operate. For example, if there were a disturbance outside the premises during for example, 'a Walk', the perpetrators would be arrested. However, if they pleaded that the frontage had provoked them to violence, and thus to their arresting, the proprietor would be charged with having incited the trouble and would be reported to the Licensing Board as being now an unfit person to hold a licence. It has been suggested that the police apparently only desisted from this dastardly behaviour when a *Scotsman* journalist took an interest in the case. However, by that time, from the police point of view, a better Celtic minded target had presented itself.

Fed up with Irish theme pubs? Plastic leprechauns, shamrock wallpaper and overpriced, badly poured Guinness do nothing for you? I could think of better. Try McCormick's in Bellshill; excellently tended Guinness, myriad supporters scarves and football strips associated with Celtic and their international rivals over the years. Also, such Irish Nationalist/Republican historical artefacts and iconography on display as; a copy of the famous 'Wanted Daniel Breen, Reward' poster, photographs of John Mitchell, Thomas Ashe, Terence MacSwiney, Thomas J Clarke, and Michael Gaughan, a laminated photograph depicting the dead 1981 hunger strikers, a montage of three photographs of the funerals of Francis Hughes, Martin Hurson and Thomas McElwee, a montage of holiday snaps of Belfast murals, including some 'IRA' murals, a large framed painting depicting the siege at the GPO (Yeats' 'A terrible beauty'), a large framed photograph depicting the executed 1916 leaders, a picture of the Provisional Government of Ireland of 1919, four Celtic scarves bearing the following messages, 'Go on home', 'Dan Breen', *Tiocaidh Ar La* accompanied by stars and a Phoenix, and *Tiocaidh Ar La*, accompanied by a phoenix and a harp.

Such a repressive approach to a culture, history, heritage, identity and politics that are not of the majority but are part and parcel of the make-up of Scotland's greatest single immigrant grouping. . .

This is the list of artefacts and iconography from a letter of complaint sent in the name of the Chief Constable of Strathclyde Police to the Clerk to the North Lanarkshire Licensing Board. According to this complaint these were not merely items that might reasonably be expected to be on display in a pub catering to an almost exclusively Irish/Celtic minded clientele (and many of them were provided by that clientele), these articles in fact provided incontrovertible evidence of the publican's 'current support for the IRA'. He was, therefore and in consequence, deemed 'by the police' to be no longer a fit and proper person to hold a Publican's Licence. Although McCormick's licence was indeed temporarily withdrawn, the respected proprietor fought his case and justice won out against the forces of the misapplication of law and order. For this upholding of democracy and seeing justice done we have to thank the Inner House of the Court of Session in Edinburgh in 2005.

You couldn't make it up, could you? Some of these items are proudly on display in some of Ireland's museums. Some of these photographs have pride of place on the walls of Bertie Aherne's office. Does Strathclyde Police deem this evidence of Ireland's Taoiseach's 'current support for the IRA'? Surely a man thought of by Republicans as being right wing, but who is also recognised as having worked earnestly for peace and harmony on that troubled island, could not be a 'supporter' of the IRA? Surely not? This accusation would make even the British Prime Minister and many a Unionist laugh. This is of course stupid and baffling. Such a repressive approach to a culture, history, heritage, identity and politics that are not of the majority but are part and parcel of the make-up of Scotland's greatest single immigrant grouping (now of course mainly second, third and fourth generation) of the past 150 years, namely the Irish, is of course standard and reflects in the attitudes of some sectarian and racist 'authorities' with regards Celtic FC and its supporters' affinities with the Irish national flag and other symbols and signatures of Irishness.

Imagine if the US authorities decided to put a stop to things like Tartan Day in New York. Stop singing Scottish songs, wearing the kilt, being proud of William Wallace etc, etc. Absurd? I think so. But just think about it logically.

The cases of McCormick's and Tully's amongst others demonstrate the difficulty Scottish society has with its so-called multicultural status. These cases also reflect the difficulty Scotland has with itself as being the creator and perpetuator of what is now called 'sectarianism', but which started off as part of the conquest and colonisation of the island of Ireland and its people and who would as a result become one of the most dispersed and displaced peoples in the world. In the past 150 years those dispersed and displaced people who exist as the Irish diaspora in Scotland have contributed wonderfully to this country; in the arts, public services, the economy, academia, education, religious life and politics, and, to the make-up of the police force itself. Of course, they even founded and continue in great numbers to support Celtic, one of the world's most famous football clubs.

Many of them have not become Scots or become British but hold their roots and origins with deep affection and high esteem. Others have become Scots and British but even some of them look proudly to what their forebears upheld and represent. Publicly this is expressed in symbols, in support for Celtic, in a variety of other ways and of course, in song and music.

> . . . reflects in the attitudes of some sectarian and racist 'authorities' with regards Celtic FC and its supporters' affinities with symbols of Irishness.

'Song and music'! Now there's another story! See what happens when you get started? See all this multi-culturalism. It might just be better to manufacture wholesale social ignorance and for us all to be the same homogenous people in Scotland? All Jock Tamson's Bairns of course. All Scots or Brits, all waving the same flag, all singing the same songs, having the same or no religion, all having the same political perspectives and all having the same morals. That would solve all the problems. Wouldn't it?

Looking in the Mirror

MICHAEL MCMAHON

My earliest memory of Celtic comes from when I was six years old and relates to that most famous of days in May 1967, although I remember nothing of the game itself. What I do recall is my late father, Pat, jumping up in our living room following Tommy Gemmell's goal and my mother frantically trying to prise my one year old brother from his grasp in case my father dropped him in his delirium.

My father was the most quiet, placid and reserved of men. He lived for another thirty-seven years and I never saw him repeat that exuberance again in his life. Perhaps that is why the memory is so vivid for me. He was a teetotaller who seldom socialised beyond his involvement with Church groups, especially the St Vincent De Paul Society. As I grew up I very seldom heard him talk about much other than his faith and Celtic.

It was not until I was in my mid-teens that I discovered another side to him. The evening news one day was reporting the Catholic Church's disapproval of a decision being made by the then Labour government. Being aware that my father supported Labour I asked him for his views on this subject. Without a moments hesitation he calmly said, 'Son, even if the Pope himself asked me I would never vote anything other than Labour.' I knew then that, for me, although faith and morality can and do infuse politics, politics and religion could also be quite distinctive journeys.

If my love of Celtic can be traced back with certainty to events of Lisbon 1967 I would have to admit that I cannot trace my politics with the same definition. Both Celtic and politics are in my blood but maybe I have two bloodstreams as I have always tried not to let my football affect my politics in terms of goals, aspirations and fairness and equality for all, regardless of what team those who I struggle for support.

A few months after my election to the Scottish Parliament in May 1999 I received an anonymous e-mail from an individual who, from the tenor of his message, clearly was no lover of the Roman Catholic Church, Celtic Football Club or the Labour Party. Accompanying his diatribe, which was easy to discount due to the sheer ignorance it exposed, was an attachment that caused me to stop and think about a wider perception that it evidently represented.

Simply put, it was a reproduction of my Party's logo but with the Red Rose that lies next to the words 'Scottish Labour' having been replaced with a Celtic Football Club crest. Of course, I am aware of the accusations often made by outsiders, sections of the media and political opponents of the Irish Catholic influence on the Labour Party in Scotland but never before had I encountered a connection being made between my Party and Celtic FC.

Donald Gorrie MSP, the much vaunted champion of anti-sectarianism, put the jaundiced perception about the Labour Party and Catholicism as well as anyone when he stated that:

> Less intellectual Catholic organisations have a grip on the party. There is a predominance within the Labour Party of Catholics. I'm amazed more hasn't been made of this relationship. We have to ask, 'Is it good for politics, democracy and society?' I'm not saying Labour is in the Church's pocket but the Catholic Church has permeated and heavily penetrated the party. In some areas it seems every Labour member you meet is a lapsed Catholic. At a local level, Labour is profoundly corrupt in terms of its relationship with the Catholic Church. In some cases, to even get a position as a school janitor you have to scratch the right backs, and that means that going to the right church helps you get on.[1]

More has not been made of it because it is an inaccurate reflection of the reality, for, as with the claim that Labour Party membership can be equated with support for Celtic, it is an invalid assertion. If the link were so easy there would be no Celtic supporters with allegiances to other political parties and no Rangers, Hearts, Hibs or Motherwell supporters in the Labour Party – and believe me, there are plenty. Quite simply, the Labour Party could not be sustained only by Celtic supporters

(1) Sunday Herald, 11/3/01

and there are more non-Celtic and non-football supporters in Labour than there are Celtic supporters.

Importantly, and many people who make these kinds of accusations conveniently forget in all their ignorance, approx- imately only one in six of Scotland's population is Catholic, the majority religion is Protestant (Church of Scotland) and many are irreligious in terms of Church and moral practice. It would be impossible for Labour to gain political power if it was dom- inated by Catholics or even the Catholic Church, which is an accusation even more fanciful.

In addition, there is a Catholic perception that often those who are lapsed Catholics can frequently be anti-clerical, anti- Church and anti-Catholic morality. Where Donald Gorrie got his ideas from is anyone's guess but they say more about him and the ignorance behind those kinds of perceptions than they do about the Labour Party or Catholicism. They also say something about stereotypes and embedded prejudice based on poor education and knowledge.

> Donald Gorrie's ideas also say something about stereotypes and embedded prejudice based on poor education and knowledge.

I would not demean anyone's intelligence by attempting to argue that the religious division which exists within Scottish society as a whole does not exist at some level within my political party but I believe that Labour could not have the electoral success that it has in Scotland if it relied only on the support of those in the Catholic Church. Conscientious and practising Catholics after all only make up less than 10% of the whole population in Scotland.

Just before I received that e-mail I experienced what for me was a far more disappointing occurrence at the hands of a Celtic supporter. At the start of the next football season following my election I attended the AGM of my supporters club, the Carfin (1948) CSC, and collected my own, my daughter's and my son's season books for the coming year. Following the meeting I was asked to pose with some of the club officials for a photograph which they hoped to send to the *Celtic View* as it is not every day that one of your members becomes a Member of the first Scottish Parliament in almost three hundred years.

Before the picture could be sent, though, an article

appeared in the *Herald* 'Diary' column claiming that members of the club had been surprised at me collecting my season book as it was sourced from a scheme set up to help unemployed members. No such scheme existed but this did not stop someone from within the club, a fellow Celt, taking the time to concoct a malicious story in order to attack me. The people involved may support the same football team as me but I would hazard a guess that they did not vote for me and if Catholic, this was hardly the action of someone whose faith had real meaning to them.

History shows that majorities are no guarantee of justice.

Being aware of the existence of the religious divide in Scotland I strenuously guard against providing any opportunity for the accusation to be made against me that I have acted with any prejudice when carrying out my responsibilities as an elected representative. To act against someone on the basis that they did not share my faith would actually put me into conflict with my faith as such an action would be wrong, indeed, 'sinful' in religious terms.

I don't consciously try to hide my religious affiliation or my Irish heritage. My faith and cultural heritage make me the individual I am and I take them with me wherever I go. They certainly led to me to supporting Celtic but I have never believed that they made me join the Labour Party, although undoubtedly in terms of Labour history, being part of a community that perceived itself as second class in many ways has become a spur to many people in that community aligning itself with a Party best seen as representing their class interests – even if the Party was given birth by Protestants, this didn't matter.

I have always appreciated the division between Church and State but I certainly cannot agree with the argument put forward by some that politicians should leave their own opinions at the door of the Parliament and simply vote to give the majority of people what they want. If we followed that advice we would bring back hanging, ban immigration and stop collecting taxes. More worryingly we would have to bow to the majority opinion in this country that we should close state funded (and therefore financed by Catholics themselves through the tax system) Catholic schools. History shows that majorities are no guarantee of justice. One only needs to be reminded that Adolf Hitler was democratically elected in Germany in the 1930s.

It has always concerned me that so many politicians who preach tolerance in society cannot seem to extend their open-mindedness to accepting the right of the Catholic community in Scotland to have their children provided with a faith based education of their choosing, especially when the State invited (indeed coaxed) Catholics to join in the State system in the first place.

As a politician I often ask the voices of tolerance why we still have racism in Scotland when we do not teach Black and Asian children separately from white children and why we still have sexual inequality and domestic abuse although boys and girls are taught side by side. I have yet to hear a satisfactory answer to those questions and am left to wonder why Catholic Schools are ever mentioned in relation to the anti-sectarian agenda. They cannot be part of the solution as they form no part of the problem. The problem of sectarianism in Scotland was part of Scotland before Catholic schools developed in response to Irish Catholic immigration to this country.

My wider concern on the anti-sectarian agenda relates to those people who insist that sectarian behaviour be eradicated from society but who cannot differentiate between legitimate political and religious opinion and manifestations of religious hatred. These same politicians will rightly defend an individual's right to take part in political campaigns, such as having British troops removed from Iraq, but at the same time will view demonstrations to have the same British Army removed from the north of Ireland as sectarian or as being supportive of perceived terrorism. Many politicians in mainstream parties in both Britain and Ireland, and who often oppose militaristic answers to this historical problem, and support Irish self-determination, are prevented from associating themselves with otherwise valid and lawful campaigns because of those who hijack these campaigns and paint them as promoting religious intolerance.

On the side of the Irish diaspora in Scotland some people

> My wider concern on the anti-sectarian agenda relates to those people who insist that sectarian behaviour be eradicated from society but who cannot differentiate between legitimate political and religious opinion and manifestations of religious hatred.

do not understand that Celtic's Catholic and Irish heritage and identity cannot and should not translate into being anti-Protestant. I cringe when I hear non-sectarian Irish tunes (and all so-called rebel songs are non-sectarian) being bastardised by a small-minded element of the Celtic faithful into containing negative chants. 'We're On the One Road' is about unity and tolerance and the achievement of a legitimate political and cultural goal, yet there are a few who chant 'soon there'll be no Protestants at all' and completely destroy the song's sentiments at a stroke. Equally, Celtic did, indeed, give us James McGrory and Paul McStay but it certainly did not create the IRA and where do the words 'God Bless the Pope' appear in that great anthem, The Soldiers Song?

I realise that for the vast majority that sing these songs they are meaningful and reflect their heritage, their country of origin and cultural distinctiveness in Scotland. In addition, often these are the people who have a real emotional stake in Celtic Football Club and culture: they are indeed Celtic's core support. Nonetheless, the numpties and degenerates who wreck these songs with their mindless chants should be marginalised by the great majority of Celtic supporters.

While there may be some who view the campaign against sectarianism as a one-sided attack on their traditions I have found that it is mostly those who simply abhor the hatred and violence which results from it who genuinely wish to fight sectarianism. Unfortunately, many of these well-meaning individuals are so removed from the reality of what the two religious traditions entail that they cannot accurately differentiate between religious prejudice and cultural and political affiliation.

I was fortunate in April 2004 to take part in a delegation from the Scottish Parliament to New York and Canada to attend the Tartan Week celebrations. On the morning of the Tartan Day parade down 6th Avenue, attired in full Highland dress, I visited the Parlour Bar to watch the home match against Hearts. I was pleasantly surprised to find a good number of the ex-patriot Celtic and Irish minded Scots-born people preparing to watch the parade that afternoon.

> The numpties and degenerates who wreck these songs with their mindless chants should be marginalised by the great majority of Celtic supporters.

Overall what struck me most was the fact that all of the official events during Tartan Week included the playing of Scottish songs extolling the patriotism of those such as Bruce, Wallace, Bonnie Prince Charlie and others who fought for the independence of Scotland or the overthrow of the British establishment of the day. It seemed to me, though a little ironic, that the Scottish Executive saw it as their role to support people with Scottish ancestry in this celebration of their heritage while at the same time the Irish community in Scotland is, at best, treated with suspicion and even some of the pubs they frequent are threatened with being closed down for acclaiming patriots who fought for Irish self determination. The people who frequent these establishments are comfortable and often knowledgeable about these patriots. It is their heritage, their culture and their identity. It is their right to express their admiration for their own patriots.

Some time ago I took Nil By Mouth to task for the contents of a newsletter in which they asked for measures to be brought in to address the problem of Orange and Catholic parades. For an organisation which proclaims itself as a prominent anti-sectarian organisation, established and financed to encourage people to refrain from the type of language which breeds hostility, to fall short of its own advice and fail to differentiate between a spiritual Corpus Christi or Lourdes Day procession and a political Hibernian or Republican march is totally irresponsible and indicates the type of ignorance which pervades the anti-sectarianism agenda. In a nutshell, apart from the odd religious ceremonial walk to a church or shrine there are 'no' Catholic marches or parades in Scotland. One would think that anyone who had a real knowledge of 'sectarianism' or who was genuinely anti-sectarian would know that.

There is clearly much work for politicians to do in this debate, not least of all to build an understanding of and between the various Protestant, Catholic, Irish, Scottish and British traditions in Scotland.

There is clearly much work for politicians to do in this debate, not least of all to build an understanding of and between the various Protestant, Catholic, Irish, Scottish and British traditions in Scotland. This is an issue that can be dealt with when those pursuing the matter understand the subject themselves before pontificating on the solution to it.

When I am amongst my fellow Celts I get irritated when

some of them, in their ignorance, belittle the Irishness and Catholic dimensions of the club and undermine the majority who, in the Celtic spirit, are proud of what they are, what they belong to and where they are from. Such Celts bear no malice towards anyone who is not part of that heritage. In this sense it is right that Celtic should be part of the attempt to eradicate sectarianism from our society and supporters should encourage that. After all, as former Celtic Chairman Robert Kelly said in a speech to a Catholic lay organisation after an ill-founded attempt by the Scottish Football Authorities to have the Club remove the Irish national flag from its stadium:

> We have no need to be ashamed of our fathers, nor have we any cause to be ashamed that those founders [of Celtic] came from that country that has provided protagonists for liberty wherever they have settled.[2]

(2) Wilson, 1988, pp. 97-98

Scotland's demon?:
Neil Lennon and Celtic

IRENE A REID

'WHO AM I TO CRITICISE. . . ' ?[1]

> O Wad some Power the giftie gie us
> To see oursels as ithers see us![2]

What connections are there between Robert Burns' musings in the eighteenth century and media narratives about Neil Lennon in the twenty-first century? The short answer is plenty, but most are unhealthy in a society that has designs on being 'the best small country in the world'.[3] This chapter reflects on the media discourses that surrounded Neil Lennon during one period of his playing career at Celtic in autumn 2005.[4] The catalyst for this was the press coverage of Lennon following his confrontation with officials at the end of the Scottish Premier League (SPL) match against Glasgow Rangers on August 20.

This critique concentrates on evidence surrounding three connected periods: (i) the days immediately after the match (August 21–28); (ii) the week surrounding the SFA disciplinary hearing on Tuesday September 20th; and (iii) the period in mid-October when, following a three-match suspension, Lennon resumed playing. The discourse surrounding these events was characterised by casting Lennon as an aggressive hard-man, unsuited to hold the responsibility of captain of Celtic FC. Although focusing on only one period, this coverage is consistent with the dominant media discourse associated with Lennon since he signed for Celtic in December 2000.

(1) J. McLean, Daily Record, 23/9/2005, p.73.

(2) Robert Burns 'To a Louse'

(3) This phrase is the marketing slogan for the Scottish Executive's Fresh Talent Initiative, launched in January 2004 to attract 'foreign workers' to Scotland.

(4) The evidence is drawn from a range of newspapers, but principally those that are defined as the 'Scottish press' and 'Scottish editions' of English-based British papers.

However, there is a further dimension to the media narrative surrounding Neil Lennon in that much of these discourses are infused with 'common mechanisms of racism'.[5] These mechanisms of racism include both explicit expressions of prejudice and more subtle and sophisticated techniques that conceal ideas and sentiments of intolerance. This can include: the use of stereotypes against a named ethnic group; the use of derogatory humour to demean and dehumanise individuals from a specific ethnic community; marking the outsider/other-ness status of particular individuals or groups; denying allegations of racism and deflecting such contentions back at those who have raised them. These mechanisms of racism are evident in discourses of racism in other countries and commun-ities.[6]

In Scotland, in both historical and contemporary contexts, these techniques are manifest as ethno-religious prejudices directed against the Irish Catholic diaspora, and the social and cultural practices and institutions that are most closely associated with them.[7] These prejudices are illustrative of the ideology of bigotry that has sectarianised Scottish society since at least the mid-nineteenth century: this bigotry is unquestion-ably a particular form of racism. Some have argued that this particular form of racism is Scotland's national demon, which in turn is commonly and collectively denied. Despite this, its presence in public and private discourses exposes as a myth Scotland's self-image as an egalitarian and inclusive society.

Herein lies the link between the media discourse concerning Neil Lennon and Robert Burns' musings. Lennon is a mirror to Scotland's demon:[8] the man whose presence evokes in some, the values and sentiments Scotland denies. For those of 'us' who are prepared to look and reflect, the popular media discourse surrounding Neil Lennon is – at least symbolically – the 'gift' the bard sought, enabling 'us' to see 'ourselves' as others do.[9]

LENNON'S JOHN MCENROE MOMENT [10]

The first match between Celtic and Rangers in the SPL in season 2005/06 took place at Ibrox on Saturday August 20th. It ended

5 G.P.T. Finn, 2000, p.55.

6 M. Billig, 2001; J.R. Feagin, V. Hern·n & P. Batur, 2001; S.J. Jackson, 2004; J.E. King, 1997; N.E. Spencer, 2004.

7 This does not deny that racism and prejudice is directed against other groups of difference within Scotland.

8 The mirror analogy is evident in A. O'Hagan, 2000 and T. Gallagher, 2000

9 My assumed shared sense of Scottishness evident in words such as 'us', and 'ourselves' can be questioned. These assumptions are explained by my biography and national identity that mark me as an outsider to – or at least on the fringe of – the 'Celtic family'.

10 I. Campbell, Daily Mirror (Scots Edition)· 24/8/2005, p.47. John McEnroe (USA) was one of the most controversial figures in tennis during the late-1970s and 1980s. His unorthodox genius in the sport earned him the nickname 'SuperMac; he was also 'Superbrat' for the furious – sometimes foul-mouthed - verbal volleys directed at officials, fans, players and himself.

in a 3-1 victory for the home side: five players were booked during the match and Celtic's Alan Thompson dismissed from the field. It was however what happened after the final whistle that dominated press reports over the next week: the reaction of Celtic captain Neil Lennon towards two match officials, referee Stuart Dougal and linesman Jim Lyon. The proceedings were broadcast live on satellite television by Setanta and the incident involving Lennon was replayed later (perhaps in edited form) on terrestrial television news and sports bulletins. A number of still photographs of the incident appeared in newspapers over the following week and again a month later when the SFA Disciplinary Committee met to consider the matter.[11]

As the players and officials conducted the post-match courtesies Lennon said something that allegedly constituted offensive personal abuse of the referee.[12] As Lennon walked away with Rangers' player Marvin Andrews the referee immediately showed the red card. The player turned back and engaged with the referee in an angry verbal confrontation. From the televised images Lennon appeared incensed; his body language was physical (in so far as whatever he was saying was punctuated with wild arm and hand gestures); his posture and stance in relation to the referee were aggressive; his face revealed his anger. The visual evidence showed that Lennon made a small degree of contact with the referee and with the linesman who intervened, although the contact was varyingly described in subsequent media coverage. The confrontation ended with the player being pulled away from the officials by two of his teammates.

Neil Lennon was not the first high-profile sports person to challenge match officials and he won't be the last – in football or any other sport. That does not condone his behaviour, or defend individuals who verbally or physically abuse or intimidate others, on the sports field or elsewhere in society. Lennon was angry and lost his temper; he confronted match officials aggressively. Clearly he should not have done so: but he did. The player apparently recognised this and apologised for his behaviour. Scottish football – like all sports, and wider society – has procedures to deal with such incidents if they happen.

> Lennon is a mirror to Scotland's demon: the man whose presence evokes in some, the values and sentiments Scotland denies.

11 The matter was dealt with by the SFA Disciplinary Committee on 20/9/2005: Lennon completed his three-match suspension in mid-October. However this incident was not far from media commentary throughout the 2005/06 season.

12 The red card was 'issued for remarks which the official ruled as 'using offensive, insulting or abusive language and/gestures' as laid down in the laws of the game.' S. Halliday, The Scotsman (Sport), 22/8/2005, p.2.

However, as this analysis of the newspaper narratives demonstrates, this was not sufficient for some football journalists and commentators.

Sport is part of the cultural fabric of contemporary modern life. For good or ill it becomes saturated with passion and emotion – for players and supporters alike. It is, in part, the role of journalists to convey something of that emotive environment in their accounts of events, but they do so from their individual perspectives and based on their interpretive judgement: both are not ideologically free.[13]

> The media demonised Neil Lennon and, to a degree, what he represented to them – and arguably, what he represented to many football fans in Scotland.

We therefore permit some creative licence in sports journalism, but it is also reasonable to expect this does not exceed the boundaries of balanced and fair reporting and, where appropriate, analysis. This caveat noted, the tenor of some accounts of the 'Lennon incident', the post-match analysis and reflections on the subsequent disciplinary implications for the player clearly indicates that these boundaries were traversed. The extensive coverage incorporated the incident into broader discourses that vilified Lennon. The nature of these media discourses do not lie simply in the language selected, but rather, in the way it developed into a concerted campaign against an individual and his character: and, in many ways more significantly, what he is seen to represent. In short, the media *demonised* Neil Lennon and, to a degree, what he represented to them – and arguably, what he represents to many football fans in Scotland.

DEMONISING THE CAPTAIN

The demonising of Neil Lennon during autumn 2005 was conducted largely through the tabloid press, though popular radio shows dedicated to football also played a significant role. It was also evident in more sophisticated forms in some broadsheet columns. In each context it was constructed using a combination of techniques and injudicious language to convey a negative image of the player. This was not a sudden development in media representations of him. Since he signed for Celtic some newspapers have constructed Lennon as an object of controversy and ridicule. In doing so the media has

13 Hargreaves, 1986; Gledhill, 1991, p.xiii.

concentrated heavily on three dimensions: (i) particular depictions of Lennon as a footballer (style of play, contribution to the team, temperament/attitude); (ii) his physique and gait, and (iii) a variety of alleged events and circumstances associated with his personal life and biography.[14] During the autumn of 2005 journalists therefore drew heavily on existing (if not necessarily accurate) perceptions of the player in order to demonise the Celtic captain following his 'McEnroe moment' at Ibrox.

Four themes dominated the newspapers' discourses that demonised Lennon.

(i) The player was stereotyped as an aggressive and bad tempered individual who sets out to cause trouble on (and off) the football field.

(ii) His behaviour was infantilised and criminalised (sometimes together) through ridiculing his maturity and intelligence.

(iii) Lennon's commitment and continued value to Celtic FC were questioned, including his willingness to work for and with the new manager Gordon Strachan.

(iv) The tabloid press 'campaigned' for the SFA Disciplinary Committee to make an example of the player by imposing a lengthy suspension.

The constraints of space in this book mean that only themes (i), (ii) and (iv) are considered, primarily because these connect in significant ways to the narrative of racism that is considered later.

To construct the stereotype of Lennon as an aggressive and bad tempered player, journalists developed strands of an existing narrative concerning perceptions about his temperament, personality and style of play. Lennon was described as a 'fiery midfielder'[15] who has 'his own hair trigger temper'.[16] References to the player as hot-headed appeared in headlines as well as within the texts of reports and post-match analyses: this was linked, both by inference and explicitly, to the fact that Lennon has red hair.[17] In addition to descriptions of his post-

Since he signed for Celtic some newspapers have constructed Lennon as an object of controversy and ridicule.

14 Lennon has acknowledged 'I'm no angel' (N. Weale, Sunday Mail (Features), 12/9/ 2004, p.12;13) but notes some press coverage is based on innuendo and half-truths (see A. Smith, Scotland on Sunday (Sport), 18/5/2003, p.2).

15 I. MacFarlane, Daily Star (Scottish Edition), 22/8/2005, p.51.

16 D. Leggat, The People (Eire Edition), 21/8/2005, p.2; 3.

17 For example, M. 58 For example, M. Grant, Sunday Herald (Sport), 21/8/2005, p.1; G. Bryce, News of the World (Score) (Scotland), 21/8/ 2005, p.2.

match confrontation with officials, the press concentrated on negative perceptions of Lennon's contribution to the match. A number of journalists and media pundits opined that during the game Lennon was 'constantly in spats off the ball';[18] 'got away with a string of kicks, shoves';[19] and involved in 'a continual spate of niggly fouls and head-to-heads,'[20] before he was cautioned late in the second-half for dissent. The dominant narrative in the press regarding Lennon's contribution to the match is encapsulated in the view:

This stereotype of Lennon. . . as aggressive and ill-tempered. . . was woven throughout newspapers' and amplified ruminations on the incident with officials.

> The volatile Celtic skipper had been in a foul mood all day, snarling, pushing and shoving his way around Ibrox, spoiling for a fight with someone, ANYONE.[21]

This description may have been true or untrue on the day. This perception does not affect the form of narrative used that is unquestionably 'pejorative'. More importantly it was bolstered with journalists' assertions that this is *characteristic* of the player. Arguably this latter point is indicative of the media discourses that typically surround Lennon. It also exposes the fact that the Rangers versus Celtic game in August 2005 cannot be taken in isolation if a more substantial understanding of what Lennon represents in the Scottish media is to be achieved. Typically, the tabloid *Daily Record* declared 'Lennon's game is to push everyone to the edge'.[22] The *Daily Express* reiterated this view with the contention that 'The Hoops skipper always treads a thin line in these games'.[23]

This stereotype of Lennon, as a naturally aggressive and ill-tempered player who causes trouble, was woven throughout newspapers and amplified ruminations on the incident with officials. The incident was described using varied tone and language particularly in communicating the nature of physical contact that occurred between the player and officials. In general broadsheet newspapers offered measured accounts to convey the emotive confrontation. One broadsheet journalist stated:

> Neil Lennon angrily barged into referee Stuart Dougal after being shown a red card . . . Lennon was so incensed by being sent off for abusive language that he pushed away assistant referee Jim Lyon in order to get at Dougal, making chest-to-chest contact with the referee and jabbing at him with his hand until being pulled away by Paul Telfer.[24]

18 Inferred view of former referee in I. King, Scottish Sun 22/8/2005, p.60

19 B. Leckie & I. King, 'You're A (Censored).' The Sun, 22/8/05, p.64

20 S. Fisher, Sunday Herald (Sport), 21/8/2005, p2

21 G. Bryce, Ibid, 21/8/2005

22 M. Mcleod, Daily Record, 22/8/2005, p.38; 39.

23 G. Clark, Scottish Sunday Express, 21/8/2005, p.111.

24 M. Grant, Ibid, 21/8/2005.

In a similar vein a *Sunday Times* columnist stated Lennon had 'reacted furiously to the red card, pushing his chest into Dougal's then shoving Jim Lyon, the assistant referee, when he attempted to intercede'.[25] Other accounts shared this tone, although at times using more loaded language. For example, in *Scotland on Sunday,* Tom English referred to 'volleys of abuse' being 'unloaded' on Dougal as Lennon 'appeared to man-handle a linesman . . . in an effort to get at the referee';[26] Stewart Fisher (*Sunday Herald*) opined Lennon was 'grabbing linesman James Lyon as he attempted to remonstrate with referee Stuart Dougal';[27] Glenn Gibbons (*The Scotsman*) referred to 'Lennon's unbridled rant at [the] referee';[28] while Darryl Broadfoot (*The Herald*) referred to Lennon's 'meltdown' and 'strop'.[29]

Tabloid journalists were predictably less restrained. The language, tone and style constructed narratives that were more graphic and intemperate. One said 'the linesman got the nippy midfielder's trademark hand-off';[30] another that Lennon had 'lashed out at the whistler and linesman'.[31] There were references to a 'physical attack on the . . . match officials'[32] and one journalist suggested Lennon was 'the most high-profile player to be charged with *assaulting* a match official' (my emphasis).[33] In keeping with the sensationalist style of the UK's tabloid press headlines they referred to him as 'CAPTAIN SCARLET';[34] 'LUNATIC; HOTHEAD';[35] and exclaimed he had 'LOST PLOT'.[36] One of the more offensive descriptions appeared in two newspapers:

> Acting like a demented animal as the last helicopter flew out of Saigon this snarling, snorting, supposed icon of a great club showed all the ugly actions of a back-street thug . . . . Face contorted, arms waving wildly this was the wee hard man you wouldn't want to meet down a dark close.[37]

A prominent place was given in the media discourse to assertions that Lennon did not have the temperament or character to be captain of Celtic FC. Graham Spiers, Chief Sportswriter in the *Herald* opined 'Lennon . . . brought himself and Celtic into disrepute';[38] Gerry McNee in *News of the World* declared, 'He's disgraced the Celtic captaincy and should immediately be stripped of it';[39] while in both the *Express* and *Daily Star* Andy McInnes proclaimed:

25 D. Alexander, Sunday Times (Scotland Sport) 21/8/2005, p.1.

26 T. English, Scotland on Sunday (Sport), 21/8/2005, p.2.

27 S. Fisher, Ibid, 21/8/2005.

28 G. Gibbons, The Scotsman (Sport), 22/8/2005, p.2.

29 D. Broadfoot, The Herald (Sport), 22/8/2005, p.2.

30 G. McNee, News of the World (Score) (Scotland), 21/8/2005, p.4.

31 M. Guidi, Sunday Mail, 21/8/2005, p.91; 92

32 I. MacFarlane, Ibid, 22/8/2005.

33 H. Keevins, Daily Record, 23/8/2005, p.5; 52.

34 A. Walker, Sunday Mail, 21/8/2005, p.88.

35 M. Guidi, Ibid, 21/8/2005.

36 R. MacLean, Sunday Mail, 21/8/2005, p.85.

37 A. McInnes, Daily Star (Scottish Edition) 22/8/2005, p.20; also A. McInnes, Scottish Daily Express, 22/8/2005, p.8.

38 G. Spiers, The Herald (Sport) 22/8/2005, p.1.

39 G. McNee Ibid, 21/8/2005 p.4.

Celtic captain Neil Lennon should today be stripped of his Parkhead commission and dishonourably discharged from Celtic Football Club.[40]

A common technique used by newspapers to substantiate their constructed narratives is to include opinions from 'experts'. The aura of expertise is often due to the connection (or previous connection) of these individuals to the sport. This technique was used extensively in the discourse that demonised Lennon in the days after the match. Former officials, managers and players in particular were given space to express their views.[41] There was unanimity amongst them that Lennon's aggressive confrontation with officials was wrong, whatever the circumstances. Some also endorsed the narrative that constructed Lennon as a football – and in some cases a social – villain.[42] This also drew on an existing narrative regarding Lennon's style of play and perceptions that he causes trouble.

In the *Sun* for example a former referee contended the trouble Lennon found himself in was characteristic and his own fault: 'Lennon creates what happens around him by himself'.[43] In contrast, match referee Stuart Dougal had offered a different view of the player on the morning of the match:

Guys like Neil Lennon and Barry Ferguson are captains and middle-of-the park competitors. They actually don't do a lot of bleating about tackles or challenges. Yeah, they complain but there are honest pros on both sides.[44]

The observations of former players (many of them regular contributors on radio and television) were prominent in the discourse and included former employees of Celtic FC. Their heaviest criticisms revolved around Lennon's suitability as captain. Murdo McLeod (a former player and assistant manager with Celtic FC, now BBC Radio Scotland pundit) stated: 'Lennon's conduct at Ibrox besmirched the club's name'.[45] *News of the World* columnist Davie Provan observed:

Lennon's rant at Dougal was that of a man with no respect for the referee and little thought for the captain's armband he was wearing.[46]

Like Provan, Andy Walker (former Celtic player and match-analyst on STV's *Scotsport SPL* highlights programme)

40 A. McInnes, Ibid, 22/8/2005, p8; also Ibid, 22/8/2005, p.20.

41 The Daily Record used a sports psychologist to give credence to the narrative that questioned Lennon's commitment and continued value to Celtic FC under the new manager (H. Keevins, 23/8/2005, p.51).

42 One journalist reflected Lennon 'has found himself firmly installed as Scottish football's Public Enemy No.1' (I. Campbell, Daily Mirror (Scots Edition), 23/8/2005, p.62; 63).

43 Inferred view of former referee in I. King, The Sun, 22/8/2005, p.60.

44 Attributed quote in S. McGowan, Daily Mail (Scots Edition), 20/8/2005, p.99.

45 M. McLeod, Ibid, 22/8/2005.

46 D. Provan, News of the World (Scotland), 28/8/2005, p.80.

acknowledged the bigotry and abuse Lennon has been subjected to in Scotland. Nonetheless, Walker cautioned, 'he's not the first Celtic player to be given this treatment' at Ibrox, and he agreed that 'Lennon's actions after the final whistle highlighted a lack of leadership on his part.'[47]

The narrative that questioned Lennon as a suitable captain compared him with previous incumbents of that office, most notably Billy McNeill. In light of the unfavourable comparisons made, McNeill's own contribution is instructive:

> This is not a thick boy, though, I know him and like him. He is an intelligent lad who has made a mistake. Right now in the heat of the moment it is easy to say 'Take the job from him.' Yet there are times when you lose the place – but you have to learn from it.[48]

This is certainly a more temperate assessment. A fatherly, or mentoring tone can also be detected in the comments. However, importantly McNeill's remark directs us to another theme in the media's demonising narrative. It is common currency in the predominantly male culture of football to refer to players as 'boys' or 'lads', irrespective of their age. This particular example conveys, in part, the camaraderie of a man's game.

However, the wider narrative that casts Lennon as a villain was peppered with analogies and metaphors associated with a badly-behaved child. Specifically, the narrative drew on stereotypes that infantilised the player. These were combined with remarks that ridiculed his intelligence. Lennon's response to infringements committed against him reinforced the narrative that he was immature;[49] he was specifically described as petulant,[50] a 'Bad Bhoy'[51] and a 'manchild'[52] who gave a 'toys out the pram performance'.[53] His behaviour was described as 'half-witted' and the 'petted-lipped strop of a playground bully who has realised no one's scared of him any more.'[54] One journalist also reinforced the narrative that this is all characteristic of Lennon:

> This was no kid throwing a tantrum but yet another seasoned campaigner who *this time* didn't have daddy Martin O'Neill to throw a protective arm around him.[55] (my emphasis)

47 A. Walker, Ibid, 21/8/2005.

48 Inferred as an attributed quote in I. King, Ibid, 22/8/2005, p.62.

49 For example Bill Leckie claimed 'Every silly little foul on him was blown up into a square go.' (Scottish Sun, 22/8/2005, p.62).

50 A. McInnes Ibid, 22/8/2005, p.20; D. Broadfoot. Ibid, 22/8/2005.

51 R. Brown, Scottish Sun, 22/8/2005, p.21; also J. Docherty, Daily Mirror (Scots Edition), 21/9/2005, p.54; 55.

52 J. Mclean, Daily Record, 22/8/2005, p.24.

53 C. Young, Scottish Daily Express, 27/8/2005, p.96.

54 B. Leckie, Ibid, 22/8/2005, p.62.

55 G. McNee, Ibid, 21/8/2005, p.4.

Analysis of the newspapers' representation of Neil Lennon exposes more loaded analogies of teenage aggression and violence. In the context of wider social and political commentary these analogies criminalised the player, and reinforced the narrative that claimed he was out of control. The criminalising codes were evident in some broadsheet newspapers[56] but were more explicit in the tabloid press. Contributors to fans' columns said he was 'no better than a ned'[57] a 'yob'[58] and a 'vicious little thug'.[59] It was said Lennon had 'launched a near-assault' on the referee,[60] and he was one of a number of Celtic's senior players accused of behaving 'JUST LIKE CONS'.[61]

Through the imagery of the misbehaving child and criminality newspaper narratives can disempower sportsmen of their adult and good citizen identities. There are parallels here with public discourses constructed round black sports men – and to lesser degree women – in other nations.[62] Such narratives dehumanise individuals. If these narratives are embedded in 'culturally sanctioned assumptions, myths and beliefs'[63] about a particular ethnic group within a specific community, then they may contribute to patterns of racism.

SUSTAINING THEIR MONSTER

The media narrative that demonised Lennon was most vociferous in the week after the match. During this period the tabloid press in particular capitalised on opinion that magnified their representation of Lennon as villain. A variety of techniques were deployed to sustain the monster they had created.

The most obvious technique was to speculate on the 'serious ramifications'[64] that his angry confrontation would have for him in terms of a probable period of suspension. In relation to this suspension some tabloid press pundits made 'demands' for Lennon to be extra-severely punished. In addition to the automatic one-match ban for being sent-off, there were calls for Lennon to be dealt with on the basis of his high profile.[65] The stereotyped characterisation of the aggressive, in-your-face hardman was also mobilised in support of calls for a harsh penalty. The frenzy reached boiling point when one newspaper declared (inaccurately) 'NEIL LENNON could end up with a

56 D. Broadfoot referred to him as 'an intelligent 34-year old man' who have behaved 'like an uneducated delinquent' (Ibid, 22/8/2005).

57 Attributed quote (a) 'Hotline' Daily Record, 22/8/2005, p.37.

58 Attributed quote (b) Ibid.

59 Attributed quote 'Fanmail,'Daily Star (Scottish Edition), 22/8/2005, p.8.

60 D. Leggat, Ibid, 21/8/2005.

61 G. McNee, Ibid, 21/8/2005.

62 Jackson, 1998; 2004; Spencer, 2004.

63 King, 1997, p.128.

64 I. MacFarlane, Scottish Daily Express, 22/8/2005, p.63.

65 See J. McLean, Ibid, 22/8/2005; H. Keevins, Ibid, 23/8/2005 B. Leckie, Ibid, 22/8/2005; I. Bell, Sunday Herald (Sport), 18/9/2005, p.6; J. Traynor, Daily Record 20/9/2005, p.54; 55; R. Martin, Scottish Sun, 20/9/2005, p.64.

mammoth ELEVEN-GAME ban'.[66] Twenty-four hours later it announced that he 'looks set to escape a massive 11-game ban – but could be out for six matches'.[67] Reflecting on these exaggerated and speculative demands one journalist reflected that although there was no justification for the player's aggressive confrontation of officials:

> Neil Lennon may have wondered if he was guilty of crimes against humanity as condemnation of his Old Firm outburst reached melting point yesterday.[68]

The use of expert opinion, as well as named and un-named sources with alleged 'inside information' continued to feature in much of the discourse. Nonetheless, not everyone expressed outright condemnation of the player. The publication of alternative opinion may have suggested an even-handed account, but this was only a veneer of objectivity. Alternative views of the incident were undermined and marginalised to ensure they did not replace the dominant narratives that demonised Lennon. One notable example in this process was to undermine the player's only personal intervention in the public discourse following the incident. Twenty-four hours after the match Lennon issued a statement, apologising for his behaviour:

> I spoke to the referee about his performance and he then showed me a red card while I was shaking hands with the Rangers players. Clearly, although I felt the red card – my first in the SPL – was totally unjustified, I understand that my reaction was wrong. I apologise for my reaction towards the referee and his assistant and I also apologise to Celtic and our supporters.[69]

The statement, issued through the website of Celtic FC, was reported the next day. Comment from the press corps was critical of the statement and the medium through which it was issued and these criticisms were incorporated into the derogatory narrative. In particular journalists reflected on what they perceived as a lack of genuine regret or contrition from Lennon.[70]

> Lennon has moved quickly to show remorse for his actions . . . but he was adamant . . . that his dismissal was the wrong decision.[71]

66 H. Keevins, Ibid, 23/8/2005.

67 H. Keevins, Daily Record, 24/8/2005, p.48.

68 I. Campbell, Ibid, 23/8/2005.

69 'Lennon apologises', celticfc.net/news/ 21/8/2005.

70 Two days before the disciplinary hearing, Martin Hannan reflected: 'His immediate apology after the match – it was genuine and the player really feels remorse for letting himself and his club down. (Scotland on Sunday (Sport), 18/9/2005, p.11)

71 S. Halliday, Ibid, 22/8/2005.

Lennon, speaking through the club's website . . . issued a terse, if not quite heartfelt apology for his behaviour'.[72]
He [Thompson] may make [his apology] more heart-rending than Lennon's brief statement . . . but I have my doubts.[73]

The narrative that sustained the pejorative representation of Lennon diminished, but did not disappear from the press over the next month. It was mobilised once again in the days immediately before the SFA disciplinary committee met to consider the matter.[74] It is probable that the negative discourse would have re-appeared: when it did it was incorporated into journalists' reactions to comments that the player should receive a fair hearing in accordance with the SFA's disciplinary procedures. The most significant person to express this reasoned view was Gordon Strachan, Celtic's manager. Strachan had been criticised in the days after the match for not censuring his captain. A month later the columnist Natasha Woods reported on an interview with the Celtic manager in which he had reflected on a range of issues related to sportsmanship, discipline and ethics in sport.[75] In the context of this broader discussion he expressed concern about the 'hysteria'[76] that characterised the media coverage of the incident at Ibrox. It was also noted that Strachan expected 'his player to be punished firmly, but fairly'.[77]

The remarks, in part, provoked further negative media discourse around the player and manager. Broadsheet columnist Ian Bell remarked:

His manager . . . can see no fault with the player. The coach has ignored suggestions that Lennon should at least be deprived of his captaincy.
Instead, we have been treated to one of football's less savoury rituals: the boss standing by one of his 'lads', even when a 34-year-old has just behaved like a five-year-old . [78]

Bell was not alone in concluding 'Neil Lennon's daft moment' should result in 'a long ban'. In *Scotland on Sunday* Jim Duffy opined, 'I firmly believe that Lennon will be hammered by the SFA'.[79] The tabloid press was, predictably, more sensationalist in its representation of Strachan's comments and the wider content of his interview. The *Sun* exclaimed 'CELTIC BOSS DEFENDS SOCCER THUGS'[80] then countered Strachan's

72 G. Spiers, Ibid, 22/8/2005.

73 J. McLean, Ibid, 22/8/2005.

74 J. Traynor asked 'How often have you watched Lennon smile, snarl, gesture and shout at opponents? That's all part of his game, and perhaps also his game-plan.'(Ibid, 20/9/2005).

75 N. Woods, Sunday Herald (Sport), 18/9/2005, p.6.

76 Woods, Ibid.

77 Woods, Ibid; also S. Halliday, The Scotsman(Sport), 17/9/2005, p.78.

78 I. Bell, Ibid, 18/9/2005.

79 J. Duffy, Scotland on Sunday (Sport), 18/9/2005, p.6.

80 A. Tolmie, 'Gord's Class War', Scottish Sun, 19/9/2005, p.11.

assessment with the views of former Scotland and Manchester United manager Tommy Docherty:

> Footballers aren't hard done by because of anything to do with being working class – they bring it on themselves by bad behaviour.[81]

On the morning of the hearing the tabloid press persisted with the narrative that demonised the player. James Traynor was not the only journalist to contend:

> The truth is Lennon is guilty and time shouldn't be wasted trying to fathom an understanding of what was going on inside his mind.

He added:

> I've always suspected the space under that ginger top might not be a good place to linger too long.[82]

This example provides further evidence then that some prominent media figures persist with a particular narrative that demeans a man who is simultaneously recognised by others as eloquent and intelligent.[83]

The discourse constructed around Neil Lennon is partly consistent with broader scholarship on media representations of gendered identities and sport.[84] In particular strands of the narrative expose how sportsmen embody certain valued attributes of masculinity. These attributes, and the men who personify them, are often celebrated. But popular media discourse turns against individuals if they are considered to transgress idealised boundaries of acceptable behaviour.[85] This, in part, might explain the media frenzy on Lennon and his character. The *Daily Record's* football writer (and BBC Radio Scotland pundit) appeared to acknowledge this:

> Maybe we're all a little to blame because we do tend to revel in the performances of players such as Lennon and there has always been a kind of dark, sneaking admiration for the game's hard men.[86]

This was a rare admonishment of his profession and its part in the vilification of Lennon although it clearly still sustained the representation of the player as one of football's hard-men. Nonetheless, it is a reminder that those who broadcast and

81 Attributed quote in Tolmie, Ibid.

82 J. Traynor, Ibid, 20/9/2005.

83 S. Halliday commented Lennon is 'a naturally intelligent character off the pitch' (Ibid, 22/8/2005). G. Spiers referred to Lennon as 'this impressive, intelligent footballer' (The Herald, 23/8/2002, p.42).

84 For discussion on gender issues and sport in Scotland see Reid, 2004.

85 Lines, 2001; Whannel, 1999.

86 J. Traynor, Ibid, 20/9/2005.

report sports are culpable in constructing narratives that reciprocally feed broader social discourses and the ideological frameworks within which they operate.

At this juncture it is instructive to reflect briefly on the responses of newspapers after the SFA had suspended Neil Lennon for three matches. The tabloid press – unsurprisingly – launched into a–'Lennon-gets-off-lightly narrative'. In some broadsheet newspapers columnists shifted their attention towards how the tabloids had demonised the player. In the *Scotsman* Glenn Gibbons suggested some newspapers had skirted close to the legal boundaries of justice, 'motivated by preconceptions – or, in today's fashionable term, an agenda – which rather body-swerve the legal concept in hot pursuit of personal satisfaction.'[87]

The *Herald's* chief sportswriter Graham Spiers was also critical. His more whimsical tone – intended perhaps to poke fun at tabloid pundits – was underscored with the jocular suggestion that the player brings this sort of frenzy on himself:

> The Celtic captain has this amazing capacity to have baying mobs and berserk tabloid columnists sounding off barmily about him. It really is a remarkable gift.[88]

Indicatively, and linking directly with the title and one of the underlying themes of this paper, it was a London based columnist who provided the most powerful critical comment on the Scottish tabloid press treatment of Neil Lennon. *The Times'* Phil Gordon reflected that some of the content bordered on contempt of court. He also suggested that it verged on a litigious attack on Lennon.[89] Given the successful legal action Lennon had brought against the *Daily Record* for defamation the press corps might have been more circumspect. In autumn 2005 the most potentially litigious elements were concentrated on Lennon's behaviour on the football field, leading Gordon to infer that where football reporting is concerned artistic licence knows no bounds – at least as far as the tabloid press was concerned. He concluded:

> The newspapers that have ganged together to pursue Lennon have treated [him] with contempt in its most literal and legal sense. There is an agenda at work. Selling more newspapers

87 G. Gibbons, The Scotsman, 22/9/2005, p.69.

88 G. Spiers, The Herald, 22/9/2005, p.32.

89 P. Gordon, The Times Online, 22/9/2005.

might be one justification, but there appears to be a darker motivation.[90]

There is an element of responsibility on footballers to conduct themselves in a manner that is consistent with the laws of the game. They must also recognise that the sports field is not a world separate from the society in which it exists and they are bound to behave in a manner appropriate in a civilised society – irrespective of the passions that are aroused. However, it is also incumbent upon those who report and interpret sport to do so in a 'responsible' manner. In the aftermath of the Ibrox match in 2005 this did not happen. The tone and substance of much of the press narrative was constructed to manipulate (or perhaps reinforce) opinion of Lennon as Scottish football's demon. Phil Gordon concluded:

> Helping to create such a public enemy . . . is irresponsible when merely kept to the confines of a football ground, but when being demonised changes the way you walk down the street it is time to think again.[91]

It is to this broader issue that attention now turns.

Elements of the discourse (surrounding Neil Lennon) are commensurate with certain common mechanisms of racism.

THE OUTSIDER IN OUR MIDST

It has been suggested that the discourse surrounding Neil Lennon has been infused within an ideological set of beliefs. These have some resonance with idealised images of (flawed) masculinity, but the evidence is more indicative of a different malaise in Scottish society. Elements of the discourse are commensurate with certain common mechanisms of racism, and have infused the evidence presented in the preceding discussion. They include:

(i) the use of racialised stereotypes of Irish people as hot-tempered/fiery;

(ii) demeaning Lennon's intelligence in ways that resonate with these racialised stereotypes; and

(iii) the use of derogatory humour to demean, dehumanise and disempower the individual and the community in Scotland he is seen to represent.

90 P. Gordon, Ibid.

91 P. Gordon, Ibid.

Such narratives are consistent with the findings of other studies on racist discourses in representations of sport.

In this case study the narratives outlined situate Lennon within the broader anti-Irish and anti-Catholic racism and bigotry in Scotland. Strands of the media discourse surrounding Neil Lennon expose the persistence of these unpalatable yet deeply embedded values in the new, post-Devolution Scotland. In Scotland the historical anti-Irish and anti-Catholic racism, and the Irish Catholic diaspora community's experience of it, has only recently been 'partly' acknowledged – although this acknowledgement may also be viewed as lacking in substance. There is however a number of commentators who assert that these sentiments and values, that were once universal throughout Scottish society, have in fact disappeared and Scotland has been cleansed of these.[92] Critics of this approach argue that although some of the most blatant structural forms of this ethno-religious bigotry have diminished, it persists in modern Scotland.[93] It persists, as in other countries, in banal, recycled and sophisticated forms as well as in those that are explicit and malign. Meredith Levine has argued cogently that in the case of Canada racist discourses operate 'subtly, covertly and insidiously'.[94] The same is also the case with ethno-religious racism in Scotland.

The media discourse examined here may be related to one individual. But the mechanisms of racism assembled in reports about Lennon contribute to broader circumstances that sectarianise the Irish Catholic-descended diaspora in Scotland, the community that has long been established as Scotland's 'other'.[95] In a related fashion, the media discourse reported here represents Neil Lennon as the embodiment of Scotland's national 'other'. In the words of one journalist Lennon is 'the outsider in Scotland'.[96]

Two further mechanisms of racism, one banal the other more sophisticated, can be considered to illustrate how the media has incorporated Lennon's outsider status.

(i) Constructing the 'Other': contentious markers of national identity status

His personal biography is testimony to the fact that Neil Lennon

> In Scotland the historical anti-Irish and anti-Catholic racism, and the Irish Catholic diaspora community's experience of it, has only recently been 'partly' acknowledged.

92 S. Bruce, 1992; S. Bruce, T. Glendinning, I. Paterson & M. Rosie, 2004; 2005.

93 Finn, 2000, p.55.

94 M. Levine 'Canadians Secretly Relieved at Johnson's Fall, New Statesman Society, 1:8, cited Jackson, 2004, p.128.

95 J.M. Bradley, 2004.

96 G. Spiers, The Herald (Sport), 17/5/2003, p.1.

is 'not Scottish', and therefore inhabits and possesses 'otherness'. He was born and grew up in Lurgan, County Armagh in the north of Ireland. Lennon's biographical facts are arguably common knowledge to most readers of the football press in Scotland, but they are regularly reinforced. In the global football market Scotland, like other countries in Europe, has its share of sports labour migrants. They too are 'marked' in relation to their non-Scottish national identity status (eg, Stilian Petrov as Bulgarian; Thomas Buffel as Belgian etc). However, the representation of Lennon's national identity status in the press is not straightforward, and is certainly not similar to that of Petrov or Buffel. It is socially constructed and reproduced in ways that affirm the complexity of history of British-Irish relations and the socio-political identities of the community from which he comes, the one that he has (perhaps temporarily) made his home and more importantly, what that is seen to represent in Scotland.

> Lennon's national identity status . . . is socially constructed and reproduced in ways that affirm the complexity of history of British-Irish relations.

The press attributes one of three national identity markers to Lennon; Northern Irish/Northern Ireland; Irish/Ireland; and Ulsterman/Ulster. All three labels may be legitimate markers of Neil Lennon's national identity status, but they are each problematic, at least in Scotland. Each label is imbued with a combination of national, ethno-religious and political meanings, that in turn are contested identities in relation to the socio-political division within Ireland and between Britain and the island of Ireland. The schisms that divide Ireland also have both historical and contemporary resonance in Scotland.

It is the use of 'Ulsterman' to mark Lennon's 'otherness' in Scotland that is the most contentious. Within the north of Ireland the term is almost always used only by those who proclaim their identity as Ulster Scots, as Protestants and as Loyalists/ Unionists and, in contemporary socio-political and ethno-religious contexts, it is associated with strands of colonial or plantation British communities (mainly Scottish) that inhabit the North of Ireland. It would not be a term used by Catholics in the North of Ireland, at least not to define their national identity in ethno-religious or political terms, though it can be used 'internally' by Catholics when referring to their nine county Ulster identity as opposed to the six county British-Northern

Ireland one, as well as within an all-Ireland context (for example in gaelic sports terms). Used in reference to someone with Neil Lennon's personal biography it is highly contentious, especially when not used by people of his community in Ireland. There are a few occasions when this term appears in newspaper narratives about Lennon. Its appearance in August 2005 in the media's racialised discourse is significant. In one instance he is 'the eloquent Ulsterman'[97], in another 'The fiery Ulsterman'[98]; but in the context of at least one depiction this use is explicitly potent and racist:

> Acting like a demented animal, this snarling, snorting, supposed icon of a great club showed all the ugly actions of a back-street thug in a game that was being transmitted live on TV throughout the world. . . Lennon was like a sewer emptying. . . His face was contorted, arms waving wildly – this was the wee hardman you wouldn't want to meet in a dark close. . . Great Celtic skippers like Billy McNeill must have squirmed at how easily *this unacceptable Ulsterman* (author's emphasis) demeaned the Hoops jersey.[99]

Space here does not permit an analysis of the socio-demographic and political identities of the readership of these newspapers in Scotland. In summary, both titles would probably be recognised as British and unionist in their editorial line, although one (*Daily Star*) falls more specifically within the cadre of 'red-tops' that is most attractive to a socio-economic 'working-class'; the other (*Daily Express*) is perhaps more 'conservative'. In both contexts, readers who renounce the cultural, social, religious and political identities of Catholics in (British) 'Ulster', and, Catholics of Irish descent in Scotland, would understand this particular reference.

97 R. McLean, Ibid, 21/8/2005.

98 R. Hepburn, Sunday Mirror(Scots Edition), 21/8/2005, p.79, 80.

99 A. McInnes, Ibid, 22/8/2005, p.8; also Ibid, 22/8/2005, p.20.

100 Bradley, 2004; Devine (ed), 2000.

(ii) Deflecting the accuser to deny Scotland's national demon

The mechanism of racism examined here is a sophisticated process. It combines denial of prejudice with deflecting racist allegations back to the accuser. Of course this mechanism is not utilised uniquely to reject allegations of prejudice in Scotland but operates in many other societies where racism is denied. In Scotland the process is partly dependent upon a national myth of egalitarianism and social inclusion. This myth is 'perceived to be, and treated as unchallengeable forms of knowledge'.[100]

The process of denial and deflection operates first by denying accusations of prejudice and then deflecting these accusations back to the complainant 'by a range of rhetorical devices'. This includes, dismissing such accusations as absurd and suggesting that the accusation is irrational or evidence of paranoia. Deflecting the allegations in this way undermines legitimate accusations and the complainant (whether an individual or a group) is blamed for being prejudiced. This process is successful and becomes the dominant mode of thinking precisely because 'substantial numbers accept and share the same system of beliefs about another group'.[101]

There is considerable evidence of this type of process of denial and deflection occurring in Scotland, particularly in the press in relation to the diaspora community of Irish descent in Scotland, Celtic FC and its supporters. The case study of print media representations of Neil Lennon in Autumn 2005 provides further evidence of this process. This included, for example, rejections of supporters' views that the referee had been harsh and/or biased as evidence of paranoia and absurd conspiracy theories. The most compelling example in this case study concerns the player himself.

Towards the end of the period of Lennon's absence from first team football some of his own views on the media's representations of the incident, his suspension and his character, began to emerge. On the official website of Celtic FC he thanked the club, and supporters, for their backing 'throughout the media witch-hunt'.[102] He stated that he believed he had received 'a fair hearing' at the disciplinary meeting which had taken the case 'on its merits and punished me accordingly'.[103]

In October 2005 the *Scotsman* published edited extracts of an interview with Neil Lennon conducted by Glenn Gibbons.[104] Gibbons also offers his interpretation of the views expressed. This article coincided with his return to first-team football after his suspension. The headline, 'I get an unfair press up here, it's totally personal', flagged up the flavour of some of the content: in particular, Lennon's view on how he has been represented 'in certain quarters of the [Scottish] media'[105], and, not only in relation to the incident at Ibrox two months earlier. Given the

> There is considerable evidence of this type of process of denial and deflection occurring in Scotland, particularly in the press in relation to the diaspora community of Irish descent.

101 Finn, 2000, p.58.

102 S. Sullivan, 'Lennon grateful for support', on celticfc.net, www.celticfc.net/ newsroom/news, 4/10/2005, downloaded 28/11/2005.

103 Attributed quotes, in S. Sullivan, Ibid.

104 G. Gibbons, The Scotsman (Sport), 15/10/2005, p.2.

105 Attributed quote in G. Gibbons Ibid.

analysis presented so far it is instructive to quote at length the player's views as they appeared:

> Whether it's my form, my body shape, the way I run, things that have happened off the field, they've always tried to pick holes in my game. There's no doubt what I did at Ibrox was totally wrong, but it was so out of character for me . . .

> . . . sometimes I read things about myself and I think, 'Are they watching the same player? . . . It's totally personal, I'm certain of it. I don't know these guys personally, I don't socialise with them, so they certainly don't know anything about me. . . There's got to be another reason – an agenda – why they write these things. And I think it's an easy get-out for these guys, or lazy journalism, just to say that I wind the crowd up. Basically they're hiding behind that kind of nonsense because none of them has the guts to come out and say what the real reason is for their hostility.[106]

The reference to an agenda is resonant of the point that journalists Gordon and Gibbons made the previous month in their assessments of the tabloid frenzy surrounding the player. Introducing the report, Gibbons was more explicit:

> . . . the Celtic midfielder expressed his conviction that he has been the object of a media-driven, concerted campaign of harassment motivated by prejudice and bigotry against a Northern Ireland Catholic playing for the Parkhead club in a predominantly Protestant environment.[107]

As with all newspaper reports this article is part of (and cannot be separated from) the discourses that surround not only Neil Lennon, but Celtic FC, the Irish diaspora in Scotland and the denial, deflection, containment and management of anti-Catholicism and anti-Irishness in Scotland.

This was not the first time Neil Lennon had referred in press interviews to the hostility directed at him in Scotland.[108] Others, including Martin O'Neill, Lennon's manager at both Leicester City FC and Celtic FC, publicly supported the player and criticised the treatment he received at football grounds throughout Scotland.[109]

For present purposes let us concentrate on the reaction to his comments in October 2005. Once again certain newspapers mobilised the mechanisms of denial, and the accusation of

106 Attributed quote G. Gibbons, Ibid.

107 G. Gibbons, Ibid.

108 See: K. McCarra, The Times(Sport), 10/11/2001, pp.18-19; G. Spiers, Ibid, 17/5/2003; A. Smith, Ibid, 18/5/2003; K. MacDonald, News of the World(Score) (Scotland),18/5/2003, p.4; M. Guidi, Sunday Mail, 30/1/2005, p.75; 79; M. Grant, Sunday Herald (Sport), 13/2/2005, p.9; B. Doogan, Sunday Times (Sport Scotland), 22/5/2005, p.8.

109 See: M. Guidi, Sunday Mail8/2/2004, p.88; I. Orr, Daily Record, 18/5/2004, p.47; 48; G. Spiers, The Herald, 23/8/2002, p.42); H. Macdonald, The Herald,19/4/2004, p.2;G. Spiers, The Herald, 24/11/2004, p.34. Others have also reflected on the hostile treatment directed at Lennon, and the capacity of the media, football authorities and sections of wider society to deny this problem, or remain silent. See also T Campbell, Keep The Faith, http://www.keep-the-faith.net/campbell/tom10.htm

prejudice was deflected back to the accuser. The absence of subtle language and a tone that conveyed feigned indignation was consistent with the tabloid press. For example Bill Leckie's report on the match that marked Lennon's return was full of these devices:

> HANDS UP if you are sick and tired of all this We Love Lenny bilge coming out of Parkhead? In fact, let's make cards up. Big red ones. Arranged right down the length of London Road to spell the message: ENOUGH'S ENOUGH. . . The rest of the country has had a bellyful of this fake rallying round a man whose last meaningful action brought nothing but shame on the game. We're weary of the fantasies of a 'campaign of hysteria' to get Neil Lennon drummed out of football. We're bored of the nonsensical accusations of anti-Irish, anti-Catholic bigotry just because the guy was criticised for behaving like a ned in an Old Firm game. Oh, and before the emails start flying about who 'we' are? We are anyone who can see beyond 'whit ye ur' and know that the reaction to Lennon's rantings on August 20 were nothing to do with nationality, religion or football allegiance. It was about decency.[110]

Leckie is, in small part, correct. There was justifiable concern over the way the player confronted the officials. It has been argued in this critique however that the tone and language used by some sections of the press, subsequent press coverage, and the techniques used to frame such criticisms, were constructed as a racist discourse. Rather than assuage some Celtic supporters and perhaps the broader community in Scotland that is descended from Irish immigrants, Leckie's comments above may have persuaded them of press prejudice that they perceive as real. Leckie's pronouncements can also in fact be seen as part of a pattern that he has long contributed to along with various other Scottish football pundits.

The same can also be said of reaction to Andy McInnes' comments that as he watched Lennon leaving Celtic Park after the match, 'it struck me that I was looking at a player who obviously considers himself a victim'.[111] McInnes resurrected some of his own the racial stereotypes and contentious markers of Lennon's national identity status to re-affirm the individual's standing as symbolic other/outsider in Scotland. For example commenting on Lennon's (alleged) claim that the media

110 B. Leckie, Scottish Sun, 17/10/2005, p.61.

111 A. McInnes, Daily Star (Scottish Edition) 17/10/2005, p.20.

campaign was 'driven by prejudice and bigotry' McInnes opined,

> Now you don't get that sort of deep thinking coming from your average footballer – Northern Irish Catholic or Billy boy Protestant.[112]

He adds:

> Maybe we should simply label Lennon an Ulsterman (no agenda there, just fact) if it helps his cause in this apparent proddy land of journalism,

Before concluding: 'Lennon a victim? Only his own head.'

In the *Daily Record* James Traynor provides a final example of this denial and deflection technique. In a tone that feigns disinterest, Traynor objects:

> Lennon, I noticed in a sorry excuse for a broadsheet the other day, was spluttering about his belief that he has been the victim of a media-driven campaign motivated by bigotry and prejudice. For God's sake have people who allow this kind of thing lost all reason and sense of responsibility?[113]

He added indignantly,

> They are adding to the diseased notion that the *majority* (my emphasis) of the people in this country are bigots and that is not the case.[114]

With these views Traynor exemplified the denials of accusations of media prejudice. In addition he lays the blame on Lennon, and the newspaper that published his views, for creating or at least fanning the flames of sentiments that are held by (as Traynor sees it) a minority of people. At this point we have to bear in mind that Catholics in Scotland are a minority and that iin number Celtic supporters are small compared to all other clubs' supporters put together. Although the biggest single ethnic group in Scotland (often itself not recognised in ethnic terms), people of Irish Catholic descent are a minority (approximately 15% of the population) in Scotland. Generally, through the dominant hegemonies of Scottish life, these three categories merge to become one of a sort. Importantly, in such views, there is an implicit suggestion that it is those who subscribe to Lennon's negative view of the tabloid press who demonstrate the real prejudice. In this way the views of the

The views of the Irish descended Catholic Celtic supporting population of Scotland are marginalised and labelled paranoiac.

112 A. McInnes, Ibid.

113 J. Traynor, Daily Record, 17/10/2005, p.24.

114 J. Traynor, Ibid.

Irish descended Catholic Celtic supporting population of Scotland are marginalised and labelled paranoiac.

Many of the reactions to Lennon's comments use humour – some of it derogatory – to ridicule the player and his comments. The conclusion in the tabloid press was that this had nothing to do with national and ethno-religious prejudices, but is all about the individual, his character, personality and the player he is. In this way the press depicted a serious and legitimate social issue, as an imagined personal 'problem' and, one only fit for humour and for, 'having a laugh'.

SCOTLAND'S NATIONAL DEMON?

This critique is instructive for social critics and popular commentators of public life in Scotland. The evidence presented is illustrative of specific aspects of the discourse that practise but simultaneously deny racism – specifically anti-Irish and anti-Catholic bigotry – in Scotland. The material considered contains examples of blatant racial stereotypes as well as more subtle and insidious racist and sectarian narratives. The analysis exposes the culpability of the press in reproducing and sustaining these through mechanisms that reciprocally uphold the underlying ideologies and sentiments that remain deeply embedded, often unchallenged and denied, and even defended, in contemporary Scottish society.[115]

The elements of media discourse examined here have been related principally to one individual. Nonetheless the mechanisms of racism assembled in reports about Neil Lennon contribute to broader discourses and everyday practices that sectarianise the Irish Catholic descended diaspora community in Scotland: the community that is 'the other' within Scotland.

This raises a number of important questions that Scotland (including the press) must face. Two are highlighted here. First to what extent is Neil Lennon a unique example of being marked as 'outsider' in Scotland? The answer of course is he is not. The evidence from all the contributors to this book and in serious and informed academic studies is testament to that. Further evidence, if any were needed, of similar media discourses that demonise particular individuals in this way has already emerged

> The mechanisms of racism assembled in reports about Neil Lennon contribute to broader discourses and everyday practices that sectarianise the Irish Catholic-descended diaspora community in Scotland.

115 The 'silence' on such sentiments, manifest in the press by absence of comment, is another device that also contributes to the persistence of these ideas.

'publicly' in relation to the young Scots-born Irishman, Aiden McGeady, following his choosing to play international football for the Republic of Ireland rather than Scotland.

Second, and perhaps more importantly for myself as the writer of this article, what does this tell Scots people like me, about 'ourselves'. James Traynor is possibly correct – the majority of people in Scotland are not overt bigots and racist. However, like dominant ethnic groups in other countries–'we' Scots are guilty of solipsism: that is, as individuals and as a national collective, often we know ourselves only from the perspective of our own 'world' – the myths, ideas, values and sentiments through which we live our everyday lives. Scotland, like all national communities, has its own national myths:[116] the narratives or stories that help us to define ourselves to ourselves, and to others. These function as part of a collective national consciousness or identity. Apart from matters such as our Protestant identity and relationship with England, part of the central element of the 'Scottish myth' is our 'inherent egalitarianism'.[117] Moreover this myth assumes Scots are 'egalitarian by dint of racial characteristics, of deep social values'.[118]

> Scotland is no different to other nations. The demeaning and dehumanising narratives of the 'negative' 'other' slip into the crevices of everyday life

Scotland is no different to other nations. The demeaning and dehumanising narratives of the 'negative' 'other' slip into the crevices of everyday life signifying, representing and vilifying difference. Over the past one hundred and fifty years, the essential 'other' in Scottish society has been the Irish Catholic diaspora: that is now in the main, Catholics born in Scotland of Irish descent. This, I would argue is the demon Scots, and others, must recognise and overcome if a better society is to prevail.

This brings me back to Neil Lennon and the media discourse considered here. It has indeed been an instructive lesson. . .

To see oursels as ithers see us!

116 D. McCrone, 2001, p.91.

117 Ibid, 2001, p.91.

118 Ibid, 2001, p.91.

Reflections on 'Sectarianism', 'Bigotry' and Bampots

TONY ROPER

At the end of 2005 I was invited by the Brother Walfrid Committee and Celtic Football Club to be a guest at the unveiling of a statue to Brother Walfrid, the most important single figure in the origins of the Celtic Football Club. It was a wonderful occasion; great speeches, great music, very colourful, lovely people. In many ways the occasion was Irish and Catholic, which ties with the very nature and identity of this great institution and its vast army of supporters. That shouldn't be such a big deal. Or should it?

These are facts of life at Celtic and to either attempt to remove them or to water them down has always seemed to me to be a mistake. As the song says, 'If you know the history, its enough to make your heart go o o o o o o . . . . . . '

However, it is important to note that Celtic and its supporters have always been proud of the fact that they have also been open to others not from an Irish or Catholic background. Next to me on match days at Celtic Park sit a Church of Scotland elder and two Muslims. Even the unveiling of the statue to Brother Walfrid reflected this ethos. In amongst the invited guests in the Celtic Boardroom that fine day was John Greig, icon of Glasgow Rangers as well as representatives from the Church of Scotland, the Jewish Community, the Scottish Premier League, the Scottish Football Association and numerous others from various walks of Scottish life – though I didn't see any referees right enough. The unveiling party had two representatives from the modern refugee community in Glasgow, a poignant statement by the Walfrid Committee that they haven't forgotten the refugee status that their own Irish Catholic forebears once embraced.

But the way that this fantastic day was ignored in the Scottish media concerned me. How on earth could it not look at this very positive occasion and join in the celebration? That made me reflect on the culture of 'sectarianism' and 'bigotry' in Scottish society. This is of course the kind of topic that invites a brick through the car window on account of a misquote or a typographical error.

My feeling has always been the same. Given that many of Celtic's best performers were not Catholics and were not from an Irish background – Johnny Thompson, Jock Stein, Kenny Dalglish, Danny McGrain, Wispy Wallace, Bertie Peacock (the list is endless so I won't go on – check for yourself if your paranoia is deep-seated enough) – I'm so very proud. Just as I'm proud of Brother Walfrid and the community that has given this great club its very lifeblood and meaning.

What does that bigotry word actually mean anyway? The dictionary gives: *'bigot – a person obstinately wedded to a particular creed'*. Hmm, let's look up *creed – 'a brief summary of the articles of Christian faith'*. Wait a minute, the Archbishop of Canterbury, the Pope, and the Moderator of the General Assembly of the Church of Scotland all fit that description. So are they all bigots? Bhoys Against the Pope? The logic of this is obviously a mite suspect, to say the least. Maybe anti-sectarian would be a better description – *one of a sect. 'Showing single-minded devotion to a party'*.

I should perhaps examine my own credentials to qualify as a bona fide non-bigoted fan. I am and have been for most of my life a fully paid-up agnostic – ie, maybe there is and maybe there isn't a God and, if there is, who knows if he's Catholic, Protestant, Jewish, Hindu, Muslim, Shinto, Mithraic. Is he a man or is she a woman? Is he or she a Celtic, Rangers, Man U, or Barcelona fan? Could be any of those, as far as my knowledge goes. However, this definitely places me in the 'not wedded to a particular creed' category. So, on strictly religious criteria, I can qualify as a non-bigot. Phew!

How about race? Am I a racist? I was brought up in the Catholic faith, I'm a Celtic fan, and I wear a religious amulet round my neck and have done for many years. Following the norm, I wear a crucifix, right? Wrong. I wear a Star of David, not for religious reasons, nor for any political reason, solely because I pay tribute to the extraordinary artistic gifts encompassing music, literature, and the arts in general that the Jewish race has given to the world. So I am also not a racist.

What about my better half? She's a 'Proddy' so no joy there. This means I qualify on two counts. This is beginning to sound a bit too good to be true: I'm starting to feel like a right wimp.

What about when I'm at work? Do I hate all other football fans other than Celtic fans? No! In fact I love the banter (so long as it is banter and doesn't disguise something else) and havin' tae think up your replies for the next day if your team gets gubbed and, even better, pinning their arses to the wall when it's their mob that get even mildly humiliated. Yessss! But that's being a fitba' fan; that's the same all over the world, that is what you pay your match ticket for; that is truly wonderful. That is not being a hate-filled sectarian bigot who's had the obligatory humour bypass.

There will, of course, be some critics who will find fault and demand that all vestiges of Christianity, Catholicism and Irishness, even Dublin Bay prawns on the menu at Celtic Park, are an incitement to riot or that green-lipped mussels are in direct contravention of the club's stand against 'sectarianism', and the singing of *The Fields of Athenry* has nothing to do with football, whereas *God Save the Queen, Paper Roses, Flower of Scotland* and *I'm Forever Blowing Bubbles* are somehow kosher.

As for Celtic and Rangers fans, cast your minds back to the World Cup in the 1990s, Holland v Ireland – the ultimate role models for the Rangers Orangemen and the Celtic Tims – and the Irish and Dutch were not even segregated, a surefire recipe for murder and mayhem, right? Wrong. They could not have been happier as they sat there, hands round each other's shoulders, singing away. So no joy there for the bigots either.

And tell me, guys, when was the last time you saw a pitched fight between the directors of Celtic or Rangers? Not too many in the casualty wards getting their cut lips stitched over something that happened in 1690. You'll have to agree!

Let's not restrict the bigot label to Celtic and Rangers fans though. What about the Jam Tarts and Hibbees fans who teach their offspring that the opposing mob eat babies and are lower than a worm's 'you know what'? Ditto Airdrie v Hamilton, Dundee v Dundee Utd, and so on.

What about Jews and Arabs, Scots and English? I went to see *Braveheart*. On the way out a guy said to me: 'Some film eh! Does it no' just want to make you go out and punch an Englishman?' As a matter of fact it did, but that's not the point. The point is that if I had met an Englishman, even a very small one, I would not have punched him. And if you need to ask why then this article and book are wasted on you and you're too sad for words.

Sadness comes in many forms and many shapes but it is certainly part and parcel of being one of them sad sectarian bigoted bampots. To those who fit that description, I am truly sorry for them. To those who do not, 'Hail Hail. I am proud to be 'Celtic Minded' and one of you.

Shame on the Shameless: Fandom and Wisdom in a Town Without Piety

Willy Maley

THERE'S ONLY ONE NED O'MALLEY

My grandfather slept three nights in a shop doorway when he arrived in Glasgow from Mayo in the 1890s. That particular immigrant experience was shared by many first-generation Irishmen and women who came to the city as well as to other towns in Scotland in search of work and a new life. They would bed down where they could and sleep rough until they could get digs sorted and work came along.

Faced with anti-Irish prejudice my grandfather did what some other Irish immigrants did – he dropped the 'O' from his name, and his children became plain 'Maley'. Some others changed their names altogether to more Scottish sounding ones while others had their names changed for them by the authorities as they couldn't write (occasionally they didn't even speak English) or that was the way their names 'sounded' to the native Scots who struggled with an Irish accent. The Irish 'Byrne' becoming the Scottish 'Burns' was one name sometimes affected and this example was highlighted in the play, 'The Celtic Story'.

I never met my Irish-born grandfather, never heard his voice, never even saw a photograph. Ned O'Malley died thirty years before I was born. Although I never knew him I believe it's true that our grandparents exert an influence over us even from the grave through what they pass down to our parents. I met a priest once from Kirby who was involved in a community history project at a local unemployed workers centre. The project was called 'The Journey', and it entailed reminding young people of Irish origin what their parents and grandparents and great grandparents had experienced on the road from Ireland to Liverpool and beyond. The African American novelist Toni Morrison has talked in a similar way, in an essay entitled 'Rootedness: The Ancestor as Foundation', about the importance of remembering the past, particularly when it helps explain present prejudice.

Ned is one of my foundations, one of the building blocks of my identity. Every time I get ideas above my station I remember that a man lay down in a doorway for three nights so that I could have a future.

SHAME ON THE SEAMUS? (OR, YOUR SECRET'S NOT A SECRET ANY MORE)

In the summer of 1999 James MacMillan, the celebrated composer, delivered a lecture entitled *Scotland's Shame?* at the Edinburgh Festival. Scotland, he announced, was an anti-Catholic country scarred by sectarianism: a media frenzy followed. A year later, a collection of essays entitled 'Scotland's Shame, edited by Professor Tom Devine was published. The subject has continued to generate debate. There was considerable controversy in February 2001 when *an Taoiseach*, Bertie Ahern, abandoned a planned visit to the Carfin Grotto and Pilgrimage Centre, a Marian shrine near Glasgow where he was to unveil a memorial to the victims of the Great Irish Famine: the proposed visit coincided with a Celtic–Rangers football match, which Ahern was also to attend that afternoon. The local MP, Frank Roy, had written to the Taoiseach's office warning that his presence at the Grotto might heighten sectarian tensions. Roy subsequently resigned as parliamentary private secretary to London's Scottish Secretary Helen Liddell. Of course Roy's concern was not the full story and a number of politicians in Scotland had began to interfere with this Irish diaspora community event once they knew of the unveiling.

Ireland was drawn further into the unfolding debate on sectarianism in Scottish society when, on New Year's Day 2002, John Reid's innocuous remarks that Celtic and Rangers draw support from either side of the religious divide in Northern Ireland got banner headlines. Reid's comments were akin to forecasting rain in Glasgow, but he was then Secretary of State for Northern Ireland (and known to be a supporter of Celtic). In Scotland, religion is a political football: in Glasgow, football is a political religion. In 2004 Aiden McGeady, a Scottish-born Celtic footballer, was pilloried in the press when he elected to play for the Republic of Ireland, the country his family and community came to Scotland from. The following spring, a BBC documentary, a Panorama special entitled *Scotland's Secret Shame* 'publicly' reopened the running sore: the programme took its title from a phrase used by Jack McConnell, Scotland's First Minister, to describe the sectarian chants and violence at Glasgow Rangers v Celtic games.[1] In short, sectarianism has repeatedly been at the centre of cultural and political debate in the seven years since MacMillan's passionate denunciation.

DEVINE INTERVENTION

An abiding curiosity of contemporary Irish–Scottish relations is that the Research Institute for Irish and Scottish Studies is located in Aberdeen, far from Glasgow, the fulcrum of Irish immigration, where its first director, Tom Devine, editor of *Scotland's Shame?*, was previously based. Approximately sixteen per cent of the Scottish population can claim Irish descent and are therefore second, third and fourth generation Irish (whether they choose to be considered as such is another matter). This figure rises to around twenty-five per cent for the West of Scotland but the North East is not famed for its Irish connections.

In his contribution to *Scotland's Shame?*, Scott Styles, who lectures in law at Aberdeen University, notes that there was only one Catholic secondary school in Aberdeen until the 1970s (now gone) and concludes that there is no 'sectarianism' in the North East. However, absence of immigration is insufficient evidence of absence of discrimination. Indeed, it may imply the reverse. There is much evidence in the USA to support this view.

On the evidence of Styles's essay, 'The Non-Sectarian Culture of North-East Scotland', the legal verdict must be the peculiarly Scottish one of 'Not Proven'. Styles's argument is a miniature

(1) BBC 1, 27 February 2005

version of the old 'Nae Problem' case against Scottish racism. We don't have many foreigners up here, so there's 'nae problem'. Just as long as they don't start taking our jobs, houses, headlines (singing their songs, supporting their football team), etc. When Styles says 'Sectarianism may be the shame of certain parts of Scotland but it is not the shame of *all* Scotland, and it has never been the shame of the north-east', methinks the laddie doth protest too much.[2]

The right response to a history of discrimination is not one of denial.

The right response to a history of discrimination is not one of denial. To borrow from Mr. Deasy in James Joyce's *Ulysses*, Aberdeen has no problem with anti-Irish racism, 'because she never let them in'. Professor Devine says, 'perhaps it's no bad thing that the Institute is located in an area with no obvious Irish links'.[3] In other words the further from the source of the inflammation, the better? Or is it a matter of emotion recollected in tranquillity?

With the advent of devolution one might have expected the exclusions and denials of the past to change, but the debate about sectarianism is one of two shameful shenanigans that marked and marred the first year of the new Scottish Parliament, the other being the furore surrounding the repeal of Clause 28 of the Local Government Act (1988). Neither issue was new, but the occasion gave both a fresh gloss.

Through Devine's intervention the first of these has been stitched up a treat in *Scotland's Shame?:* a volume aimed at naming and shaming the stiflingly singular Scotland that refuses to acknowledge its mixed and multiple origins and identities. Inevitably, the academic angle has led to the introduction of a question mark, but the complexion of the collection, diverse though its individual contributions are, suggests shame is unquestionable, and that the question mark should come after Scotland, whose status as a homogenous and unified country (and concept) is what's in doubt. There is Devine argues, a 'lack of consensus' over the exact nature of the problem, as well as its current extent, but also a general awareness of the need for an enlarged and more accommodating notion of Scottishness. From the outset, it's clear that defining the nature of the shame – naming it – isn't easy. In his preface, Devine

(2) Scott Styles, 'The Non-Sectarian Culture of North-East Scotland', in T. M. Devine, ed., *Scotland's Shame? Bigotry and Sectarianism in Modern Scotland* (Edinburgh, 2000), p122

(3) Tom Devine, cited in Trevor Royle, 'Northern Lights Illuminate Celtic Past', *Sunday Herald* (30 July 2000), http:// www.sundayherald.com/ print9829

touches on race, religion, national identity and class, all issues that interconnect, a cross-hatching evident from the outset:

> This book is concerned with prejudice in modern Scotland. Prejudice can take many forms, perhaps the most obvious of which is racism in today's world. But this collection of essays takes a much narrower focus. It seeks to examine in more detail than ever before considered in a single volume, the specific and controversial issue of anti-Catholic bigotry and discrimination in present-day Scotland.[4]

This preface rules racism out of court by narrowing the terms of the debate to 'the specific and controversial issue of anti-Catholic bigotry and discrimination in present-day Scotland'. In the next paragraph we learn that:

> The historical record demonstrates unambiguously that Catholics in Scotland, the vast majority of whom were descended from Irish immigrants, experienced routine discrimination in the labour market.

This reads like 'racism in today's world', only it's not 'present-day Scotland'; it's 'The historical record' – rather than the *Daily Record* – that demonstrates discrimination by descent. Being of Irish provenance is at least as important as being of the Catholic faith. In Scotland the two tend to go together. This descent from Ireland is a long and winding affair, for Devine reminds us that:

> As late as the 1920s and 1930s. . . the General Assembly of the Church of Scotland waged a relentless campaign against the supposedly malign effects of Irish Catholic immigration which was judged a 'menace' to 'our Scottish nationality'.[5]

There you have it, nation and religion coming together as one to exclude another nation, another religion. The story of the twentieth century, particularly the post-war period, purports to be a progressive narrative of inclusion. With the decline of heavy industry (allegedly the main locus of sectarianism), and the rise of a significant Catholic middle-class, the 1980s were expected to have witnessed the demise of such outdated discrimination:

> A formerly despised ethnic group had apparently become fully integrated into the mainstream of Scottish life in the space of two generations.[6]

(4) Tom Devine, Preface to T. M. Devine (ed.), Scotland's Shame?: Bigotry and Sectarianism in Modern Scotland (Edinburgh: Mainstream, 2000), p7

(5) Tom Devine, Preface to Scotland's Shame, p7

6 Ibid.

A 'despised ethnic group' suggests racism rather than religious discrimination; but once again the lines blur, for it emerges that class is the key, both to the end of sectarianism (implicit in the model of social mobility mapped out by Catholic schools), and to its persistence (implicit in the 'tribalism' of the 'Old Firm' and the 'underclass' attracted to Orange marches). This last point is compromised, as football in Scotland is a less exclusively working-class pastime than it was a few decades ago, yet, 'sectarianism' survives, nay, thrives.

MacMillan put his finger on the racialised character of so-called 'sectarianism'.

Thus, the story goes – and Devine's probing preface is precisely designed to unpick this complacent narrative – that social mobility for a section of the Irish Catholic minority rendered sectarianism 'a subject which was not discussed in polite circles', or at least not in mixed company. This conspiracy of silence was broken by one of Scotland's brightest stars. 'MacMillan', as Devine puts it, 'did not mince his words'. In the essay that gave the book its name, MacMillan identified 'a very Scottish trait – a desire to narrow and to restrict the definition of what it means to be Scottish'. More to the point, MacMillan put his finger on the racialised character of so-called 'sectarianism':

> The obsessive attempts, historically and contemporaneously, to peripheralise and trivialise the Catholic experience in Scotland (and in particular the Irish Catholic experience) is a self-defeating tendency. It represents the very opposite of the enriching multicultural pluralism which I crave for this country'.[7]

The Irish character of the Catholic experience in Scotland is crucial. Some Scottish Catholics are not Irish, some Irish in Scotland are not Catholic, but where Irishness and Catholicism coincide, discrimination is discernible.

Ironically, the debate around anti-Catholicism in Scotland, and with it resistance to an Irish identity viewed by some as un-Scottish, occurs at a time when Ireland and Scotland are engaging with each other on a more structured basis. Failed devolution in Northern Ireland preceded devolution in Scotland, and the emergence of new (or renewed) political institutions went hand-in-hand with the opening of an Irish Consulate in

(7) James MacMillan, 'Scotland's Shame', in Devine (ed.), Scotland's Shame?, p16

Edinburgh and, a Council of the Isles, an element in the Good Friday Agreement. The Council of the Isles, aka the British–Irish Council (BIC), a body set up under the Good Friday Agreement, consists of representatives of the British and Irish governments, the Northern Ireland Assembly, the Welsh Assembly, the Scottish Parliament, and the democratic institutions of Jersey, Guernsey and the Isle of Man. Its principal aim is to promote links between the various governments, assemblies, and institutions.

This process of institutional innovation found an echo, culturally, in the establishment of the Irish-Scottish Academic Initiative (ISAI), from which sprang the Aberdeen Centre so far from the crucible of Irish identity in Scotland. The appearance of a major new anthology of Scottish writing, *Across the Water*, in which authors expounded on their Irish influences, enriched understanding of Irish-Scottish relations, showcasing a generation of writers in Scotland from an Irish Catholic background, including Des Dillon, Chris Dolan, Anne Donovan and Andrew O'Hagan.[8] There is evidence of growing interest in this dynamic cultural crossover, but evidence of problems too. The failed Scottish-Irish bid to host the 2008 European Championship was blamed in part on crowd trouble at an Old Firm match in the period leading up to UEFA's decision.

Ireland was always much more successful at representing itself globally, even managing to secure a postcolonial passport. Devine sums it up when he says, 'Ireland's on a roll, culturally and economically. It's cool to be Irish'. Irishness is sexy, and big in America, and for a long time Scotland lagged behind like a huffy wee brother, utterly uncool, fearful and resentful, resistant and forgetful.

One marker of the maturity of a culture is its attitude to minorities, to the marginalised or excluded. Ireland is currently undergoing problems and tensions as for the first time in its modern history it welcomes immigrants to its shores. Scotland has a long way to go in terms of maturity. Damaged cultures, those with a history of colonialism, are susceptible to extremes of bias and bigotry. In Scotland, where the dark forces of the past still busily concentrate negative energies around matters

> Scotland has a long way to go in terms of maturity. Damaged cultures, those with a history of colonialism, are susceptible to extremes of bias and bigotry.

(8) Argyll Publishing, 2000

of religion, the national question, having been partially resolved by devolution, has given up the ghost to some of the demons from the country's past.

Anti-Irish racism cannot be openly acknowledged in Scotland, but has to be closeted with the spectre of sectarianism. It is a form of prejudice addressed more directly in England. A recent report into discrimination against the Irish community in Britain failed to give due consideration to its vexed Scottish context. Professors Mary Hickman and Wlater Bronwen compiled the report, entitled *Discrimination and the Irish Community in Britain*, for the Commission for Racial Equality in 1997. There is ignorance on both sides of the Border, for this key work on anti-Irish feeling, an invaluable resource for any scholar interested in the subject, is not alluded to in the volume edited by Devine, who laments the lack of evidence for Scotland without taking a hard look at the work of Hickman and Bronwen.[9] Further, there are virtually no references in Scottish newspapers to this report or its serious nature. The resistance to opening up about Irishness within a Scottish milieu derives from a deep-lying discrimination, reluctant to show its true colours.

'Sectarianism' is just a lazy slogan, a euphemism for an underlying racism about which Scotland remains in deep denial, a fear and loathing that dare not speak its name.

When the Irish-Scottish Academic Initiative was first discussed, it was suggested the word 'Celtic' be used as the connecting term. This was rejected on the Irish side as a rather obvious attempt to avoid using 'Irish' in a Scottish context. For make no mistake about it, 'sectarianism' is just a lazy slogan, a euphemism for an underlying racism about which Scotland remains in deep denial, a fear and loathing that dare not speak its name. Devine admits as much when he says of so-called 'sectarianism' that:

> Academic studies of the subject are still few and far between. Racism, the problems of ethnic minorities and gender inequalities all attract systematic attention and investigation; not so sectarianism.

Maybe that is because the term is a specious swearword, a tabloid totem, concealing a continuing denial of Scotland's implication in the colonisation of Ireland. Devine gets to the heart of the matter when he observes that the vast majority of

(9) This work has been partly added to, even surpassed, via the *Irish 2 Project* carried out by a team comprising Walters, Hickman, Sarah Morgan and, the editor of this collection of works, Joseph M Bradley. Although much of the findings are yet to be published they also offer evidence of discrimination against Catholics of Irish descent in Scotland.

Catholics in Scotland 'were descended from Irish immigrants'.[10] Devine acknowledges that Scotland is an increasingly secular society. How does this square with the continuing virulence of 'sectarianism'? Either old habits die hard, or the religious flag of convenience has slipped to half-mast. How can Devine or MacMillan account for the fact that non-Catholics with Irish surnames – Maley culpa – are subject to 'anti-Catholicism'? This can only be achieved by conceding that more than Catholicism is at issue.

The storm around 'sectarianism' is about Ireland as much as Scotland. While the outsider's view, even that of many insiders, is that anti-English feeling is the dominant expression of exclusivist or aggressive nationalist feeling in Scotland, the most reported form of discrimination revolves around religion, specifically and predominantly discrimination against Catholics – not Italian or Polish but primarily Irish Catholics. Denied or dismissed as–'sectarianism', anti-Irish racism is arguably the strongest of national antipathies. The 'Lesson of Ireland', for some Scottish commentators, is like the 'Lesson of Bosnia', in which the dangers of nationalism are laid bare in all their violence and vexation. This is blaming the victims. A whole tradition of Scottish historiography does one of two things – ignores Ireland completely, except for occasional hand-wringing and insincere allusions to 'sectarianism', or blames Ireland for all that's negative. The history is selective and short-sighted. Irish immigration after the Famine depressed wages and introduced an 'alien culture' (or so the story goes). Mention is rarely made of the British state-sponsored Anglo-Scottish plantation of Ulster in the early seventeenth century, or to the so-called Irish problem in the twentieth century as also being a Scottish problem. In addition, it should be noted that it was these Scottish and English planters in Ulster that gave birth to Orangeism. Critics are inclined to compare Scotland to Quebec, Estonia, or Catalonia, rather than to Ireland, which it most closely resembles – too close to home for comfort?

The renewed concern with Scottish-Irish connections marks a change. The phrase 'Scotland and Ireland' can imply that a United Ireland and a separate Scotland would break English hegemony over both. Conversely, some commentators, such as

> A whole tradition of Scottish historiography does one of two things – ignores Ireland completely, except for occasional hand-wringing and insincere allusions to 'sectarianism', or blames Ireland for all that's negative.

(10) Tom Devine,
    Preface to Scotland's
    Shame, p7

the sociologist Steve Bruce, speak of 'Ulster and Scotland', by which they mean the six counties partitioned off in 1920. Ulster of course is nine counties (three in the 'south') while Northern Ireland is six. Here, the subtext is that Northern Ireland, threatened with a change of constitutional status, better align itself with Scotland rather than be absorbed by the Irish Republic. Coincidentally, Liam McIlvanney and Ray Ryan, in their introduction to *Ireland and Scotland: Culture and Society, 1700–2000* (2002), acknowledge that:

> Within Irish studies, the Irish/Scottish comparison is viewed by some as unionism's answer to postcolonial studies, and there may, indeed, be some justification for viewing Irish-Scottish studies in this light.[11]

According to Professor Patrick Reilly, 'Scotland has ceased to be a Protestant country without ceasing to be an anti-Catholic one.' With due respect to my former colleague, I'd like to stretch his terms: 'Scotland has ceased to be a religious country without ceasing to be a racist one.' Reilly admits as much when he points out Catholics in Scotland are the country's oldest and largest immigrant community.[12]

The cul-de-sac of 'sectarianism' is the last refuge of scoundrels unwilling to face up to the reality of a racist Scotland. It's not a term taken seriously by academics precisely because it's a bogus media concoction, intended to close down discussion of Irish–Scottish relations or of the Irish in Scotland. One only requires to view the evidence for this in numerous publications from the Scottish middle class secular academic and journalistic brigade who resent any research offering contrary perspectives to their views, especially on the part of academic or journalistic Catholics of Irish descent. MacMillan calls at the close of *Scotland's Shame?* for the 'airing of hidden perspectives'.[13] Let's start with the perspective hidden by the one-size-fits-Patrick cloak of 'sectarianism' – anti-Irishness.

We live in a time of darkness and denial. In an interview in the *Sunday Herald* in the wake of his Edinburgh lecture, MacMillan said:

> There's a fantastic phrase at the end of *The Tempest*: 'This thing of darkness I acknowledge mine'. I think Scots need to

(Sectarianism) is not a term taken seriously by academics precisely because it's a bogus media concoction, intended to close down discussion of Irish–Scottish relations or of the Irish in Scotland.

(11) Introduction in Liam McIlvanney and Ray Ryan, eds., Ireland and Scotland: Culture and Society, 1700–2000 (Dublin, 2005), p14

(12) Patrick Reilly, 'Kicking with the Left Foot: Being Catholic in Scotland', in Devine, ed., Scotland's Shame?, p38

(13) MacMillan, 'I Had Not Thought About It Like That Before', in Devine, ed., Scotland's Shame, 265

look in the mirror sometimes. We in Scotland need to see that something like anti-Catholic prejudice – or something like racism, or rampant sexism, or our various other things that plague us but we are in denial of – are all things we need to take on board'.[14]

It is an interesting allusion. Paul Brown, in an essay that takes the same quotation from *The Tempest* as its title, reads Shakespeare's play as a colonial allegory of the Ulster Plantation: and the Irish playwright Frank McGuinness has adapted it. Even four hundred years ago Ireland was the unspeakable other, imagined only through some distant relative. In *Ulysses*, Joyce spoke of 'Patsy Caliban, our American cousin'.

IRISH–SCOTTISH MINDED: BIGOTS, LITTER LOUTS, AND LAZY JOURNALISM

In January 2002, I was asked by Kevin McKenna, Deputy Editor at the *Herald*, to do a piece responding to the remarks made by John Reid about Celtic and Rangers attracting Irish supporters. I submitted 1,000 words but the piece did not appear. I am convinced that it had been pulled for pointing out that the newspapers were manufacturing controversy and fabricating in a sensationalist fashion in order to cultivate silence. Someone (not Kevin) didn't like it. Does that make me paranoid?: terrible problem, litter. Being a green writer, environmentally friendly, dutifully recycling material, I tried to place the piece elsewhere. The article was an abbreviated version of an essay for the book *Celtic Minded*, whose aim was to map out, explore and record in the face of insular, ignorant, sectarian and racist opposition, the Irish Catholic context of Celtic Football Club from its founding to the present day: that longer essay duly appeared.[15]

One of the things implied in the phrase 'Celtic minded' is an understanding that Celtic Football Club has its roots in the Irish Catholic immigrant community. No matter how the club develops, those roots and that identity remain. Being mindful and minded of them is very far from being sectarian. It guards against the mindlessness of that amnesia induced by enforced assimilation. The majority of supporters of Celtic Football Club are of Irish-Catholic extraction. This is in line with the club's

(14) Quoted in Pat Kane, 'Defender of the Faith', Sunday Herald, 15 Aug. 1999

(15) 'Shut Up' and 'Trouble': The Nonsense Over 'Sectarianism'', in Joseph M. Bradley, ed.,'Celtic Minded: Essays on Religion, Politics, Society, Identity ... and Football (Glendaruel, Argyll, 2004), pp195-201

origins and history and is known the world over. Yet, for reasons that have more to do with prejudice than progress, in Scotland, the Irish dimension of Celtic and its support has caused discomfort for many commentators. Football and religion (and cultural and national origins?) don't mix, the story goes, especially where the religion in question is considered 'foreign'. Some say this has changed, that anti-Catholic/anti-Irish discrimination is dead and gone. This is either wishful thinking or wilful censorship.

In Scotland, the Irish dimension of Celtic and its support has caused discomfort for many commentators.

Despite periodic coverage of 'sectarianism' in the media, there are relatively few public discussions of the importance of the Irish contribution to modern Scottish history and culture. The title of my own contribution to the first volume of *Celtic Minded*, 'Shut Up and Trouble', points to the double bind of muteness or mayhem. Say nothing or start a fight. The right of Celtic supporters to identify themselves as Irish or Catholic, or both, and to celebrate that fact, seems straightforward. In a modern multicultural Scotland such affiliations are part of the many-sided make-up of this country. The notorious Celtic paranoia often turns out to be paranoia about Celtic. There's nothing to be afraid or ashamed of in a tolerant and inclusive society that welcomes its immigrant communities and recognises the input of its minorities. Nothing, that is, but the bigotry that can't be put to rest simply by ignoring it, or by telling its victims to shut up or there'll be trouble.

The great thing about football – and the grievous thing too – is the nature of fandom or fanhood. 'Fan', short for 'fanatic', refers to 'a person filled with excessive and mistaken enthusiasm, especially in religion', from 'fanum', meaning 'temple'. Not all Celtic fans are as open to the other, the outsider, as they should be, given the club's origins in an immigrant community. I have a few experiences of my own of the decidedly unwelcoming nature of some Celtic supporters. We would be ostriches to ignore this. Like all peoples, communities or cultures, we cannot say we are without sin. However, we must aim to be precisely that.

Apart from that problem, I'm dead against the doubting Tims, the Uncle Tims, who'd try to airbrush Irishness or

Catholicism from the history and present reality of Celtic. With my name, my background, my history, how could I be otherwise? I'm Glaswegian. My grandfather was Irish-born. My father, raised as a Catholic, converted to Communism. He fought for the Republic during the Spanish Civil War and was a POW in Spain for six months. His nine children had no religious schooling, but grew up bearing an Irish name and supporting Celtic Football Club. I'm not a Catholic but 'Tim' – short for 'Timothy' and synonymous with Celtic supporters – is my middle name.

A balanced preview of *Celtic Minded* appeared in *Scotland on Sunday*, but the headline ran: 'Celtic Supporters Sing Praises of Sectarian Anthems'. An obvious explanation may exist for the misfit between the actual article and the headline. I'm still waiting to hear it. A couple of weeks later *Celtic Minded* was reviewed in the *Herald* by Graham Spiers, who describes himself as 'hailing from a liberal Protestant tradition'. Spiers jerked his knee so much he could have damaged his cartilage. He spoke of *Celtic Minded* being marred by a 'drooling, dripping Irishness', and 'dripping with a bitter, molten Irishness' that made him 'queasy' (just like Mr Deasy). Now, if you substitute 'Jewish' or 'Asian' for 'Irish' in that review you'd get a red card for racism. *Celtic Minded* might make it harder for people to be so blithely anti-Irish: the more that read *Celtic Minded* the more we may have a window of opportunity to fight the racism and sectarianism in our midst: that was one of the book's original intentions. Spiers's review suggests it's failed.

It might also have helped of course if he'd read the book – his piece being a lazy review conducted after reading only three chapters from a total of twenty-two. I'm actually from the 'liberal Protestant tradition' myself, and if it wants to claim that title it has to be a lot more liberal, and abandon the casual racism of anti-Irishness.

Football and religion can be separated in a lot of cases. Growing up, I saw most religious feeling as 'fundamentalist'. Anyone who went near a place of worship was a 'bible-thumper' to me. I darkened the door of neither church nor chapel. When it comes to Celtic Football Club, though, I'm faithful through and through. I'm glad to live in Glasgow, where the streets have no shame, though it's sad sometimes to live in a city where Irishness is too often viewed as a problem rather than as an enriching aspect of Scottish culture. I'll never forget the journey I took, and the journey that others took, for me to be here.

POSTCARD FROM THE NEW SCOTTISH PARLIAMENT

A few years ago, someone sent me a Scottish Parliament promotional postcard entitled 'Voices of Scotland'. The organisation behind the card was the Holyrood Project Team, and the purpose was to invite suggestions for 'phrases and quotes summing up what they believe it means to be Scottish'. A selection of these was to 'be wrapped around the huge hoardings surrounding the new Parliament building site'. Suggestions were to be submitted to the Edinburgh Book Festival. To get the ball rolling, the card offered some for slogans for starters.

On one side was a picture of a large building site with three quotations printed over it. First, there was a quote from former US President Woodrow Wilson: 'Every line of strength in American history is a line coloured with Scottish blood'. The second quote was from Robert Burns: 'Scot, wha hae wi' Wallace bled, Scots wha Bruce has often led, Welcome to your gory bed, Or to Victorie'. The third quote was a back page belter from the *Sun* newspaper. Yes, you've guessed it, our old friend the Mary Poppins putdown: 'Super-cally-go-ballistic-celtic-are-atrocious'. Can anyone spot the odd one out?

In fact they're all odd. The Holyrood Project Team was out of its league. Woodrow Wilson's observation might have pleased the Ku Klux Klan, the hillbillies and the rednecks, but do we really want to celebrate the new parliament with a quote from an American President who supported racial segregation? Wilson believed segregation was 'not humiliating, but a benefit.' A couple of years ago there was controversy surrounding two massive bronze medallions cast in Wilson's honour that have marked the midpoint of the Wilson Bridge over the Potomac River near Washington for over forty years. A new bridge was being built and some locals didn't like the old Medallion Man.

The Director of Public Works for one of the local counties involved said of Wilson: 'On racial issues, he was a throwback, and I don't think we here are that interested in celebrating that part of his record.'

The Burns quote is better, but of all the lines that might have been chosen, this seems a strange selection. On top of the bloodline ballyhoo of an American President with a poor record on race relations we get more blood with a bit of gore thrown in for good measure, and a call to victory. That sets us up nicely for the third quote, which is about a humiliating defeat for what might be considered a Scottish institution and Irish football club. I'm partial to a bit of wordplay myself, but what you think of this particular pun depends on your perspective. It's either a cringe-inducing headline from an English tabloid or a wonderful tribute to the triumph of the underdog that had its day in the Scottish Sun (or rain, in this case).

The 'Voices of Scotland' include an Irish brogue – and many other accents. I'd have thought the new Scottish parliament might want to celebrate Celtic's famous victory in the European Cup. There was a Wallace there too, among a team of eleven Scots-born players whose names are legend from Holyrood to Hollywood. Apparently that headline had been used before. 'Super Cally Goes Ballistic' was a headline used by the *Daily Star* in relation to Liverpool's Ian Callaghan. This proves that there's nothing new under the sun, and nothing new in the *Sun* either. Except for 'Freddie Starr Ate My Hamster'. That really is a *Sun* exclusive. I tell my students not to believe anything they read in the papers, especially if it's by me!

Great minds think alike, but being Celtic-minded means begging to differ. I was irked when one Celtic supporter wrote to me when I was a columnist for the *Celtic View* to take me to task for mentioning that my father fought the fascists in the Spanish Civil War. But I got over and over it. I know there are forty shades of green and white and of course, like any group or community, not all Celtic supporters are totally like-minded. Certain common frames of reference and ways of seeing things do prevail in the Celtic environment but I also know that as well as a strong socialist republican tradition running through the Celtic support there are also some small-minded 'right-wingers' there too. But for most Celtic supporters, the club's history and origins provides our greatest singular attraction.

Being a Celtic supporter isn't all in the mind. You feel it in your bones, and not just when you're sitting in the stand on a winter's night wishing you'd worn your long johns. I, being of Celtic mind and body, believe that it's all about inclusion and advancement for all. For me, being Celtic minded can mean Irish and Catholic but not exclusively so, it also importantly means social inclusion and internationalism. It definitely means not just tolerating immigrants and others, but welcoming them with open arms, seeing them as part of our history. It means rooting for the underdog, and holding the door open for others. If you know the history, it's not a closed book, but a doorway to the future.

Contributors

Dr Joseph M Bradley, the editor of this collection of essays, is the author of 'Ethnic and Religious Identity in modern Scotland' (Avebury 1995), 'Sport, Culture, Politics and Scottish Society: Irish Immigrants and the Gaelic Athletic Association' (John Donald 1998) and joint author of 'Sport Worlds: a sociological perspective' (Human Kinetics 2002). Dr Bradley has published widely on sporting matters in relation to religion, ethnicity, diaspora and politics. His publications include works on Orangeism in Scotland, Scotland's international support, politics in Scottish football and the Irish diaspora in Scotland. He is currently exploring the culture of football in Scotland with a view to a published book in 2007/8. He is lecturer in Sports Studies at the University of Stirling.

Tom Campbell was born in Glasgow. His first Celtic V Rangers match was an 8-1 defeat by Rangers during the Second World War, but he persisted and has remained a Celtic supporter ever since. He emigrated to Canada in 1956 and became a teacher in 1958, acting as Pribcipal of St. Paul's Separate School in Alliston, Ontario. After marriage he moved to Ottawa as Head of the English Department at Sir Wilfrid Laurier H.S. and later at Glebe Collegiate. Since retiring in 1989 Tom has moved back to Scotland, settled in Edinburgh and writes books about Celtic including the soon-to-be-published 'Tears in Argentina', an account of Celtic's quest for the World Club Championship in 1967.

Roisìn Coll lectures at the University of Glasgow in the Department of Religious Education. Her research interests are in the field of Catholic Education and in particular the relationship between Church and state. She is a keen musician and, with a particular interest in Irish music, enjoys performing at festivals throughout Scotland and Ireland. Like many Celtic supporters Roisìn's family originates from Ireland She†spends much of her free time†in Ireland and has a particular love for†Donegal. She†has a season ticket at Celtic Park and rarely misses a match; home, away or European.

Gerry Coyle is a freelance writer and journalist. Gerry was born and lives in Glasgow. His earliest memory of watching Celtic was a European Cup tie against Benfica at Celtic Park in season 69/70. Celtic went on to reach the final in Milan where they were beaten 2-1 by Feyenoord.

Dr Robert A Davis graduated from the University of Strathclyde with a BA and from the University of Stirling with an MLitt in English Literature and Anthropology. He is head of religious education at the University of Glasgow and has taught and written widely on many aspects of Scottish education, childhood and literature. First Celtic game was in October 1966 against Airdrie when Celtic won 3-0.

Tom P Donnelly left Glasgow for Canada in the 1970s. After a long struggle to maintain his love for Celtic far away from Glasgow he led from the front in moves that finally saw the establishment of the North American Celtic Supporters Association in the 1990s. Tom is currently vice President of the Association, is a full time Union activist in Canada and travels back to Glasgow often to see Celtic.

Stephen Ferrie is a communications professional working in the financial services industry in Scotland. He is married with two teenage children and lives in Coatbridge where his love of Celtic has been carefully nurtured since the 1960s. This is his second contribution to the Celtic Minded collection. Stephen attended his first Celtic match in a league game versus Raith Rovers in November 1968. Celtic won 2-0 and 31,000 attended.

Karen Giles graduated from the University of Stirling's Department of Sports Studies in the 1980s. She is the English football correspondent for the Herald newspaper in Glasgow. Her penetrating analysis and commentary mark her as one of the best sports journalists around.

Eddy Grady was born in Glasgow in 1967 and began going to Celtic matches in the late 1970s. Since 1994 he has collected Celtic FC memorabilia specialising in the triumphant season of 1966/67, Celtic's 1987-88 Centenary Year, the Lisbon Lions 25th Anniversary and the UEFA Cup Final in Seville in 2003. He has items on loan at the Celtic FC museum and on occasion has displayed items from his collection at organised events.

Michael Kelly was born in Armagh in 1975 and is a solicitor in Belfast. He attended his first Celtic match in August 1988 – a 4-1 victory over Ayr United. A former president of the Queen's University CSC, he was elected secretary of the Association of Irish Celtic Supporters' Clubs shortly after its inception in 1998 and remains in that position today. He is currently a member of Belfast Shamrock CSC, of which he was the founding chairman.

George McCluskey was born in Hamilton in 1957. He signed for Celtic in 1973 and played in the hoops for ten years. He is fondly remembered by Celtic fans throughout the world for scoring the winning goal against Rangers in the 1980 Scottish Cup Final. He moved from Celtic in 1983 to play for Leeds and subsequently played for Hibernian, Hamilton and Kilmarnock. He currently works for Celtic in youth development and outreach. Married to Ann, George has three daughters and one son and is also a patron of the Irish Christian Brothers Third World charity 'Project Zambia'.

Hugh McLoughlin attended Our Lady's High School in Motherwell and graduated from Glasgow University with a degree in Life Sciences. Is a retired school teacher, a regular contributor to the Catholic press in Scotland and a lifelong Celtic supporter. He attended his first Celtic match in season 1964/65. While still at Motherwell, Hugh remembers celebrating the European Champions Cup win with special interest in two former pupils, Billy McNeill and Bobby Murdoch.

Michael McMahon attended his first Celtic match in April 1974 and witnessed a 2-0 victory over Aberdeen. He was educated at St Teresa's Primary School, Newarthill and Our Lady's High School, Motherwell. He spent 17 years as a welder and became active in the trade union movement before going to Glasgow Caledonian University in 1992 where he gained a Bachelor of Arts (Hons) in Politics and Sociology. He was first elected a Member of the Scottish Parliament for Hamilton North & Bellshill in 1999. He is a member of the Carfin 1948 Celtic Supporters Club and a season ticket holder at Celtic Park, as are his two daughters, Siobhan and Mairead, and son, Gerard.

Dr James MacMillan is a composer whose music is played all over the world. He studied as an under-graduate in music at the University of Edinburgh, and completed his doctoral studies at the University of Durham. He has numerous honorary doctorates and fellowships from various British universities and colleges. He was awarded a CBE in 2004. His Edinburgh Festival speech 'Scotland's Shame: anti-Catholicism as a barrier to genuine pluralism', was delivered in 1999 provoking a bout of national soul-searching. While alienating him from many of the Scottish commentariat, it has attracted much more objective and thoughtful reflection elsewhere. He composed the music, 'Walfrid at the Gates of Paradise' for the unveiling ceremony of a commemorative sculpture of Brother Walfrid at Celtic Park in 2005. His first Celtic game was the Scottish League Cup Final in April 1969 v Hibernian at Hampden.

Celtic won 6-2 and 74,000 attended.

Professor Willy Maley teaches at Glasgow University. He is an award-winning playwright. He co-wrote with Ian Auld – brother of Lisbon Lion Bertie – The Lions of Lisbon (1992), a play marking the silver anniversary of Celtic FC's celebrated European Cup victory, which attracted an audience of 10,000. Willy, who shares his name with one of the club's foundation pillars, is a season ticket holder in the Lisbon Lions Stand and was a columnist with the Celtic View 2003/05.

Andrew Milne is Editor of More than 90 Minutes: a Celtic fanzine and a columnist for the Daily Ireland Newspaper. He comes from Drogheda, Co. Louth and is secretary of St Margaret's Celtic Supporters Club. Together with his fellow club members he has helped raise thousands of euros for local and national charities. He attended his first Celtic game at Celtic Park in January 1989 when Celtic beat Dumbarton 2-0 in the Scottish Cup.

Richard Purden is a freelance writer born and brought up in Oxgangs, Edinburgh. He has been writing about Celtic since 2002 combining his passion for the club alongside faith and rock n' roll. He has been contributing to the Celtic View since 2002 and writes a weekly column on all things Celtic for the Irish Post. He also writes regulary for Scotland on Sunday's Review section. When not writing about Celtic he plays in folk duo Purden and McKenzie.

Professor Patrick Reilly was educated at the University of Glasgow and the University of Oxford where he completed his research degree on Jonathan Swift. Head of Department of English at the University of Glasgow before retiring as Emiritus Professor in 1997. A journalist and broadcaster, he has published books on literary criticism including studies of Swift, Orwell, Golding, Fielding, Conrad and Joyce. He lives in Glasgow. The first game he remembers attending was a wartime league match (southern) against Albion Rovers in Coatbridge in November 1941. The match ended 4-4 and Jock Stein, playing centre-half, either made his debut or played as a trialist for Rovers.

Dr Irene A Reid was born and raised in Renfrewshire. She completed a BEd degree in Scotland, then graduated with an MA in Sociology of Sport from Queen's University, Canada and PhD from the University of Stirling. She has worked in teaching, sports development and administration. She is currently a lecturer in Sports Studies at the University of Stirling. Her research focuses on issues of nationhood and cultural identity in Scotland and also sport and gendered identities. She is from a Scottish Protestant background with an infusion of influence from the north of Ireland on her father's side. Although interested in football for most of her life, she is not a Celtic supporter and has yet to attend a Celtic match.

Tony Roper was born in the Anderston district of Glasgow in 1941. Along with 60,000 others he attended his first Celtic game in May 1953 in the Coronation Cup against Arsenal at Hampden Park. Celtic went on to beat Manchester United in the semi-final and Hibernian in an all-green and white final nine days later. Tony is an actor and director and authored the famous 'Steamie' play and TV production of the late 1980s. Along with fellow Celtic supporter Phil Differ, he has written and produced 'Ricky and Me', a tribute to Scottish actor and comedian, Ricky Fulton.

Edward Toner was born in 1963 in the east end of Glasgow. First Celtic game attended in the late 1960s. Joined his first Celtic Supporters Club as a teenager and has been a member of the Dennistoun No1 CSC since 1983. Has been active member of the Celtic FC Supporters Association for many years. Was elected as General Secretary of the CSA in October 1999. In 2003 he represented Celtic supporters in receiving the FIFA 'Fair Play' Award in Switzerland. Has lived and worked all his life in the east end of Glasgow. Currently employed as a Welfare Rights Officer.

Brian Warfield has been a Celtic supporter since as far back as he can remember. He was one of the founding members of the Wolfe Tones in the 1960s. The band takes its name from Wolfe Tone, one of the leaders of the 1798 Irish Rebellion. Brian Warfield has proved to be as prolific and committed composer of songs, mixing traditional and contemporary material. The band continues to play to huge audiences all over the world and their music CDs continue to sell millions of copies each year.

Bibliography

Ahluwalia P & Zegeye A, 'Frantz Fannon and Steve Biko: Towards Liberation' in Social Identities, 7, 3, pp455-46, 2001

Allison L. The Politics of Sport, Manchester University Press 1986

Anderson B. Imagined Communities: Reflections on the Origins and Spread of Nationalisms, Verso, London 1991

Archer I. & Royle T. (Eds) 'We'll Support You Evermore: The Impertinent Saga of Scottish 'Fitba', London: Souvenir Press 1976

Armstrong G. and Giulionotti R. (Eds). Entering the Field: New Perspectives in World Football, Oxford: Berg, 1997

Audrey S. Multiculturalism in Practice: Irish, Jewish, Italian and Pakistani migration to Scotland, Ashgate, Aldershot 2000

Bairner A. Football and the idea of Scotland, in G Jarvie and G Walker (Eds), Scottish Sport in the Making of the Nation, Leicester University Press, 9-26, 1994

Bar-On T. The Ambiguities of Football, Politics, Culture and Social Transformation in Latin America', Sociological Research Online, vol, 2, no 4, 1997

Billig M. Banal Nationalism, London: Sage 1995

Blain N. & Boyle R. Battling along the boundaries: The marking of Scottish identity in sports journalism, in G. Jarvie & G. Walker (Eds) 'Scottish Sport in the Making of the Nation', Leicester University Press, 125-141, 1994

Boyle R. & Haynes R. 'The Grand old game': football, media and identity in Scotland, in Media, Culture and Society Vol.18, No.4, pp.549-564, 1996

Boyle R. & Haynes R. Power Play: Sport, the Media and Popular Culture, London, Longman 2000

Bradley J.M. Ethnic and Religious Identity in Scotland: Politics, Culture and Football, Aldershot: Avebury 1995

Bradley J.M. 'Intermarriage, Education, and Discrimination' in T. M. Devine (ed) 'St Mary's Hamilton: A Social History 1846-1996' John Donald pp.83-94

Bradley J.M. 'Profile of a Roman Catholic Parish in Scotland' in Scottish Affairs No 14, Winter, pp.123-139 1996

Bradley J.M. 'Identity, Politics and Culture: Orangeism in Scotland' in Scottish Affairs No 16, Summer, pp.104-128 1996

Bradley J.M. 'Facets of the Irish Diaspora: 'Irishness' in Twentieth Century Scotland' in Irish Journal of Sociology Vol.6 1996

Bradley J.M. 'We Shall Not Be Moved'! Mere Sport, Mere Songs?: a tale of Scottish Football' in 'Fanatics' London: Routledge, pp.203-218 1998

Bradley J.M. 'Sport, Culture, Politics and Scottish Society: Irish immigrants and the Gaelic Athletic Association in Scotland' John Donald, Edinburgh 1998

Bradley J.M. 'Imagining Scotland: nationality, cultural identities, football and discourses of Scottishness' Stirling Research Papers in Sports Studies, University of Stirling 2001

Bradley J.M., Maguire J., Jarvie, Mansfield L. Sport Worlds: A sociological perspective, Human Kinetics, USA 2002

Bradley J M, 'Images of Scottishness and Otherness in International Football', Social Identities: Journal for the Study of Race, Nation and Culture, 9, 1, pp.7-23 2003

Bradley J M Celtic Minded: essays on religion, politics, society, identity and football, Argyll Publishing 2004

Brah A., Hickman M.J., & Mac an Ghaill M. Thinking Identities: Ethnicity, Racism and Culture, London: MacMillan Press 1999

Brown A. (Ed) Fanatics: Power, Identity and Fandom in Football, London: Routledge, 1998

Brown C. The Social History of Religion in Scotland Since 1730, Methuen, London 1987

Brown C. Did Urbanisation Secularize Britain, Urban History Yearbook 1988

Brown C. Religion and Society in Scotland since 1707, Edinburgh University Press 1997

Brown S.J. 'Outside the Covenant: The Scottish Presbyterian Churches and Irish Immigration 1922-1938', The Innes Review, Vol.XLII, No.1, Spring pp.19-45 1991

Brubaker R. 'The return of assimilation? Changing perspectives on immigration and its sequels in France, Germany, and the United States' in Ethnic and Racial Studies, 24, 4, pp.531-548 2001

Brubaker R. 'Cognitive Perspectives', Ethnicities, vol 1, part 1, 2001, pp15-17

Bruce S. No Pope Of Rome: Anti-Catholicism In Modern Scotland, Mainstream Publishing, Edinburgh 1985

Bruce S. 'Out of the ghetto: the ironies of acceptance' The Innes Review, Vol.XLIII, No.2, pp.145-154 1992

Bruce S. 'Comparing Scotland and Northern Ireland' in Scotland's Shame: Bigotry and sectarianism in modern Scotland, Mainstream, Edinburgh 2000, pp.135-142

Bruce S. 'Catholic Schools in Scotland: a rejoinder to Conroy', Oxford Review of Education, vol 29, no 2, pp.269-277 2003

Bruce S, Glendinning, Paterson I & Rosie M. Sectarianism in Scotland, Edinburgh University Press, Edinburgh, 2004

Buckley M. 'Sitting on your politics: the Irish amongst the British and the women among the Irish' in J. McLaughlin (ed) Location and Dislocation in Contemporary Irish Society, Cork University Press, Cork, pp.94-132 1997

Burdsey D and Chappell R, ' 'And If You Know Your History. . .' An Examination of the formation of football clubs in Scotland and their role in the construction of social identity', Sports Historian, No.21, pp.94-106, 2001

Burdsey D. 'One of the lads'? Dual ethnicity and assimilated ethnicities in the careers of British Asian professional footballers', Ethnic and Racial Studies, Vol 27, No 5, pp757-779, 2004

Campbell T. and Woods P. The Glory and the Dream, the History of Celtic FC, 1887-1986, Mainstream Publishing 1986

Canning Rev B.J. Padraig H Pearse and Scotland, published by Padraig Pearse Centenary Commemoration Committee, Glasgow 1979

Cassidy L. 'Faded Pictures from Irish Town' in Causeway, pp.34-38, Atmn1996

Coakley J.J. Sport in Society: Issues and Controversies, Mosby, Colerado 1990

Coakley J.J. Sport in Society: Issues and Controversies, USA, Irwin, McGraw-Hill 1998

Cooney J. Scotland and the Papacy, Paul Harris, Edinburgh 1982

Conroy J. 'Yet I Live Here. . .' A Reply to Bruce on Catholic Education in Scotland', Oxford Review of Education Vol.29, No.3, Sept pp.403-412, 2003

Crabbe T, 'Englandfans – A New Club for a New England? Social Inclusion, Authenticity and the Performance of Englishness at 'Home and 'Away' ', Leisure Studies, vol 23, no 1, pp63-78, Jan 2004

Curtis L. Ireland The Propaganda War, Pluto Press 1984

Curtis L. Nothing But The Same Old Story: The roots of Anti-Irish Racism, Published by Information on Ireland, 5th edition 1988

Curtice, J. & Seawright, D. 'The Decline of the Scottish Conservatives and Unionist Party 1950-1992: Religion, Ideology or Economics?' in Journal of Contemporary History, 2, 2, pp.319-342 1995

Davis G. The Irish In Britain 1815-1914 Gill and Macmillan 1991

Devine T.M. (ed) Irish Immigrants and Scottish Society in the Nineteenth and Twentieth Centuries: Proceedings of the Scottish Historical Studies Seminar: University of Strathclyde, 1989/90' John Donald Ltd 1991

Devine T.M. Scotland's Shame: Bigotry and Sectarianism in Modern Scotland, Edinburgh: Mainstream 2000

Devine T.M. (ed) St Mary's Hamilton: A Social History, 1846-1996, John Donald, Edinburgh 1995

Devine T.M. & Mitchison R. People and Society in Scotland: Vol.1, 1760-1830, John Donald, Edinburgh 1988

Dickson T. (ed) Capital and Class in Scotland, John Donald Ltd 1982

Docherty D. The Celtic Football Companion, John Donald 1986

Donovan R. 'Voices of Distrust: The Expression of Anti-Catholic Feeling in Scotland 1778-1781', in The Innes Review Vol.XXIX, 2, pp.111-139, 1978

Doyle A. 'Ethnocentrism and History Textbooks: representation of the Irish Famine 1845-49 in history textbooks in English secondary schools' Intercultural Education, Vol.13, No.3 2002

Dunning E. Sport Matters: sociological studies of sport, violence and civilization, London, Routledge pp.130-158 1999

Eitzen D. Stanley & Sage, George H. Sociology of North American Sport, 5th ed. Dubuque I.A., Brown and Benchmark 1993

Esplin R. Down the Copland Road, Argyll Publishing 2000

Feagin, J. R., Hernén, V. and Batur, P. White Racism: The Basics, New York: Routledge, 2001

Finley R.J. 'Nationalism, Race, Religion and The Irish Question in Inter-War Scotland' in The Innes Review, Vol.XLII, No.1, Spring, pp.46-67 1991

Finn, G.P.T. 'Racism, Religion and Social Prejudice: Irish Catholic Clubs, Soccer and Scottish Society – I The Historical Roots of Prejudice' in The International Journal of the History of Sport, 8, 1, pp.72-95 1991

Finn G.P.T. 'Racism, Religion and Social Prejudice: Irish Catholic Clubs, Soccer and Scottish Society - II Social Identities and Conspiracy Theories' in The International Journal of the History of Sport 8, 3, pp.370-397 1991

Finn G.P.T. 'Faith, Hope and Bigotry: Case Studies of Anti-Catholic Prejudice in Scottish Soccer and Society' in Scottish Sport in the Making of the Nation: Ninety-Minute Patriots' Leicester University Press 1994

Finn G.P.T. 'Sporting Symbols, Sporting Identities: Soccer and Intergroup Conflict in Scotland and Northern Ireland' pp.33-55 in Scotland and Ulster, I.S. Wood (ed), Mercat Press, Edinburgh 1994

Finn G.P.T. Series of papers lodged with Jordanhill Library, Strathclyde University on the role of conspiracy in anti-Catholicism in Scotland and Northern Ireland, 1990-1994

Finn G P T & Dimeo P. 'Scottish Racism, Scottish Identities: The case of Partick Thistle' in Fanatics: power, identity and fandom in football, Routledge 1998

Forgacs D. The Antonio Gramsci Reader, Lawrence and Wishart, London 1999

Forsyth R. in Linklater M. and Denniston R. (eds) Anatomy of Scotland: how Scotland works, Chambers, pp.334-353, 1992

Fraser T.G. (ed) The Irish Parading Tradition: Following the Drum, Macmillan Press, 2000

Gallagher D.J. 'Neutrality as a Moral Standpoint, Conceptual Confusion and the Full Inclusion Debate' Disability & Society Vol.16, No.5, pp637-654 2001

Gallagher T. Glasgow The Uneasy Peace, Manchester University Press 1987

Gallagher T. 'The Catholic Irish in Scotland: In Search of Identity' in T.M.Devine (ed) 'Irish Immigrants and Scottish Society in the Nineteenth and Twentieth Centuries' John Donald Ltd 1991

Gilley S. & Swift R. eds The Irish in the Victorian City, Croom Helm, London 1985

Giulianotti R. Game Without Frontiers: Football, Identity and Modernity, Aldershot, Arena Ashgate 1994

Giulianotti R. 'Built by the Two Varelas: The Rise and Fall of Football Culture and National Identity in Uruguay' in Finn G.P.T. and Giulianotti R. 'Football Culture: Local Contests, Global Visions' Frank Cass, London (originally from Galeano E. 'Football: in Sun and Shadow' London p.42 2000, 1997

Gledhill, C. (ed) Stardom: Industry of Desire, Routledge, 1991

Gramsci A. Selections from prison notebooks of Antonio Gramsci, New York, International Publishers 1971

Greely A.M. McCready 'Does Ethnicity Matter' in Ethnicity Vol.1, No.1, April, pp.91-108 1974

Gruneau R. & Whitson D. Hockey Night in Canada, Toronto, Canada, Garamond Press 1993

Handley J.E. The Irish in Scotland, John S Burns & Sons, Glasgow (this book incorporates both 'The Irish in Scotland 1798-1845' and 'The Irish in Modern Scotland' 1943 & 1947, Cork University Press) 1964

Handley J.E. The Celtic Story, Stanley Paul, London 1960

Hargreaves J. Sport, Power and Culture – A Social and Historical Analysis of Popular Sports in Britain, Polity Press 1986

Hargreaves J. (ed) Sport, Culture and Ideology, Routledge, pp.30-61 1982

Hargreaves J. & McDonald I. 'Cultural Studies and the Sociology of Sport' in

J. Coakley & E. Dunning 'Handbook of Sports Studies' Sage, pp.49-60 2000

Hickman M. 'A study of the incorporation of the Irish in Britain with special reference to Catholic state education: involving a comparison of the attitudes of pupils and teachers in selected Catholic schools in London and Liverpool' unpublished PhD, University of London 1990

Hickman M. Religion, Class and Identity: The State, the Catholic Church and the Education of the Irish in Britain, Avebury, Aldershot 1995

Hickman M. 'Reconstructing deconstructing 'race': British political discourses about the Irish in Britain' Ethnic and Racial Studies, Vol.21, No.2, pp.289-305 1998

Hoberman J. Sport and Political Ideology, Heinemann, London 1984

Hobsbawm E. Nations and Nationalism Since 1780: Programme, Myth, Reality', Cambridge University Press 1990

Holmes M. 'Symbols of National Identity: The Case of the Irish National Football Team' in Irish Political Studies 9, pp.81-98 1994

Holt R. 'Sport and History: The State of the Subject in Britain' in Twentieth Century British History Vol.7, No.2, pp.231-252 1996

Hopkins P. Everyday Racism in Scotland: A Case Study of East Pollockshields, Scottish Affairs, No 49, pp88-103, 2004

Horne J. 'Racism, Sectarianism and Football in Scotland' in Scottish Affairs 12, pp.27-51 1995

Horne J, Tomlinson A, Whannel G. Understanding Sport, London, E&FN Spon 1999

Huckin T, 'Textual Silence and the discourse of homelessness' in Discourse and Society, vol 13, part 3, pp347-372, 2002

Hughson J. 'The Croatian Community' in Sporting Immigrants, edts Philip A Mosely, R Cashman, J O'Hara & Weatherburn, Walla Walla Press, Australia, pp.50-62, 1997

Inglis J 'The Irish In Britain: A Question Of Identity' in Irish Studies in Britain No.3, Spring/Summer 1982

Isajiw W. W. 'Definitions of Ethnicity' in Ethnicity Vol.1, No.2, July, pp.111-124 1974

Jackson J A, The Irish in Britain, London, Routledge and Kegan Paul, 1963

Jackson, S. J. 'A Twist of Race: Ben Johnson and the Canadian Crisis of Racial and National Identity', in Sociology of Sport Journal, Vol.15, No.1, pp.21-40, 1998

Jackson, S. J. 'Exorcizing the ghost: Donovan Bailey, Ben Johnson and the politics of Canadian identity', in Media, Culture & Society, Vol.26, No.1, pp.121-141, 2001

Jacobs S L. Language death and revival after cultural destruction: reflections on a little discussed aspect of genocide in Journal of Genocide Research, 7, 3, pp423-430, 2005

Jarvie G. & Reid I. 'Sport, Nationalism and Culture in Scotland' in The Sports Historian, 19, 1, pp.97-124 1999

Jarvie G. Walker G. (eds) Scottish Sport in the Making of the Nation: Ninety Minute Patriots, Leicester University Press 1994

Jones R L, 'The Black Experience within English Semi-professional Soccer', Journal of Sport and Social Issues, vol 26, no 1, pp47-65, 2002

Kendrick S. 'Scotland, Social Change and Politics' in 'The Making of Scotland: Nation, Culture and Social Change' D. McCrone, D. Kendrick & P. Straw (eds), Edinburgh University Press 1989

Kelly E. 'Challenging Sectarianism in Scotland: The Prism of Racism' in Scottish Affairs, No.42, Winter, pp.32-56 2003

King, J. E. 'Dysconscious Racism: Ideology, Identity, and Miseducation' in R. Delgado and J. Stefancic (eds) Critical White Studies: Looking Behind the Mirror, Philadelphia: Temple University Press, pp.128-132, 1997

Kircaldy J. 'Irish Jokes: No Cause For Laughter' in Irish Studies in Britain, No.2, Autumn/Winter 1981

Kinealy C. This Great Calamity: The Irish Famine 1845-52, Gill & Macmillan,1994

Lewis G, 'Welcome to the margins: Diversity, tolerance, and policies of exclusion' in Ethnic and Racial Studies, vol 28, no 3, pp536-558, 2005

Lines, G. 'Villains, fools or heroes? Sports stars as role models for young people', in Leisure Studies, Vol.20, No.4, pp.285-303 2001

Logue P. (ed) Being Irish: Personal reflections of being Irish today, Oak Tree Press, Dublin 2000

Long J. A. & McNamee M. J. 'On the moral economy of racism and racist rationalizations in sport' in International Review for the Sociology of Sport, 39/4, pp405-420, 2004

Mac an Ghaill M. 'The Irish in Britain: the invisibility of ethnicity and anti-Irish racism' in Journal of Ethnic and Migration Studies, no 1, pp137-147, 2000.

Mac an Ghaill M. 'British Critical Theorists: The Production of the Conceptual Invisibility of the Irish Diaspora' in Social Identities, vol 7, no 2, pp179-201, 2001

Mac an Ghaill M. & Haywood C, 'Young (male) Irelanders: postcolonial ethnicities – expanding the nation and Irishness' in European Journal of Cultural Studies, Vol 6, 3, pp386-403, 2003

McCaffrey J. 'Roman Catholics in Scotland in the nineteenth and twentieth centuries', in Records of the Scottish Church History Society, 21, 2, 1983

McCrone D. The Sociology of Nationalism, Routledge 1998

McCrone D. Rosie M. 'Left and Liberal: Catholics in modern Scotland' in Boyle R. & Lynch P. (eds) Out of the Ghetto: The Catholic Community in Modern Scotland Edinburgh: John Donald, 67-94 1998

McCrone D. Understanding Scotland: the sociology of a nation, 2nd edition, Routledge 2001

MacDonald C.M.M. Unionist Scotland 1800-1997, John Donald 1998

McFarland E.W. Protestants First: Orangeism in nineteenth Century Scotland, Edinburgh University Press 1990

McKenna Y. 'Forgotten Migrants: Irish Women Religious in England, 1930s-1960s', in International Journal of Population Geography, 9, pp.295-308 2003

MacLaughlin J. 'Pestilence on their backs, famine in their stomachs: the racial construction of Irishness and the Irish in Victorian Britain' in 'Ireland and Cultural Theory, The Mechanics of Authenticity' C. Graham, R. Kirkland (eds), Macmillan

McPherson B.D., Curtis J.E. & Loy J.W. The Social Significance of Sport, Human Kinetics, Illinois 1989

Maguire J. & Poulton E. K, 'European Identity Politics in Euro 95: Invented Traditions and National Habitus Codes', International Review for the Sociology of Sport, 34, 1, 1999, pp17-29

Maver I. 'The Catholic Community in Scotland in the Twentieth Century' in T.M. Devine & R.J. Finley (eds) Edinburgh University Press, Edinburgh, pp.269-284 1996

Miller D. (ed) Rethinking Northern Ireland, Culture, Ideology and Colonialism, Addison Wesley Longman, Essex 1998

Mitchell J. 'Religion and Politics in Scotland' unpublished paper presented to Seminar on Religion and Scottish politics, University of Edinburgh 1992

Miles R. & Muirhead L. 'Racism in Scotland: a matter for further investigation?' in Scottish Government Yearbook, pp.108-136 1986

Miles R. Racism, Routledge 1989

Mitchell M.J. The Irish in the West of Scotland 1797-1848: Trade unions, strikes and political movements, John Donald Ltd 1998

Moorhouse B. 'Professional Football and working class culture: English Theories and Scottish evidence' in Sociological Review, 32, 285-315 1984

Moorhouse B. 'Scotland Against England: Football and Popular Culture' in International Journal of the History of Sport, 4, 189-202 1987

Moran R. 'A Victim's Perspective in, The Future of Football' in Garland, Malcolm and Rowe, edts, Racism in Football, pp190-200, 2000

Morley D. & Chen K.H. (eds) Stuart Hall: Critical dialogues in cultural studies, Routledge, London 1996

Morrow S. The People's Game?: Football, Finance and Society, Palgrave Macmillan, Basingstoke 2003

Muirhead Rev. I.A. 'Catholic Emancipation: Scottish Reactions in 1829' Innes Review, 24, 1, Spring 1973

Muirhead Rev. I.A. 'Catholic Emancipation in Scotland: the debate and the aftermath' Innes Review, 24, 2, Autumn 1973

Murray B. The Old Firm: Sectarianism, sport and society in Scotland, John Donald Ltd 1984

Murray B. Glasgow's Giants: 100 years of the Old Firm, Mainstream 1988

Murray B. Bhoys, Bears and Bigotry: The Old Firm in the New Age, Mainstream 2003

Nixon H. L. & Frey J. H. A Sociology of Sport, London, Wadsworth 1996

O'Conner K. The Irish in Britain, Torc, Dublin 1970

O Tuathaigh M.A.G. 'The Irish in Nineteenth Century Britain: Problems of Integration' pp.13-36, in Gilley and Swift 'The Irish in the Victorian City' 1985

Phiney J S, Horenczyk G, Liebkind K, Vedder P. 'Ethnic Identity, Immigration, and Well-Being: An Interactional Perspective', Journal of Social Issues, Vol 57, no 3, pp493-510, 2001

Reid I.A. 'Nationalism, Sport and Scotland's Culture' in Scottish Centre Research Papers in Sport, Leisure and Society, Vol.2 1997

Rosie M. & McCrone D. 'The Past is History: Catholics in Modern Scotland' in 'Scotland's Shame: Bigotry and sectarianism in Modern Scotland' Mainstream, Edinburgh, pp199-217 2000

Rosie M. The Sectarian Myth in Scotland: of bitter memory and bigotry, Palgrave Macmillan, 2004

Rowe D. & Wood N. (eds) Editorial of Media, Culture and Society, Vol.18, No.4 1996

Said E. Culture and Imperialism, London, Vintage, 1994

Schlesinger P. 'Media, the Political Order and National Identity' in Media, Culture and Society, Vol.13, No.3, pp.297-308 1991

Shaw S. M. 'Discrimination is a Societal Issue Too: Moving Beyond Individual Behaviour', Leisure Studies, 27, pp37-40, 2005

Spencer, N. E. Sister Act VI: Venus and Serena Williams at Indian Wells: 'Sincere Fictions' and white racism, in Journal of Sport & Social Issues, Vol.28, No.2, pp.115-135 2004

Sugden J. & Bairner A. 'Northern Ireland; Sport in a Divided Society' in Allison L. (edt) The Politics Of Sport, pp.90-117, Manchester University Press 1986

Sugden J. & Bairner A. Sport, Sectarianism and Society in a Divided Ireland, Leicester University Press, 1993

Sugden J. & Tomlinson A. (eds) Hosts and Champions: Soccer Cultures, National Identities and the USA World Cup, Aldershot: Arena, Ashgate 1994

Walker G. & Gallagher T. (eds) Sermons and Battle Hymns: Protestant Culture in Modern Scotland, Edinburgh University Press 1990

Walls P. & Williams R. 'Sectarianism at work: Accounts of employment discrimination against Irish Catholics in Scotland' in Ethnic and Racial Studies, Vol.26, No.4, pp.632-662 2003

Walter B. Morgan S. Hickman M.J. & Bradley J.M. 'Family Stories, public silence: Irish identity construction amongst the second-generation Irish in England' Scottish Geographical Journal, Special Edition on 'The Fate of 'Nations' in a Globalised World', Vol.118, No.3, pp.201-218, 2002

Walvin J. The People's Game: The History of Football Revisited, Mainstream 1994

Werbner P. 'Our Blood is Green': Cricket, Identity and Social Empowerment among British Pakistanis, in Sport, Identity and Ethnicity, Ed by J Clancy, Berg, 1996, pp. 87-112, 1996

Whannel G. 'Sport stars, narrativization and masculinities', in Leisure Studies, Vol.18, No.3, pp. 249-265, 1999

Wilson B. Celtic, A Century with Honour Willow Books, William Collins Publications, Glasgow 1988